ABERFELDY
PAST AND PRESENT

THE AUTHOR

ABERFELDY
PAST AND PRESENT

THE
STORY OF A SMALL HIGHLAND TOWN
AND
SOME NOTES ON THE DISTRICT
IMMEDIATELY SURROUNDING

By N. D. MACKAY,

M.D., B.Sc., D.P.H., F.S.A.Scot., &c.

Illustrated
with
Photographs, Maps, &c.

PUBLISHED IN 1954 BY
THE TOWN COUNCIL OF ABERFELDY
As Administrators of the Common Good Fund

PRINTED IN SCOTLAND BY
WM. CULROSS & SON LTD., COUPAR ANGUS, PERTHSHIRE

To My Fellow Townsfolk

CONTENTS

ILLUSTRATIONS

For the use of the following photographs, etc., I express my sincere indebtedness to :— (A) Mrs Clow, Alma Villa, Aberfeldy : (B) the late Mr William G. Folkarde, M.A., Riverlea, Aberfeldy : (C) Mr James A. MacGregor, Belleville, Aberfeldy : (D) Mr Nelson D. Macnaughton, Bridgend, Aberfeldy : (E) Mr John C. Menzies, Culdares, Aberfeldy : (F) Mrs C. J. D. Munro, late of Murthly Farm : (G) Mr Andrew Reid, Printer, Aberfeldy (for use of blocks) : (H) Mr Ian M. Thomson, L.D.S., F.R.P.S., Edragoll, Aberfeldy.

Those marked (J) and (K) are from illustrations which have appeared from time to time in local Guide Books and from my own negatives respectively.

Maps, Line Drawings, etc.

FOREWORD

In the following pages notes accumulated over a long period of years are gathered together to form an Account of 'Aberfeldy and One Mile Around'—an Account which, it will be found, moves about in a somewhat random manner from place to place in space and from point to point in time. It is not meant for the hustling Baedeker-minded American 'doing Europe' or anyone of his type but for the Aberfeldy-ite who, from the comfort of his own armchair, may wish to survey some of the past and present of the town in which he lives, and for the native who, though no longer resident, may still be interested. It is not a 'guidebook,' and still less a 'history.' The true Aberfeldy-ite requires no guidebook, while, as for history —well, Aberfeldy has no history in the real 'historical' sense at all.

* * * * * *

For many years I have felt that Aberfeldy deserved to have its story in print. There is no book extant which sets out to meet this need, so, with a view to doing what I could to fill the gap, I have for almost as long as I can remember kept on gathering material on the chance that, some day, I might find time to write such a book. Since I retired from active life five years ago I have found that time, and this book is the result. I have no doubt that others could have done it better ; possibly in time someone will, but, till then, I hope this one will serve the purpose intended.

I was born and have lived most of my life in the town so that much of what has happened here during the last sixty or more years is a matter of my own personal recollection. It may be said that much of that part of the Account which covers the past few years is of little interest to anyone, being merely a repetition of what is common local knowledge. I quite agree —common local knowledge *at the present time*—but, I would ask, how much of what was common local knowledge one hundred years ago lives on to-day? A certain amount, no doubt, has come down to us by word of mouth and such of it as I have been able to collect is included here, but this method of passing on information is dying out; the bards are dead, and the seannachies all but extinct. A certain amount too, but not nearly as much as one would wish, is to be found in pamphlets, etc., written by one-time residents who have now passed on, and in articles lying forgotten in the files of newspaper offices, but these, helpful as they are, are few and hard to come by. When I add further that what is 'present' to-day will be 'past' in another fifty years I feel that the inclusion of what may be common local knowledge in 1952 calls for no apology.

For material covering a varying period prior to my appearance on the scene in 1882 I have to thank residents of longer standing than myself and others, now dead, who were well up in years while I was yet young. For information dating further back I have had recourse to records left by people who lived in the times of which they wrote or had access to sources of information perhaps not generally available, and to all these I express my sincere indebtedness.

I also wish particularly to express my indebtedness and thanks to Miss Dickson of the Reference Department of the Edinburgh Public Library (for valuable help given in searching through old records, etc.), to Messrs, C. R. Allister, of the Commercial Bank of Scotland Head Office, Edinburgh (for notes on the story of the Branch in Aberfeldy), R. S. Brydon, M.A., Ph.D., Strathbraan, late Rector of Breadalbane Academy (for help in checking and correcting proofs), George Craik, Bank of Scotland, Aberfeldy (for supplying some points of information on the local Branch), J. D. Haggart, O.B.E., C.B.E., J.P., ex-Provost of Aberfeldy (for permission to examine and make use of certain old Building Leases, Feu Charters, and Plans of the Town), Alexander Low, Union Bank of Scotland, Aberfeldy (for notes on the history of the Branch under his care, and for collecting information and for keeping me right on a number of other matters bearing on present day activities in the Town), John B. Lowson, Savings Bank of the County and City of Perth (for details concerning the Branch in Aberfeldy), Malcolm MacCallum, Dundee (for reminiscences of his father, the late Mr Donald MacCallum— see below), James Macdonald, 15 Kenmore Street, Aberfeldy, Session Clerk (for some particulars regarding the Free Church of Scotland in Aberfeldy), James A. MacGregor, Belleville, Aberfeldy, Registrar, etc. (for many interesting stories of the old 'worthies' of the Town during the latter half of last century, and much else besides—see below), William MacLean, Bigrow, Kenmore (for some notes on Borlick and Pitilie), Rev. Ian MacLellan, Parish Minister of Weem, a native of Islay (for some information he has been able to supply, and for checking and correcting my spellings in Gaelic, a language of which, I am ashamed to confess, I know little or nothing), Ian Macnaughtan, Road Surveyor Highland District of Perthshire, Aberfeldy (for notes on roads and bridges), John C. Menzies, Culdares, Aberfeldy (for access to certain old documents, etc., in his possession), Henry M. Paton, Editor of the Proceedings of the Society of Antiquaries of Scotland, Edinburgh (for the use of the blocks of the illustrations of the Glassie and Margmore Stones), Andrew Reid, Printer, Aberfeldy (for the use of three half-tone and two line blocks), John Shaw, Scotston, by Dunkeld (for information, etc., on Borlick and Pitilie), to the Registrar General, New Register House, Edinburgh (for various census returns, etc.), to the members of the Town Council of Aberfeldy, as Administrators of the Common Good Fund, but for whose generosity and public-spiritedness the publication of this book would probably not have been possible, and, lastly, to my Wife but for whose patient forbearance with me in my preoccupation over a prolonged period it would probably never have been written.

The help of others, willingly given and gratefully received but not mentioned here, is acknowledged as occasion arises in the main text of the work.

PERSONAL NOTES on some of the local authorities quoted in this Account :

REV. JOHN KENNEDY, D.D., born in Aberfeldy in 1813, died 1900, was the son of Rev. James Kennedy, first Congregational Minister in Aberfeldy. He was a well-known divine who did much good work in the East End of London and became known as the Non-Conformist Bishop of Stepney. He left reminiscences, *Old Highland Days*, which tell of Aberfeldy as he remembered it as a boy, and a *Memoir of Rev. James Kennedy* in which a few of his father's recollections are given. One son, Sir Alexander Kennedy, became a leading electrical engineer in the City of London.

REV. HUGH MACMILLAN, D.D. LL.D., F.R.S.E., F.S.A.Scot., born in Aberfeldy in 1833, died 1903, was the son of an Aberfeldy merchant. He was Moderator of the Free Church of Scotland, editor of *Good Words*, author of *The Highland Tay* (1901), etc., and contributed to the *Proceedings of the Society of Antiquaries of Scotland* articles on Cup-marked Stones in the Aberfeldy district. His son, who died in September of this year, became Lord Macmillan of Aberfeldy, a Lord of Appeal who at one time was Solicitor General and Lord Advocate of Scotland.

REV. JOHN MACLEAN, Pitilie, born 1829, died 1911, was Parish Minister of Grantully for many years. He was a recognised authority on local lore but could never be persuaded to commit his knowledge to paper. He was a fine Gaelic scholar, a real old worthy, and a great favourite with everyone.

MR JAMES A. MACGREGOR, Belleville, Aberfeldy, though not native born has lived in Aberfeldy for about 80 years. He was our first uniformed male postman and acted in this capacity from 1883 to 1928. As editor and producer of *The Aberfeldy News*, a paper which appeared weekly during the summer months for four years until the First World War put a stop to its publication, and as reporter and correspondent to various newspapers, journals, etc., and as District Registrar, he has kept his finger on the pulse of the town and is a mine of local information. Born 1868, and still going strong !

MR DONALD MACCALLUM was born in Dunkeld in 1862 and came to Aberfeldy at the age of three ; six weeks later, from the vantage point of his father's shoulder he watched the first railway train steam into Aberfeldy station. He left school and started work at the age of nine and, in course of a long life, as house boy, man-servant, valet, butler, and house steward, travelled far and encountered many famous people. He had a wonderful memory, was a keen observer and deeply interested in the lore of the town, but unfortunately left few written notes ; these few however, re-enforced by others supplied to his son Malcolm, have been a helpful addition to those I had gleaned from him directly during his lifetime. He spent his latter years in the Factory, and died there in 1947.

MR ALEXANDER GOW, a native of Duntaylor and a classical scholar of some repute, in the third quarter of last century conducted a school in Kenmore Street known as Gow's Secondary School. He wrote a brochure on *Aberfeldy in the Eighteenth Century*.

MR J. C. CAMPBELL who, if still living would now be aged about ninety, but who died some six or seven years ago, was a native of Aberfeldy and spent his youth in the town. In his later years he was engaged in writing down his recollections of Aberfeldy together with what other notes he had been able to gather covering a period from about the middle of last century onwards. When he died his notes were in manuscript form. I was fortunate, however, in that during his lifetime I was permitted to see some of these notes and after his death, through the kindness of Mr James A. MacGregor to whom he had made them over, to see and make extracts from them all.

In the following Account I have not hesitated to draw an all these sources as required, and here make due acknowledgment. If there are errors I assume responsibility and express my regret ; omissions there are bound to be and no one regrets them more than I do, but if anything is preserved that otherwise might have been lost then I shall feel that my time has not been wasted.

Now, just one final note on the set-up of the book itself : To my mind cross references and footnotes are a constant interruption to easy reading, so, they have been cut out altogether, the only references being to appropriate passages in the Appendix (*e.g.* (*A*), (*B*), etc.), for the benefit of readers who wish to know a little more about the subject of the reference than is contained in the main text. For the benefit of those who disagree with me on the matter of cross references a copious Index is provided.

N. D. MACKAY.

ABERFELDY,

PERTHSHIRE.

31st December, 1952.

ABERFELDY
PAST AND PRESENT

"Aberfeldy is a favourite resort on the Tay, well known for the Falls of Moness mentioned in Robert Burns's song 'The Birks of Aberfeldy'."

Thus casually and almost callously does the *Encyclopedia Britannica* dismiss the subject ; but there is more to it than that, a lot more, for Aberfeldy was on the map long before Burns's day, and long before the *Encyclopedia Britannica's* day too, for that matter. Less in the eye of History perhaps than some other localities in Perthshire—Ardoch, Scone, Dunkeld, Killiecrankie, to mention only four—the town has played its part, a humble one possibly, in the sometimes turbulent life of the Highlands in the past, and nowhere in that county referred to by no less an authority than Sir Walter Scott as probably the most varied and beautiful in Scotland is there a finer centre for the Nature lover.

* * * * * *

Though Aberfeldy, as such, may be said to have had no 'personal' history before 1787 when the three small hamlets which then occupied the site came together under the lairdship of the Breadalbanes it stands before a common background with the rest of the Highlands, the background of a past which has left its mark on our race and its monuments on our countryside.

Far back in prehistoric times, some 4,000 years ago, men of the Neolithic or Later Stone Age—a Mediterranean stock—spread northward into Britain at a time when it was still probably part of the mainland of Europe, and for centuries were its only inhabitants.

For a period covering many thousands of years before their coming, apart from some remains found in the 1890's in one or two caves on the 25 feet beach terraces near Oban and identified as probably belonging to the Palaeolithic or Early Stone Age, the men of which vanished from Europe at a very remote period, there is no evidence to suggest that Scotland had any human inhabitants. The Palaeolothic Age covered that era in the earth's history which followed the second Great Ice Age which is estimated to have occurred between 100,000 and 250,000 years ago and extended over at least two lesser glacial periods. It included various types and races of men differing widely from each other in physical development and culture, but it is very doubtful whether any of them lived in what is now known as Central Perthshire.

In contrast to the men of the Early Stone Age, who were in the main powerfully built, Neolithic men were of small stature, from 5 ft. to 5 ft. 6 in., having long narrow (dolichocephalic) heads and no great muscular development, indeed not unlike the Lapps who may be their present day descendants. They lived in pit houses, 8 or 9 feet in diamenter, formed partly by excavation and probably roofed. They did not burn their dead as did the Early Stone Age men but buried them in 'barrows' or 'tumuli'—artificial mounds 10 or 20 feet high containing stone coffins or 'cists' usually about 4½ feet long and 3 feet wide, in which the dead were placed with the knees drawn up to the chin.

Some, though not all, of the Standing Stones and Stone Circles which are scattered about the country are believed to date from Neolithic times, but the commonest remains of the period, apart from the burial mounds, are the Cup- and Ring-marked Stones which occur not only in Great Britain and Ireland but in the pre-historic jungle mounds of India and across Asia and Europe. These Stones are commoner in Scotland than in any other part of Britain, and commoner in north Perthshire than in any other part of Scotland. Though numerous in the Tay Valley they are, oddly enough, rare in the Tummel Valley.

The stone arrowheads and finely polished stone 'axe-heads' or 'celts' which are still picked up from time to time also date from this period. (These stone arrowheads in more credulous days than the present used to be called 'elf-shots' and were supposed to be weapons shot by fairies at cattle to produce certain disorders. To cure such disorders the affected cow had to be touched with an elf-shot or made to drink the water in which one had been dipped. A hair of the dog——!).

* * * * * *

The peaceful times which the Neolithic people enjoyed here as in other parts of Britain ended with the Celtic invasions, the date of the first of which can only be conjectured. It is known however that when the Phœnicians traded with Britain for tin so early as B.C. 600 the inhabitants were Celtic and that when the Romans came to Scotland they were already a powerful nation.

Probably the earliest migration to Britain of the Celtic peoples took place between B.C. 1300 and 1000. On their arrival of course they found the Neolithic people already in occupation ; these they called 'Sithe,' pronounced 'Shee,' meaning 'the peaceful people.' This term is still applied to fairies, and the old burial mounds 'Sithean,' pronounced 'Shian' meaning 'the places of the peaceful people,' are called fairy knowes to this day. Three of these knowes or knolls are still to be seen between the road and the Tay-Lyon confluence on the farmlands of Tirinie.

The Neolithic people would seem not to have been exterminated by the invaders as burial mounds have been found containing the graves of both races, but, be this as it may, there are to-day in our own Highlands some types of short dark people who show certain affinities with Neolithic man, which would suggest that possibly, even after the lapse of many centuries, the strain still lingers on.

One thing that is certain however is that, long before the

coming of the Romans, Scotland was populated by three principal races, all tall and fair and all of Celtic origin, with their source in Asia, viz : The Britons in the South, the Cruithnich or Picts (generally referred to as the Northern Picts) in the north and east, and the Gaidhil (Gaels), often referred to as Southern Picts, in the centre and west.

These last, the Gaels, the purest of whom held as part of their territory the Highlands of Perthshire, came from Asia via Greece, Spain, Portugal ('Port-nan-Gaidhil'), and France to Ireland, and so to the west coast of Scotland.

Unlike the people of the Neolithic Age who lived in more or less settled communities and led an agricultural life, the Celts were in the first instance nomadic and pastoral races but, by the time the Romans invaded Britain, they lived in 'hut circles,' often congregated into 'towns' with earthen ramparts. In Perthshire there are numerous remains of these 'hut circles,' formed of sods and stones, of a height of about 4 feet and diameter of 20 to 40 feet. For centuries they had no houses in our acceptance of the term but lived in the open air. The sunken roofed chambers of this period are believed to have been for the storage of grain though, in a few cases, fireplaces have been found which might suggest that on occasion they served as dwelling places or as refuges for women, children, and old men in times of trouble. Latterly, however, as weather conditions got colder, small huts were erected, probably roofed with turf and measuring about 12 feet by 16.

Housing conditions among the poorer classes in the Highlands must have continued more or less unchanged for centuries, as will be told later.

The hill and other forts of which there are many in this district and Glenlyon date from the Celtic period of our history, and there is evidence to suggest that some of these were occupied as dwellings so late as the 8th century.

* * * * * *

When in A.D. 84, the Roman General Julius Agricola, 'the best of generals under the worst of Emperors, Domitian,' invaded Scotland north of the Forth he found himself confronted with the combined forces of the Gaels and the Picts who, despite their internecine quarrels, were prepared to unite in face of a common enemy.   In the battle of Mons Granpius which ensued though Agricola won the day, it is significant that he did nothing to follow up his victory.

What Roman remains there are in Perthshire are attributed to the Emperor Septimus Severus who, in A.D. 208, about 125 years after Agricola, fought his way up the east coast as far as the Moray Firth.   Any actual occupation by his forces of the Highlands proper were confined to the fringes and entirely sporadic, while to the north and west of the country he never penetrated at all.

From the time of Constantine (died A.D. 337) till the overthrow of society which followed the fall of Rome in A.D. 410 barbarism, paganism, and Christianity had marched side by side in the Highlands for even before the days of the 'Saints' Christianity had been finding its way into Scotland north of the Forth, doubtless through the agency of refugees fleeing from the Roman occupied and partly Christianised regions of the country further south.   In addition it has to be remembered that many of the Scots were already Christians when they came over from Ireland.

*   *   *   *   *   *

While Saints came and went during the second half of the first Millennium secular history was being made.   In 860 Kenneth the son of Alpin, now referred to as Kenneth Mac-Alpine, son of a father belonging to a Galloway branch of the Scoti and a Pictish mother, became King of the united Scots and Picts and assumed the title of 'King of the Scots,' not, be it noted, 'King of Scotland.'

The country lying north of the firths of Forth and Clyde was still known by its old Celtic name of Alban—a name which it had borne from a very remote period—and Kenneth's kingdom was restricted to that part of it occupied by the two races from which he was sprung.

Under the line of kings founded by Kenneth, the Scoti or Scots migrating from Ireland, gradually added to the territories under their sway in Scotland, so much so that, towards the end of the 10th century a transference to Scotland began of the name 'Scotia,' till then applied to Ireland, a transference to be completed in the 11th, though it was not till after the 12th that it came to cover the whole of the districts which formed the later Kingdom of the Scots, *i.e.*, the area between the Firths of Forth and Clyde in the south and the Spey and Drumalban in the north.

About the time of King David I (1107-1153) the form 'Scotland' was beginning to come into use, but it was not until the reign of Alexander III (1249-1286) that that use became general and co-extensive with the utmost limits of the country.

It was David I who, on his return from England in 1136, introduced feudalism into Scotland. Before this the people in the Highlands appear to have lived in a patriarchal form of society, in tribes or clans each comprised of families or groups of families living together or near each other. The Gaelic word 'clann' means simply 'family,' 'children,' 'offspring.' A number of these groups might fall within the jurisdiction of a 'Mormaor' who was the hereditary ruler, and under whom was the 'Toiseach' the military leader. The office of Mormaor was hereditary in the limited sense that it passed not necessarily from father to son but to him chosen from the three nearest in descent to the founder. This gave the members of the clan the power to refuse to elect anyone who might be objectionable. Under the feudal system, based on military service, in which occupiers of land became vassals of the landowners or Mormaors who became their feudal superiors and who, in turn, directly or through mid-superiors, became vassals of the Crown, the already existing tribal or clan system was widened and strengthened.

With the disappearance of the supremacy of the Crown after 1286, when Alexander III died childless and the succession was in dispute, the clans, cut off from all central authority and protection, were thrown largely upon their own resources and the people forced for their self-preservation to turn to and gather round their superiors or, when these were non-resident, chiefs chosen by themselves.

The introduction of clan names as it were 'compacted' these groups but this did not come for some time. They were unknown up to the 13th century and not common until the 14th when the name of the superior (or chief) was taken as their surname by his vassals. They had none before. In some cases, where the superior, generally of non-Scottish extraction, already had a surname, as in that of the Laird of Weem,— de Meyners of Norman descent—the vassals took this as their own.

The bonds of a common name and common interests bound the members of the clan still more closely together and, in time, led to the adoption of distinctive tartans so that, in the clan feuds and battles so frequent in those days, men might know who were their friends and who their enemies.

The clan system, in its feudal aspect, died out after the Union of the Crowns in 1603 when Parliament became able to make its power felt but the tartan, which by then had become established as part of the National dress, continued to be worn in the Highlands until after The '45 when it was proscribed by law. In the 1746 Act 'For the more effectual disarming the Highlands in Scotland—' etc., it was laid down "That from and after the first day of August, 1747, no man or boy within that part of Great Britain called Scotland—shall, on any pretence whatsoever, wear or put on the clothes commonly called Highland clothes—that is to say, the plaid, philabeg or little kilt—" etc. "and that no tartan or party-coloured plaid or stuff shall be used for great coats or for upper coats—" etc. Anyone offending under the terms of this Act was liable on a first conviction to "suffer imprisonment, without bail, during the space of six months, and no longer," and, on a second, to "transportation to any of his Majesty's plantations beyond the seas......there to remain for the space of seven years."

It was not until 1782 that this iniquitous Act, described even by Dr Johnson as rather an exhibition of "an ignorant wantonness of power than the proceeding of a wise and beneficent Legislature," was repealed. After thirty-six years it was not surprising that some time should elapse before the Highland garb began to return to favour ; young men had never known it, and older men had grown away from it, but surely, if slowly, it regained its popularity and to-day the Highlander is as proud of his Clan and tartan as ever were any of his forefathers.

*   *   *   *   *   *

The very early history of the Highlands, even after the commencement of written records in the time of the 'Saints,' is difficult to piece together, the annalists of these days, generally members of the various religious bodies, being inclined to colour their writings with much of the obviously fabulous and to alter dates and distort facts to suit their own particular contentions. It is not remarkable therefore that on many points even experts disagree and the laymen who is wise keeps out.

After the departure of the Romans Scotland for centuries had many troubles, not all of her own making, to contend with. Scandinavian pirates ravaged her shores and for a time occupied her seaward and island territories ; later, her fertile Lowlands were a continued temptation to the rapacious English, and it was not until Bannockburn (1314), and Scotland was recognised as an independent kingdom, that the way seemed clear. But it was not clear, as anyone who has read the history of Scotland in the Middle Ages, knows well. Nor did the Union of the Crowns in 1603 bring peace, for we had Cromwell warring on our soil in the late 1640's, and in the reign of Charles II we find the two countries at grips again. The Union of the Parliaments in 1707, which largely deprived Scotland of a proper say in the management of her own affairs was not popular north of the Border at the time, nor, in the opinion of a large proportion of our population, is it now. The Jacobite Risings of 1715 and 1745 are too well remembered in the Highlands to require more than a passing mention here, but events of these stirring times so far as they touched Aberfeldy and its immediate surroundings will be noticed later.

I have not attempted to give even a condensed history here, not even the skeleton of one, at most one or two odd bones perhaps. The few points noted however, particularly that of the birth and growth of the Clan system, do appear to have some bearing on the past history, not only of the Highlands in general, but of our own district if not of Aberfeldy specifically and others no doubt will crop up in the course of the Story now to be told.

* * * * * *

It may be a source of satisfaction to some to be able to pin-point our little town on the map of Scotland by working out its position on latitude 56.37 N. and longtitude 3.52 W. but there is a much easier way open to anyone with a pencil and a ruler, for lines drawn from Cape Wrath to the uppermost reaches of the Solway and from Duncansby Head to the Mull of Galloway intersect at a point so near Aberfeldy as scarcely to matter—so it must fall out that the Heart of Scotland cannot be far away.

From this it happened, therefore, when about the middle of last century a plantation in the shape of a heart was laid out on the hillface behind the town to the south, that the local people were quick to label it The Heart Wood and to decide that it truly marked the Heart of Scotland. I say 'marked' in preference to 'marks' for the Heart Wood no longer exists as such for now, what with storms, the woodman's axe, and the obliteration of its eastern boundary through the rapid spread of thickets of self-sown alders, willows, birches, etc., the stranger within the gates may well be forgiven if he fails to note the site.

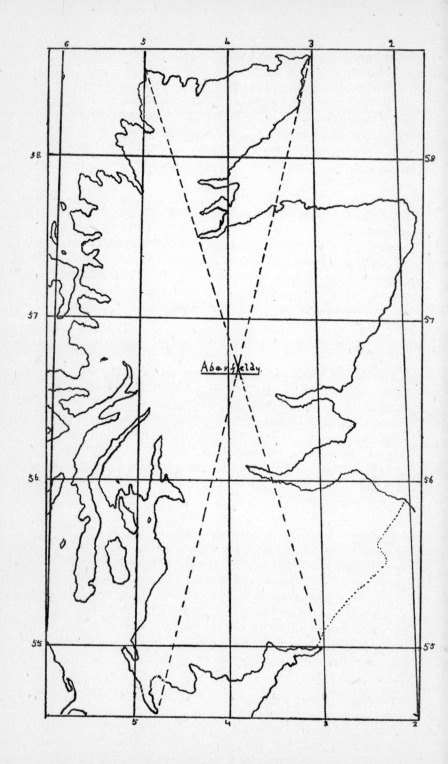

Aberfeldy.

Despite the denial by the then land steward (William Dunn) of the Breadalbane Estates that there was any 'geographical' idea in the minds of the foresters at the time of planting, or that the heart shape was anything other than fortuitous, the name, 'The Heart Wood,' still clings to the site just as the belief in the significance of the name still clings to the minds of the people, and seems likely to persist there as part of the local lore of Aberfeldy long after the land steward's denial is forgotten.

*   *   *   *   *   *

Probably every town and village in the land has its own store of lore, traditions, and legends ; they are part of our heritage from the past and the country would indeed be a poorer place without them.   Some, like that concerning the Heart Wood, are no doubt based on false foundations ; others may rest or seem to rest on surer ground, but all, from their very nature, must carry with them an element of uncertainty, for, where there is no uncertainty, tradition ceases to be tradition and becomes history.

Aberfeldy's legend of St. Palladius, however it arose in the first instance, having little or no historical foundation or background, must therefore remain a legend.   Though his name appears in several of the *Calendars of Scottish Saints*, there are many anachronisms with contradictions and obvious fabrications in the records of the early Christian Church in Scotland, and Skene (*History of Celtic Scotland*), in referring to what he calls "the fabulous mission of Palladius to Scotland," states that there is reason to doubt whether this Saint was ever in Scotland at all.   In the opinion of authorities competent to judge, the belief that he came to this country arose out of two errors committed by John of Fordun, the Scottish Chronicler who died in 1384.   Fordun would seem to have been misled by the recorded facts that the Saint's mission was to "the Scots who believed in Christ," and that Scotland has not always been called 'Scotland,' the Scots at the time of Palladius being inhabitants of Ireland.   The second error lies in his identification, apparently without justification, of the word 'Paldy' with ' Palladius,'

Be all this as it may, however, the local story runs as follows :
Some time about the middle of the 5th century Pope Celestine,
dissatisfied with the state of the Catholic Church in Ireland,
ordained Palladius, a deacon, as first bishop to that country.
So far the story is more or less according to the old records.
The *Encyclopedia Britannica* carries on the tale, but on
thinner ice : Failing in his mission in Ireland, Palladius is
said to have retired 'to the land of the Picts in North Britain'
where he worked as a missionary and ultimately died. Local
tradition now steps in : Palladius on his retiral from Ireland
came to the Den of Moness in A.D. 469, where he took up his
abode and built a cell from which he attended to the spiritual
wants of the people in the district ; a hamlet grew up in the
neighbourhood of the ecclesiastical site, and so Aberfeldy was
born. His cell is said to have been in a field, still known as
'Raghair-na-h-eaglais,' or 'Field of the Church'—the low-
lying field on the Moness side of the burn, the lower part of
which is cut through by the embankment which carries the
main road to Crieff just beyond the bridge.

In view of the legend Palladius has been canonised in the
minds of the people and adopted as Patron Saint of Aberfeldy,
though, and this is unusual, his 'Day' in the Calendar, 6th July,
has never been commemorated by any local 'Fair,' (The
'Fair' or 'Festival,' for this was the original meaning of the
term, was always held on the Saint's 'Day' and named after
him). (*A*)

By those who hold to this legend it is stated that his name,
'Peallaidh' in Gaelic, persists in the old name of the Moness
Burn, 'the Faldy,' sometimes 'Paldy,' and in 'Aberfeldy,'
Gaelic 'Aber' or 'Obar Faldy' 'At or near the mouth of the
Faldy,' or Gaelic 'Obair Pheallaidh' 'the work of Peallaidh.'
('Pheallaidh' is the genitive or possessive form of 'Peallaidh,')

*   *   *   *   *   *

There is another claimant for 'Aberfeldy honours' however,
and thereby hangs a tale which, with possibly an air of greater

probability about it, has to be told : Long ago when people were more credulous than they are now, the gorge of the Moness Burn was believed to be the abode of two 'urisks' ; one, Peallaidh an Spuit—Peallaidh of the Spout — was said to have frequented the region of the Upper Fall, and the other, Brunaidh an Easain, the region of the Lower Fall. These two urisks used to enter the houses of Aberfeldy at night and play tricks on the inmates. It is the first mentioned of these whose claims to have given his name to Aberfeldy contest those of St. Palladius.

For the benefit of the uninformed a word or two about urisks in general may not come amiss here. According to Macalpine's Gaelic Dictionary 'uruisg' (Anglicised form 'urisk') in Perthshire signifies 'hobgoblin'. The Gaelic 'uisg' 'water' gives the clue, for the urisks were believed to be supernatural beings who haunted ravines, waterfalls, lonely hill lochs, and, in some cases, fords, etc., where people had to pass going to or from markets and fairs. The urisk, though occasionally reported to have been seen by others, was as a rule visible only to those who had the second sight. In habit the urisk, bigger and stronger than an ordinary mortal and of a rougher aspect, seems to have combined the qualities of a man and a spirit and, though generally preferring solitude, was wont at the end of harvest time to hover about farmyards, meal mills, cow sheds, etc. In return for kindnesses such as offerings of milk and so on the urisk would often prove helpful by way of performing arduous duties in and around the farm but, on the other hand, if treated with neglect or disrespect, was liable to become wantonly mischievous. To prevent dogs and cats from stealing the milk offering, etc., it was customary to chalk a ring of weird design round the bowl.

Such a being then was Peallaidh an Spuit and, in view of the fact that other urisks in the district (though outside the scope of this Account) have left their names attached to the burns the recesses of which they used to frequent—*e.g.*, Paderlan of 'Allt Paderlan,' 'the burn of Paderlan' near Fearnan —his claim to have given his to the Moness Burn and Aberfeldy cannot be ignored.

Incidentally, there has been referred to in old guidebooks a rock in the Den of Moness called 'Caisteall Pheallaidh.' Its exact location seems to be uncertain now ; it might commemorate either the Saint or the urisk.

How Peallaidh an Spuit came ultimately to forsake his old haunts is told in a tradition of Lochtayside : Appparently he and his brother urisks in the surrounding parts were wont to forgather in an old sheep-house on the farm of Callelochan, on the south side of Loch Tay between Acharn and Ardtalnaig. At these meetings Peallaidh acted as tyler or doorkeeper and, when all had been recognised and admitted, the Brethren proceeded to business. On one occasion a local shepherd, getting wind of a projected meeting and being anxious to see what transpired, concealed himself in the sheep-house beforehand. Disappointed, however, to find that the discussion was in a language unknown to him, he made a slight movement in order to see better what was going on. In doing so he betrayed his presence by upsetting a shearing-stool ; thoroughly startled, the urisks fled helter-skelter through the door and vanished from the district for ever.

*   *   *   *   *   *

The spelling of the name 'Aberfeldy' is now stabilised probably for all time, but this has not always been so. The earliest instance which I have been able to trace of the present form occurs in the Taymouth Estates Accounts, 1781 ; prior to this date, from 1771 when the Breadalbanes took over most of the town, the usual form was 'Aberfaldy.'

It would seem that the first mention in written records of the town, or hamlet as it was then, as a definite place with a name of its own, is in a Charter of about 1296 (to be referred to later), the spelling given being 'Abyrfeally' or 'Abyrpheallaidh.' Some of the other early spellings, as given in *The Red Book of Grantully* (by W. Fraser, 1868), are as follows :

1. In the Charter of the Lands of Garnetully (Grantully), Kiltullyth (Cultullich), and Abirfally (Aberfeldy), granted to Alexander Stewart (or Steuart) by the Earl of Douglas, 30th March, 1414.
2. In papers dated 15th March, 1525 —'Obbrefeally,'
3. In papers dated 5th July, 1525 —'Obbirfeally,'
4. In papers dated 14th May, 1526 —'Abirfealdy,'
5. In a Charter by Queen Mary in favour of William Stewart, the lands of 'Abirfaldy,' dated 2nd January, 1545.
6. In another Charter by Queen Mary, dated 22nd April, 1552, 'Abirfeldy,' and also 'Abirfeldye.'

It is only right to state at this point in connection with the origin of the name that the old name of the Moness Burn, 'Paldy' or 'Faldy', has been taken by some to have nothing to do with either Palladius or Peallaidh an Spuit but to mean 'the burn of the pools,' of which there are very many in its course ; 'Aberfeldy' would then come to mean simply 'at the mouth of the burn of pools.'

Before passing on from this vexed question however it may be worth noting the following : According to Duncan Campbell in *The Book of Garth and Fortingall* tradition has it that, long ago and before the time of St. Columba and written records, three 'goblin saints'—'uruisgean'—came to Glenlyon. One of these, Peallaidh by name, had his Glen headquarters on the mountainside above Slatich in a sheiling still known as 'Ruidhe Pheallaidh,' and, at the highest point of the Rock of Craigeanie, pressed his foot and left the imprint which is known as the Footprint of St. Palladius to this day. According to the same tradition he founded Aberfeldy and gave it his name. It would seem interesting to speculate whether Peallaidh the Saint of Aberfeldy and Glenlyon and Peallaidh the urisk of the Den of Moness were not one and the same individual.

* * * * * *

The word 'Moness' means either 'waterfall foot' or 'den foot' according to the meaning taken from the final syllable 'eas.'

In Gaelic, in general, 'eas' signifies 'waterfall' but, in this district, it is usually taken to mean 'den' or 'narrow valley.' The first syllable derives from the Gaelic 'bun,' 'foot,' the 'm' being due to ellipsis in the phrase 'i mbun easa.' In *Bleau's Atlas*, based on Timothy Pont's Surveys, (1654) Moness is spelt 'Buness.' The late Rev. John MacLean suggested the derivation 'Monadh-n-eas,' the 'Hill of the Waterfall,' but that just given is probably more likely to be the true one.

Moness House, which is nearby and which during the 1939-45 War served as a hostel for school children evacuated from Glasgow and now functions as an hotel, was originally the mansion of the Flemyngs, Barons of Moness, a family who held land on the east side of the burn for 300 years. At the end of this period the line ran out in a female whose son had perforce of debts to sell the property, retaining his patrimony of Killiechassie which in turn however came to be sold in the next generation. The Flemyngs then disappeared entirely from the district, leaving not a sign behind them but their sculptured coat of arms, minus their somewhat boastful motto LAT THE DEID SCHAW (Let the Deed Show), which is to be seen high up on the south-east wall of the house below a stone bearing the initials R.S.F. and Æ.F. over the date 1753, and one or two names on tombstones in the old burial ground by the roadside in Killiechassie.

Though the Flemyngs are now practically forgotten in the district, time was when they played their part in the activities of their period here and elsewhere. The earliest references which I have been able to trace, however, go back only to about the middle of the term of their lairdship of Moness. Two concern the then laird, Alexander Flemyng, the first with regard to the safeguarding of his own life and the second with regard to the disposal of the life of another :

1. Jan. 12., 1607 : Petition by Alexander Flemming of Moness and John dubh Kessan, his servant, for a summons against John dubh McKeane and Thomas John McEwenson who have on several occasions lain in wait for their slaughter —etc.

Moness House.

2. In *Pitcairn's Criminal Trials* Alexander Flemyng of Moness is mentioned as one of the Atholl lairds amongst the members on the assize at a murder trial in which Alastair Stewart McGillichallum was sentenced 'to be tane to the Mercat Croce of Edinburgh and their to be hangit vpoun ane gibbet quhill he be deid—' etc.

In 1622 one of the family, a young son possibly ! seems to have been had up for poaching : November 1622. One of a number of persons who were proceeded against for having worn hagbuts and pistolets and shot wildfowl and venison was 'Robert Flemming apparent of Moness.'

In 1685 another 'Robert Fyleming' of Moness was Governor of Inverary Castle.

In a letter from Lord Nairne to the Duke of Atholl, dated 29th September, 1707, the Laird of Moness is referred to. As this letter is amusing, part of it is worth quoting : "I am very well, I thank God, after our Highland progress, but if I were not you should have heard on't, for I would have sent to desire ye. favour of a visit from you, who's sight imediately curs ye. sick & made Brodalbane, whom Balgowan and Moness swears is past four score, hop down his green steps faster yn. we could follow."

Moness was sold for £9,600 to the Breadalbanes in 1787 in the time of John, the fourth Earl and first Marquis, and held by them for 134 years, till 1921 when the eastern part of their vast estates was broken up and came under the hammer. It is now in the hands of the Moness Estates Ltd., into which Company it was converted by the Russells, the real owners.

* * * * * *

In 1772 the Flemyngs caused to be built what was until recently the oldest building in Aberfeldy, Factory Buildings or, briefly, the Factory. Four years ago (1948) the Burgh boundary was extended, taking in Moness House which, on the evidence of the dated tablet, is older by 19 years.

The Factory, at the top of what is now Tayside Place, was set up by the Flemyngs to give living and working accommodation to a number of lace and muslin makers they brought over from Flanders to teach the local people the secrets of their craft, but apparently the venture was not a success—possibly the local people were not interested—and after a time the foreign workers were returned to their own country.

Till then cotton was unknown in the district and linen was in general use, the flax being grown locally and all stages of manufacture carried out on the spot. During the 18th century, largely owing to the improvement in communications wrought by General Wade's road-making, the market in England for flax raised and dressed and spun in Scotland was opened up, with beneficial effect on the general welfare and prosperity of Aberfeldy and district. Prior to this time there had been practically no outlet for linen made in the Perthshire Highlands but for more than one hundred years thereafter the management of flax was the most important industry in Aberfeldy. A larger crop was grown and profitable work was found not only for the wives and daughters of the cultivators but for cottar women and indeed for all women who chose to be industrious. During the quarter century between 1725 and 1750 flax was spun with the rock and reel and it was only about the time of Thomas Pennant's "Tour" in 1769 that spinning wheels were introduced. These machines were commonly called 'little wheels' to distinguish them from the large wheels that had long been in use for wool.

The bleaching of the Aberfeldy flax spinners was done in a field above what is now known as Bank Street and many of those engaged in the industry lived in a street which was built in 1775 on the site of the present Kenmore Street. The houses there were on short leases and the adjacent land was parcelled out into crofts for the lease-holders.

The Factory, though now two-storied with access to the upper storey dwellings by the original outside stone stairs, at first showed three stories, the ground floor containing the looms of the lace makers from Flanders, the next above their living quarters, and the top a large loft. The bleach-fields attached to the Factory were where Market Street now is.

About this time there was in operation a venture called The Moness Manufacturing Company ; whether this company had any connection with the Flemish lace makers is not clear and little seems to be known about it, the only direct reference to it extant apparently being in the form of an entry which was afterwards found in a ledger that had belonged to an Alexander Stewart, a merchant of that time, but Dr. Garnett, who visited the district in the latter part of the 1700's, wrote of "a considerable muslin manufacture carried on by some Glasgow merchants ;" it is possible though not certain that he was referring to this Company.

After the departure of the Flanders lace makers the top storey of the Factory was used by the town's folk as a dance hall, etc., and was the only one then available, whilst the ground floor, divested of its looms, was converted for use as dwelling houses. This was in the early 1800's. In 1890 further reconstruction took place, the ceilings of the middle floor being raised 18 inches. The level of the old ceilings is still indicated by markings on some of the walls; the thickness of the walls, by the way, is noteworthy.

* * * * * *

Now the flax industry is dead, and wool, which used to be spun and woven in many of the cottages, is worked only in the Breadalbane Woollen (Tweed) Mills though, in one or two of the older houses, the thud of the hand loom was still to be heard by the passer by well on into the last quarter of last century, in fact well on into my own time.

The Breadalbane Woollen Mills (Messrs. P. & J. Haggart) are worthy of inspection for here the visitor may see wool in all stages of manufacture, from the raw as it comes from the sheep's back to the finished article, tweed or tartan, ready for the tailor. In the lower of the two mills some of the old wooden hand looms are still preserved and, though now more or less museum pieces replaced (though only a few years ago) by modern machinery, they can still function and do very fine work indeed. This building, situated on the west side of the Moness Burn almost directly opposite the Factory used to be known as the Dyer's Mill. It was approached from the east at a point just riverward of the northern end of the Factory by a crazily constructed foot bridge the piers of which were discarded retorts from the neighbouring gasworks. This bridge, called the Dyer's Bridge, finally becoming unsafe, was removed several years after the erection of the Alma Bridge a few yards upstream. The Dyer's Bridge had two alternative titles of obvious significance, the Lovers' Brig and the Trysting Brig.

The Dyer's Mill was run latterly by an Alexander MacDonald known in his time as The Dyer, for many years a manufacturer of tweeds and blankets. In addition to the mill under mention he ran a second, in which the washing and dyeing of the wool was done, in a block of houses now called Tayside Cottages a little way further down and on the opposite side of the burn. This second and older mill, built about 1804, was in that part of the block which backs on to the golf course and, in a sketch in my possession dating from about the middle of last century, is named simply 'the Dyeworks.' It's wheel, of the under-driven type, was inside the building, power being supplied by water carried from the upper mill via first a tunnel under the burn and then by an open channel running down through ground now occupied by the gardens of the houses on the west side of Tayside Place. The effluent lade as it flows from behind the building towards the river now serves only as a golfers' 'hazard.'

Though the last 'Dyer' MacDonald did not die until 1882, for some years prior to 1880 the mills were worked by a Mr Walker, but in 1880 the Haggarts (Messrs. P. & J.), then of Keltneyburn Woollen Mills, had already acquired the un-expired portion of the lease in order to be nearer the rail-head and by 1890 had moved their entire business to the Aberfeldy premises, which they enlarged. They quickly built up an extensive business with a world wide reputation for tweeds and tartans of a very high quality, and have had and have as patrons the late Queen Alexandra, King Edward, King George V and Queen Mary, King George VI and Queen Elizabeth (now the Queen Mother), and other members of the Royal Family—by Royal Appointments dating back to 1899 when Queen Alexandra was Princess of Wales.

In 1899 they moved their show-rooms from rather cramped premises in Bank Street to a fine new building in Dunkeld Street. The present proprietor of the firm, which dates its foundation back to 1801, is ex-Provost James D. Haggart, O.B.E., C.B.E., J.P., past President of the Royal Warrant Holders Association, etc.

The mill in Tayside Cottages was given up by the Haggarts but near by, in Mill Street, a lint mill, was taken over by them and rebuilt to suit the purposes of their trade. Here the wool is washed and dyed before being taken to the lower mill to be carded, spun, and woven.

* * * * * *

Mill Street, incidentally, owes its name not to the woollen mill nor to a sawmill which operated close by but to a meal mill which at one time stood almost on the site of the present one just behind the shops on the north side of Bank Street. In times gone by it was a practice for charitable people to put meal into bags which were hung for the purpose outside the old mill, as outside others elsewhere in the country, for the benefit of the poor. In 1796 the emolument of the miller in Aberfeldy, one Hugh Cameron, was 'a lippie of meal run from the mill's eye.' (A lippie was an old Scots dry measure equal to $\frac{1}{4}$ peck). He also got a mutton ham from every tenant, which they called Christmas dues or 'Bonnag.' Upon these terms he was 'obliged to buy mill-stones and keep in proper repair all the machinery upon his own proper charges.' The present meal mill itself is not modern as buildings in Aberfeldy go, for, on a gable facing the burn, until it was concealed by a brick extension erected during improvements within the past year or two, could be seen carved the date 1826. Inside the mill the date is repeated and may still be read.

As a point of interest it may be noted that the Alma Bridge, when first built (round about 1900), was an all-concrete erection. Apparently faultily constructed, it collapsed shortly after it was opened for traffic and was replaced by the present iron girder structure, the only parts of the original bridge now remaining being the two ends on which the girders rest. The job was under contract and the architect (Mr William Bell, who was also Burgh Surveyor) found himself between £300 and £400 out of pocket by the time it was completed.

The roadway leading from this bridge to the higher level of Taybridge Terrace runs along an artificial embankment which was gradually raised by the simple expedient of dumping a lot of the town rubbish.

Power is supplied to the Woollen Mills and the Meal Mill by water conveyed from the Moness Burn higher up by a lade which at one point passes under Bank Street near the top of Mill Street. In the early 1870's a yacht (like the bridge, named 'Alma' after the then Marchioness of Breadalbane), while being towed by traction engine from Glasgow, whither it had been brought by sea from the Isle of Wight, broke through the road surface at this point and lay there, as it were, shipwrecked in the middle of the town for the better part of a week before it could be jacked up and taken the remainder of its journey to Loch Tay. It had arrived from the south the preceding evening and spent the night 'at anchor' in The Square, an object of such interest to the townsfolk that many of them turned out to see its early morning departure. After its 'wreck' the operations set afoot to get it back on an even keel and under way were keenly watched and when ultimately it was safely out of the town on the final lap of its long overland journey the people of Kenmore Street sighed in relief, for a repetition of the acci-

"Shipwreck" — Yacht 'Alma' — in Bank Street. 1873.

dent in their narrower thoroughfare might have proved a serious matter. As it was, the salvage was not carried out entirely without incident for one of the three stout tree trunks, which had been set up in the form of a tripod to carry the lifting tackle, snapped under the strain and, shooting as from a catapult, crashed through the window of a shop on the south side of the street, narrowly missing the shopkeeper, Mr Alexander Robertson, who fortunately was stooping down at the the time and so escaped injury, if not worse. Mr Alexander Robertson was a member of the firm of Messrs. W. & A. Robertson who built the large business premises on the east side of The Square in 1881, a firm whose name, shortened usually to simply "W. & A's", was almost a household word in Aberfeldy and district for over half a century.

* * * * * *

Opposite the upper of the two woollen mills the left bank of the burn is seen to be faced with a concrete wall extending for about 100 yards. The average annual rainfall in Aberfeldy over the last 44 years is 37.4 inches, *i.e.*, a monthly average of 3.11 inches, that for the month of June being 2.10, but in the great storm of 24th June, 1935, which wrought the damage which called for the erection of this embankment, 4.25 inches fell in the course of about 6 hours (over 400 tons of water per acre!)

Of this phenomenal fall the following account appeared in *British Rainfall*. 1935 : "At about 1h. 30 m. on the 24th the first drops of rain commenced to fall. Soon after thunder and lightning commenced and the rain got heavy. The thunder and lightning continued till about 5h. 30m. and were pretty incessant and very near. The heaviest of the rain fell by 5h. 30m. and subsequently eased off gradually although it did not actually stop until just after 8h. The flooding in Aberfeldy was due to the extraordinary rise of the Moness Burn which flows through the centre of the town. In the town it tore down one of its banks and carried away for about thirty yards throughout its whole width one of the roads—"

(Mill Street). "—The bank was cut up to such an extent that about 100 yards of it have had to be built up with concrete facing and about 600 loads of stone, etc., were required to fill in the space behind the new wall. The bank opposite was partly undermined. Lower down where the burn runs through level ground to join the Tay an iron girder bridge—" (the Alma Bridge) "—with a normal level of about 5 or 6 feet above the water was submerged, but this was partly owing to trees, etc., brought down by the flood and damming the water back. At this point much of the water was diverted from the bed of the burn and flowed into nearby houses—" (Factory Buildings) "—which were rendered uninhabitable for some weeks. A considerable sized wooden bridge further down the burn—" (a wooden bridge which occupied the site now occupied by the more substantial one in the golf course) "—was swept into the Tay and carried some 5 or 6 miles downstream. One or two other hill streams were also affected, but, beyond altering the appearance of their beds and bringing down trees and rocks there was little damage."

Since the concrete facing was set up the burn has dug, and is still digging a trench for itself along the base of the wall to the extent almost of undermining it. Trouble would appear to be brewing in the near future but, at the time of writing, treatment in advance seems to be nobody's business.

Whether the bank that was torn down by the spate was one of those which the fourth Earl of Breadalbane caused to be set up is not certain now, but the following items taken from the Estates Accounts for the years 1788/89 and 1789/90 are of interest :—
"Planting the Den of Moness   £30 9 0"
"To Munro and McIsack for building the dyke
on both sides of the burn at Aberfeldy   £182 16 6"
Paving of the water channel below the bridge connecting Bank Street with Bridgend was carried out about the same time, but there is nothing to indicate that the cost was included in the "£182 16 6!"

(It may be noted that the McIsacks or McIsaacs are entitled to wear the Macdonald tartan).

BLACK STREET — NOW BURNSIDE.

Down the opposite side of the burn from Mill Street runs Burnside, the old name of which was Black Street. Up to 1874/75 a complete row of single-storied thatched cottages extended here right down from behind the back of the Breadalbane Hotel old stables, now a garage, almost to the Factory. All but one of these faced the burn and were on the east side of the road, the odd one, standing between the road and the burn where Achnacarry now stands, faced south; here, in my young days, dwelt an old couple known to everyone as 'Cherry Jock' and 'Cherry Jean'. There were one or two heavy-cropping cherry trees in their garden and, in season, no child with a taste for this fruit was turned away empty handed! During the last quarter of the century these cottages were all cleared away, the last two to go, in 1896, being the one which stood where Annesley Cottage now is, and Cherry Jock's.

* * * * * *

From near the top of Burnside a short street, which oddly enough bears no name, strikes off to pass behind the garage to enter The Square between, on the right, the Commercial Bank Buildings (dating from 1886) and, on the left, the Congregational or Independent Church the Foundation Stone of which was laid on 28th August, 1877, by The Hon. Arthur Kinnaird, M.P., and The Rev. John Kennedy, D.D., the so-called Nonconformist Bishop of Stepney (London) who was a native of Aberfeldy. The Stone, bearing an inscription to this effect, is in the wall of the church by the doorway.

The 160th anniversary of the formation of the Independent Church in Aberfeldy was celebrated on 6th August, 1950. The formation in 1790 was the result of the evangelistic labours of the Haldane Brothers, two Scottish missionaries who lived during the latter half of the 18th century and the first half of the 19th. J. A. Haldane, the younger of the two, was ordained pastor of a large Independent congregation in Edinburgh, their meeting place to begin with being a circus. This was the first Congregational Church known by that name in Scotland. Aberfeldy's was the second.

In connection with the building of the predecessor of the church in the Square, the old Chapel in Chapel Street, the following note appeared in the *Sunday Dispatch*, 11th November, 1934 : "By many in the 19th century the wearing of the kilt suggested a lack of genuine religion. At Aberfeldy a chapel was being built. Dr John Kennedy persuaded the carpenter to don the trews whilst at work on the sacred building. The carpenter wore the trews for one day only, the excuse being that the trousers made the wearer feel cold!"

The journalist responsible for this story would seem not to have verified his facts. Dr Kennedy, whose age at the time of the erection of the Chapel was only seven, used to tell it of his father, the Rev. James Kennedy. Dr Kennedy, in his booklet *Old Highland Days*, states that in his young days practically no one wore the kilt, the carpenter, a man named M'Intyre, being one of the few exceptions.

Dr Kennedy, a son of the manse where his father was Aberfeldy's first Congregational minister, was born in 1813 and spent the first twelve years of his life here, and also, while a student at Aberdeen University, some time as tutor at Moness to the son of Campbell of Glenorchy, who had retired there from London. His reminiscences were published by one of his sons, Howard Angus Kennedy, after his death in 1900.

The church in The Square was built to take the place of the old Chapel, just mentioned, which on its erection gave its name to Chapel Street ; before this the street was known as Factory Street. This old Chapel still stands on the right half way down from The Square to the Factory and serves as a store belonging to a business firm whose main premises occupy buildings set up in 1881 on the east side of The Square. Some time after it ceased to be used as a place of worship a well was sunk close by, the water being used in the manufacture of aerated and mineral waters.

It was the first church of any denomination to be built in Aberfeldy and could accommodate between three and four

OLD INDEPENDENT CHAPEL IN CHAPEL STREET IN 1856 (*From a drawing*).

INDEPENDENT MANSE, THE SQUARE, IN 1856 (*From a drawing*).

hundred persons. Dating from 1820, it occupies a site granted by the then Earl of Breadalbane who, for some reason or other, had held out for a considerable time against a building under this denomination being set up in the town. In the early days the "Independents," or "Missioners" as they were called at that time, met with many difficulties and much opposition in the country, it being even said that on some estates the lairds threatened with eviction farmers who dared to associate themselves with the sect. Lord Breadalbane himself appeared to share in this prejudice and when he finally granted the site he stated that he was moved to do so as he had "received an excellent character of Mr Kennedy and a good account of his people." In addition to granting the site he promised fifty pounds worth of wood towards the building of the church.

The Rev. James Kennedy came to Aberfeldy in 1806 and for the first few years of his ministry his chapel was but an apartment in a private house. When his early application to Breadalbane for a site on which to erect a church was refused a house in The Square was acquired (1810) and the congregation met in a ground floor room reserved for the purpose. It was a modest enough house but about the best in the town at the time. On occasion, when the numbers who turned up for worship were beyond the capacity of this room and the weather was suitable the meeting adjourned to The Square. The first part of the service was in English and the second, and longer, in Gaelic ; there was no break between the two addresses and the session sometimes went on for so long as three hours. This building, the upper storey of which was occupied as a manse by the minister, was removed to make way for the new church of which, as stated, the Foundation Stone was laid in 1877, the work of erection being completed the following year. The last service in the old Chapel was held on 28th July, 1878.

In July 1859 a native of Aberfeldy then in business in Glasgow —John Anderson, founder of the Glasgow Polytechnic—was the means of bringing Charles Haddon Spurgeon to address a meeting in the Chapel in Chapel Street but it seems that the coming of the great preacher was not adequately announced owing to the town crier, or bellman, who could not read, giving out the notice from memory in an almost incomprehensible mixture of Gaelic and English, and very few people turned out. This came as a great shock to Spurgeon who, though as yet a young man of 25, had been addressing audiences of thousands in Glasgow, Edinburgh, and elsewhere, and he began his discourse by stating that he was not in the habit of addressing so few people. (My informant had this from one who was present at the meeting).

There was no Established Church of Scotland building in the town in these days ; the people though belonging to two parishes, Dull and Logierait, were three miles distant from the church of the former and nine from that of the latter ; the nearest, though not their own, was one mile distant, at Weem.

When in 1843 the Disruption split the Church from top to bottom and what became known as the Free Church of Scotland broke away, John, the Second Marquis of Breadalbane, himself an ardent Dissenter, granted lands for the erection of a Free Church in Breadalbane Villas, as Taybridge Road was then called, and a manse in the Crieff Road. The Foundation Stone of the Church was laid by him on 13th November, 1843 and, during the time taken in building, the congregation met for communion, etc., in a field west of Tomghiubhais—a field which has served various purposes in its day, as will be told later—and only about a quarter of a century ago there passed away in Aberfeldy an old women who had been baptised there.

In 1900 the original Free Church (which I shall refer to as Free Church A.) was itself in a state of upheaval, for this year marked the union of the Free and United Presbyterian Churches of Scotland. Though the latter Church had neither place of worship or following in Aberfeldy a small minority of members of the former stood out against the Union and carried on under the old name (which I shall distinguish as Free Church B.).

To begin with their claim to the local church buildings and property seemed just, and those who supported the new combined Church, the United Free Church of Scotland as it was called, were evicted on a House of Lords decision, 4th August, 1904, and met for service in the Town Hall. Ultimately the Kirk Commission which was set up under the Earl of Elgin to adjudicate on cases throughout the country awarded the buildings, etc., to the United Free and in August 1906 the Free Church B. folk in turn found themselves roofless. Nothing daunted however, and while carrying on in the Town Hall as the United Free had done before them, they set about providing a church for themselves. This building, on the right near the top of Chapel Street, was opened for public worship on 8th September 1907, free of debt, the money being raised by purely local effort.

It is interesting to note that the United Free Church congregation in Aberfeldy was the second in Scotland to be evicted from and the first to be re-instated in the local pre-existing Free Church A. buildings, and that the local Free Church B. adherents were the first in the country to erect for themselves a new building as a result of the decisions of the Kirk Commission.

Further evidence of these stirring times is to be found in Aberfeldy. Following the decision of the Commission, whereby the objectors to the Union in Glenlyon continued possession of the church and manse at Cambusvrachan, the members of the old congregation who went with the Union were turned out. They thereupon erected for themselves a substantial wood and iron church on a site by the river near the Lyon bridge at Cambusvrachan. This building, with the coming of the union of the United Free and Established Churches in 1929 and in view of the proximity of the existing Parish Church at Innerwick, became redundant and was sold for use as a store, etc., to an Aberfeldy contractor who re-erected it behind Breadalbane Terrace, where it still stands.

The Established Church of Scotland in the Crieff Road, dedicated 31st August, 1884, and originally a Chapel of Ease, was disjoined from the parishes of Dull and Logierait and became a *quoad sacra* Parish Church on 19th March, 1897. When the union of the Established and United Free Churches took place in 1929 the local churches assumed the names of St. Andrew's Established Church (in the Crieff Road) and Breadalbane Established Church respectively. To begin with the congregations carried on each with the minister then officiating but, in 1951, after the retiral of one incumbent and the death of the other, they came together and now one minister holds the double charge and conducts services in the two buildings on alternate Sundays.

When I was a boy the Thursday before Sacrament Sunday (in February and July) was observed as Fast Day, or Little Sunday as it was sometimes called, and the school and all places of business were closed ; church services were held in the forenoon and the evening. Preparatory service was held at 11 a.m. on the Saturday, and Thanksgiving service on the Monday following.

The wood and iron Roman Catholic Chapel in Home Street, 'Our Lady of Good Counsel,' was built by the Marquis of Bute a year or two after the Established Church was built in the Crieff Road, the officiating priest being resident in Strathtay, where he also conducts service in the 'Church of the Holy Cross' ('*Santa Croce*'). A number of years ago the short spire of the Aberfeldy Chapel was blown down ; it has never been replaced.

St. Margaret's Scottish Episcopal Church in Kenmore Street dates from 1906, the officiating clergyman, resident in Aberfeldy, having the additional charge of the Scottish Episcopal Church in Strathtay.

The Plymouth Brethren, a company with a small following in the town, have their Meeting Room in a house at the top of Chapel Street. The local branch was founded in 1896.

For a period of years in the 19th century Baptist services were held in a barn belonging to a blacksmith in Mill Street, the officiating clergyman being the Baptist minister from Milton Eonan. There is now no Baptist ministry in Glenlyon.

It may be remarked that, whatever it was in the past, Aberfeldy is now well 'churched.' It is, but I fear that the religious fervour which possessed our forebears of the early 1800's, and was not to be measured by the number of churches in their midst, is at the present time a waning force.

When the Independent or as it is now called the Congregational Church was built on the site of the old manse and meeting house in The Square the successive ministers had no fixed 'official' residence for about thirty years till the present manse was acquired near the west end and on the north side of Kenmore Street almost opposite one of the many old toll-houses which used to dot the countryside until de-moted in 1878 under the Roads and Bridges (Scotland) Act.

* * * * * *

This old toll-house, known locally as the West Toll, with its bow window projecting into the footway and commanding the approaches from both directions, is now called The Armoury having at one time served as Headquarters of the Aberfeldy (A) Company of the 5th V.B.R.H. (Volunteer Battalion Royal Highlanders—The Black Watch). Behind it are the drill hall of the local branch of the Territorial Army and a miniature rifle range.

The 5th V.B.R.H., the "Volunteers" as they were popularly known, used to drill twice weekly in season, in the old Breadalbane Academy playground (now the Town Hall Yard) when in mufti, and in the Weem Park when in uniform.

Annually the Aberfeldy Company with the rest of the Battalion went under canvas for a spell and it is told that on one occasion, when in camp at Bolfracks, the men, possibly after too much of the wet canteen the night before, failed to respond to the reveille. Sir Robert Menzies, their colonel at at the time, felt that this could not be allowed to pass so he got some of his own men to bring secretly one of the 12-pounders from his battery at Castle Menzies and, next morning, personally supervised its loading and firing. There was a deafening report and in an instant 800 startled men were out of their tents with nothing on but their shirts. A collie dog that was looking on got such a fright that it swam the river and, it is said, never stopped running till it got to Logierait, and a rabbit trapper working ten miles away declared that he heard the noise distinctly!

When in 1906 the Volunteers were being fitted into the new Territorial Army a proposal was made that the 5th V.B.R.H. should be converted into a Cyclist Corps. This was bitterly opposed by the men concerned and the proposal was dropped. As one of them said at the time, "If I am to be killed I would rather be shot in my kilt than knocked off a bicycle!"

Until the time of the 1939/45 War two other toll-houses would have come within the ambit of this Account, one, known as the East Toll, on the Dunkeld Road on the right as one goes east about a quarter of a mile out of the town some 20 paces beyond the further end of the stone bulwark where the river approaches the road, and the other at the point of junction between the road which runs from east to west from Strathtay to Coshieville and that going north across the valley from Wade's Taybridge. The Weem Toll, as this latter is called, is still standing—and lived in—a menace to the fast moving traffic of the present day, but the other has vanished.

It is told how once a keeper of the Weem Toll was urgently summoned from bed by a man who appeared to be in a violent hurry. Not taking time to slip on some clothes he hastened out and opened the gate. The traveller, without waiting to pay the fee, immediately whipped up his horse and sped on his way to Aberfeldy. Not to be beaten the keeper, barefooted and clad only in his shirt, gave chase and, catching up with the delinquent on the slope of Taybridge where the horse had slowed down to a walk, exacted his dues—and went home to bed !

The East Toll for some years before the 1939-45 War stood tenantless and crumbling to ruin and when the war came it was found to be a convenient object on which to stage a Civil Defence practice operation. Most of the stones of which it was constructed were removed a year or two later. This wrote *finis* to a long life and now only the flagstone that lay outside the door, the weed-covered old garden clearing, and a few stones scattered about remain to mark the site. Within the past months an attempt to reclaim part of the old garden has been made by a family of the tinker-tramp class who, for the time being at all events, have come to anchor in a wooden hut erected on the knoll that rises between the road and the railway at this point.

On the small platform at the Aberfeldy end of the bulwark stood for some years a stone blockhouse which was built during the 1939-45 War as an anti-German-invasion precaution.

* * * * * *

East of the bulwark the road crosses the Borlick Burn or Pitilie Burn as it is sometimes called ('Pittiely' on the Ordnance Map) and ascends about 200 yards to pass the Aberfeldy Cemetery. One of the first burials here, if not actually the first—that of a schoolboy—took place in 1893, the stone bearing this date standing with its back to the west wall about halfway along it in the direction of the river quite near the entrance gate.

When a suitable site for the proposed cemetery was being sought, the field west of Tomghiubhais was one of those suggested, but it was found that there was not sufficient depth of soil for the purpose. Before the present ground was acquired by the Aberfeldy Cemetery Company interments from the town took place in various churchyards in the surrounding district—Logierait, Pitcairn, Weem, Fortingall, and Kenmore. At the moment the question of the acquisition of further ground is under consideration.

Just opposite the cemetery, on the south side of the railway, in 1896 the erection of a large whisky distillery was commenced by Messrs. John Dewar & Sons, Ltd. ; it started operations in 1898. It now bears the name of A. & A. Crawford, Ltd., one of the firms, of which John Dewar's is another, of the big whisky combine known as the "D.C.L."—Distillers' Company Limited.

The ground occupied by the cemetery and the distillery used to be one of the town's Cow Parks. It was called the East Cow Park. In addition to this park there were other grazings set aside for the local cow population. These were necessary for at one time probably as many as 150 cows were owned and housed in Aberfeldy ; to-day, apart from those on the farms of Moness and Duntaylor recently brought within the burgh boundary, there is not one.

The other cow parks may be mentioned here in passing ; further reference will to them be made later :—
The West Cow Park : the Torr : and the 'Cour' and the East Park, west and east of the Moness Burn respectively where the golf course now is. The Cour is rarely referred to as such nowadays but in the name of a house, Courbank, overlooking it from Taybridge Terrace its memory is preserved. ('Cour,' Gaelic 'Cuir' 'curves,' *i.e.*, fields lying in the curve of the river). There was yet another park in use at one time by the local crofters, the Laichan, on the hill-slope south of the Crieff Road about ¾ mile from the town centre.

Rising to the south-east of the distillery and over-looking it is a wooded hillock called Tom Challtuinn—Hazel Mound— where fairies used to dance and revel on moonlight nights and whence they made their periodic visits to Creag Scriadlain. Creag Scriadlain ('the craig of crumbling slaty rock'), to the east of Farragon, was said to be the real home of the fairy folk in this part of the world. To the immediate east of this hillock lie the ruins of Tomchaldon or Tomchaldane, once a small hamlet of four or five cottages ; though now scarcely one stone stands on the top of another, only thirty or forty years ago several old people died in Aberfeldy who were born here. One of these, (1840-1913), was the late Mr Peter MacLaren, father-in-law of Mr James A. MacGregor. It is interesting to note that Mr MacLaren started his working life as a journeyman joiner at 16/- per week *and* no Saturday half-holiday !

A few yards riverward of the ruins of Tomchaldon there is an old lime kiln, one of the many dotted about the countryside and now derelict. The kiln at Tomchaldon, hardly discernible to-day, was one of the seven which were once operated within the area covered by this Account ; the other six will be noticed in due course, but all speak of the days when farmers requiring lime for their fields had to depend for supplies on their own endeavours. The output of these kilns was limited, not by the quantity of lime available, which was always ample in the district, but by the shortage of fuel. Prior to the 1700's lime did not appear to have been used as a soil dressing in Perthshire.

Access to the distillery is by means of a road which passes under the railway in company with the Borlick (or Pitilie) Burn and, leaving on the right the dam the water of which is used in the distillery for cooling purposes and supplying power, proceeds onwards up the hill to the farms of Borlick and Mains of Murthly.

Borlick long ago, like Murthly, was owned by the Steuarts of Grantully and, later, by the Menzieses of Weem. It is interesting to note in the Borlick Estate Accounts when Sir Robert Menzies was Laird that the change over from pounds Scots to pounds sterling took place between the times of the entries dated December 1762 and November 1763. The switch over led to some curious figures in the cash columns, noted particularly in the more carefully kept accounts from Murthly after the Breadalbanes took over both properties in 1771, *e.g.*, Cash received in 1773 was £67   2 11 and $\frac{8}{12}$ of a penny.

When the change took place Scots money was equal in value to only $\frac{1}{12}$ that of English of the same denomination, which, of course, explains the $\frac{1}{12}$ fractions appearing in accounts of the day.

Currency depreciation is no new thing in Scotland. In Bruce's time the shilling Scots stood level with the shilling English by but the time of the Accession of James VI it had fallen to $\frac{1}{4}$ and by the time of the Union still further to $\frac{1}{12}$, at which level it continued. During much of the period covered by these changes, however, money as such was scarcely known in the Highlands, most of what trading there was being by barter, with cattle as the main form of transportable wealth. It was almost inevitable from this that cattle raiding should go on on a large scale. In fact it did so to such an extent that it would seem to have been, in the lawless state of the country in the 16th and 17th centuries, almost the chief occupation of the people. In an attempt to check the traffic in stolen beasts bonds were taken from landowners who controlled the numerous ferries, including that at Aberfeldy which was on the line of one of the main drove roads from the north and west to the great Falkirk Trysts.

The name 'Borlick' ('Borlig' in an old map of 1763) is a form of 'Boreland' or 'Board Land,' in other words a home farm producing crops for the use of the laird. In an old statement of rentals, etc., the following lands were listed in the Barony of Borlick :—

Borlick	£22	6	1½	Mid Straid	£ 9	5	4
Piteily	£ 7	2	6	West Straid	£12	2	6½
Erichil	£14	17	0	Dundaie	£ 8	10	10
Croftdow	£ 5	8	10	Brucecroft	£ 6	3	9

It was in the neighbourhood of Borlick that, to quote from *The Highland Tay* by the late Rev. Hugh Macmillan, D.D., "the famous Andrea Ferrara—" of Belluno, Italy "—is said to have had his smithy in the 16th century. He made his splendid broadswords, which rivalled the blades of Damascus and Toledo, out of iron dug from the surrounding hills and smelted by the help of native birch woods ; and he tempered them with the water of the stream which had qualities for this purpose as rare as those of the Abana and the Tagus. The trademark of the swords made in Breadalbane by Andrea Ferrara has a St. Andrew's Cross and sometimes the hilt is composed entirely of St. Andrew's Crosses."

So wrote Dr Macmillan and so runs tradition, but unfortunately we live in an iconoclastic age when traditions as well as idols of the past are liable to be shattered, for modern research has shown that there is no authority whatever for supposing that Andrea Ferrara ever visited Scotland at all, far less that any of his swords were made here. It is true that his blades were greatly sought after in Scotland, but so they were in every country in Europe. The Scottish swords attributed to him are all broad-bladed transformed claymores ; at the sale at Taymouth in April 1922, at the time of the break-up of the eastern lands of Breadalbane, one of these swords fetched 19 guineas. In the old days these weapons were known as Andrew Ferraras ; thus, Sir Walter Scott writes in *Waverley* (Chap. I) "We'll put him in bail, boy ; old Andrew Ferrara shall lodge his security."

* * * * * *

The farm of Mains of Murthly at one time formed part of the small estate of Murthly (Gaelic, 'Mor Thulaich,' 'Great Tullich'), which for many years was an adjunct of the Cistercian Monastery which was founded and endowed at Coupar Angus by Malcolm IV in 1164, being granted to the monks there by Isabel, Countess of Atholl, so long ago as 2nd February, 1232. When the abbey lands became secularised the property passed through various hands and finally, via the Menzieses of Weem, to the third Earl of Breadalbane in the 1770's. It, with Borlick, was held by the Breadalbanes till 1921 when it was sold to the Russells along with Moness.

Prior to the alteration of parish boundaries in 1891 Murthly formed part of the parish of Weem, and was anciently known as a 'five pund land, of old extent, in the lordship of Coupar.'

In 1642 the mansionhouse and mill were both standing. This was in the time of the Campbells of Murthly, the first of whom, a son of James Campbell of Lawers and grandson of Sir Colin Campbell of Glenorchy, was John Campbell whose name appears as witness to several charters of dates prior to 1569 and who is known to have been alive in 1525. Robert, the 8th and last Campbell laird 'served as heir to his father, 9th March, 1666.'

The old possessions within it comprised (1) Burnfoot, (2) Tomchaldane, (3) Mains of Murthly, (4) Tominella, (5) Duntaggart, (6) Tombane, (7) Croftmarquis, (8) Byrecroft, and (9) Brae of Murthly. Most of these names are now obsolete and of some of the places that bore them scarcely a trace remains.

Burnfoot, as its name suggests, lay down near the junction of the Borlick Burn with the Tay. Only the oblong outline of the turf covered foundations of the walls of one of its buildings is to be seen now in the field between the Dunkeld Road and the railway, about 40 yards east of the Murthly Road.

(Across the main road from the site of Burnfoot, within the memory of the late Mr Donald MacCallum, there were still signs of an old wayside inn which once stood there ; Tigh-an-Seanair, 'the House of the Grandfather,' it was called).

Tomchaldane has already been noticed.

Mains of Murthly : This name is now applied to the farm as a whole. Near the upper boundary of the field directly behind the steading there is a large boulder, smoothed and rounded by the passage of the great glaciers of the Ice Ages, which shows on its upper surface several of those so-called 'cup-markings'—though they are more like shallow saucers than cups—which are so common in this part of the country and the significance of which is such a puzzle to archæologists. This boulder, estimated to weigh about 14 tons, is of coarsely granular diorite and would appear to have been transported by glacial action from a mountain range to the north-east of Glenlochay, 40 miles distant, where intrusive sheets and dykes of this mineral of considerable extent are found *in situ* among the crystalline schists. Travelled boulders of this type, known technically as 'erratics,' are not uncommon in districts over which glaciers have passed.

In the next field up the hill slope, at a few yards distance, is the site of Tominella ('the mound of the first ploughing').

Looking Westward from the Grantully Road.

Old Cottages at Boltachan, now derelict.

Here in the middle of last century stood a tiny hamlet and, though there is little trace of it to-day, the late Rev. John MacLean (born in Pitilie, 1829) used to tell how he had received his early schooling in a small schoolhouse near by. At that time there were twenty-four families living on the brae-face around here ; now there are only two farms—three if Pitilie be included.

Thomas Pennant in his *Tour in Scotland*, 1769, in writing of the habitations of the "Highlanders" on Lochtayside, states that they occur "not singly, but in small groupes, as if they loved society or clanship..........As the farms are very small it is common for four people to keep a plough between them, each furnishes a horse, and this is called a horse-gang." In these days, and even as late as 1813 in some parts of the country, the old Scottish plough was in general use with the four horses, or more often ponies, yoked abreast and led by a man walking backwards. According to the Rev. David Duff, Parish Minister of Kenmore, in the M.S. he prepared in 1837 for the *New Statistical Account* "the iron plough is becoming quite common with our tenants," the presumption from this being, of course, that at an earlier date wood was the material used.

In the few lines quoted above Pennant summarised the clachan or hamlet system and its communal character in the middle 1700's, but even then the change was beginning to show which was to have the result a century or so later of having in the country districts only considerable villages and isolated farms where hitherto almost every inhabited place was a cluster of dwellings inhabited by farmers and mechanics, together with cottars who maintained a precarious existence by working at what they could find to do.

Aberfeldy itself is merely one result of this change for, as will be told, it was at one time comprised of three (or four) hamlets, near, yet distinct from each other.

Only Boltachan and Tighchraggan on the other side of the valley are left now of the many clachans which in the past were dotted round Aberfeldy within the radius of one mile, and even these are not true hamlets in the old sense of the word. Certainly one may see there a few of the real old cottages, some inhabited, some derelict ; those still inhabited have been, as it were, 'revised and brought up to date' as far as conditions have allowed, one even being connected up with the electric mains. Formerly thatched, they are now, with the exception of one in Boltachan and one in Tighchraggan, roofed with slates or sheet metal—less picturesque, no doubt, but more serviceable.

But, to return to Tominella : This site is of further interest in that here are to be seen the well known cup-marked stones of Tominellow (as it is more often spelt nowadays) ; of these stones one shows upwards of forty cups, some of them very distinct.

*   *   *   *   *   *

From the Mains of Murthly the road continues as a rough track up the hill to Duntaggart, 'Dùn-an-t'sagairt' 'the priest's fort,' or, as oftener translated, 'the priest's hillock,' a name which might seem to suggest roots reaching deep into the past perhaps even to the days of the Cistercian monks who held Murthly so long ago.

The present house served at one time as the residence of the excise officer on duty at the neighbouring distillery at Pitilie, and was then commonly known to the people round about as The Exciseman's House. To its immediate east lie the scattered stones and crumbling ruins of yet another now vanished hamlet. The outlines of some old buildings may still be traced, but of the lime kiln which once stood near by practically nothing remains.
In the field immediately above Duntaggart is another fine specimen of glacially rounded rock.

The other names on the list—Tombane 'the white mound,' Croftmarquis 'Croit-Mharcais' 'the croft of Marcus or Mark,' Byrecroft, and Brae of Murthly—refer to sites outside the

REV. JOHN MacLEAN — PITILIE.

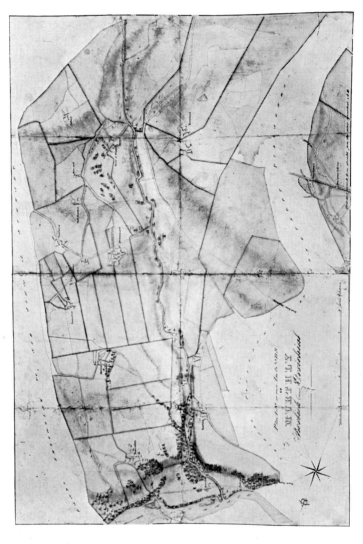

For Key to this Plan, See Opposite.

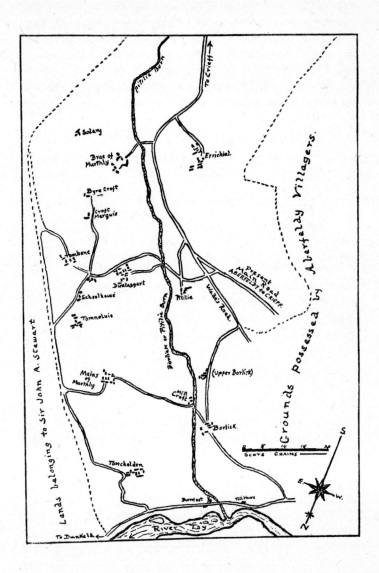

THE LANDS OF MURTHLY, BORLICK AND ERRICHIAL
IN THE EARLY PART OF LAST CENTURY, FROM AN OLD PLAN.
(*Spellings as in Original*).

range of this Account but they, together with those described, are shown on the accompanying Plan of the Lands of Murthly, Borlick, and Errichill, a Plan which dates from the time of Sir John A. Stewart 6th Baronet who was Laird of Grantully from 1827 to 1839. The old schoolhouse of Tominella (spelt 'Tomneluie' on the Plan) is also shown—on the central vertical fold about one inch from the top.

About 150 yards west of Duntaggart the road crosses the Borlick Burn where, beside a small cottage, stand the the ruins of the old Pitilie Distillery with its dam and lade, It is said that it was the knowledge that the water of this burn was suitable for the processes involved in whisky distilling that led the Dewars to build where they did lower down, but that, not long after, they found that water from the Tay was even more suitable, and for a time the necessary water was forced up by a ram pump sunk in the ground near the river bank. Burn water is now in use again. Pitilie distillery ceased operating about 15 years before Dewar's was built. In the *New Statistical Account*, 1845, it is stated that in active operation it 'distils annually over 6,000 gallons and pays about £1,320 duty.'

The malt used here was prepared at Borlick, in that building which backs to the farmhouse some twenty or thirty yards away. Here may still be seen the upstairs lath-and-plastered kiln room with the lower part of its wide funnel-shaped chimney-ventilator, and, downstairs, the outline of the now filled in pit into which the dried malt was shot and in which it was allowed to lie until ready for spreading on the specially prepared clay floor where in due course it began to sprout. Whether the final crushing process was undertaken here or elsewhere is not now clear. The construction of this clay floor must have been interesting to watch : First the clay was spread evenly over the area to be covered ; sheep were then driven over it slowly, to and fro, until it was tramped and packed to a hardness as of concrete ; simple, yet effectual. The Borlick floor is still where it was and as it used to be, and makes a good sound floor in the farm tractor house.

Upstairs beside the kiln room was the holy of holies ; the name, 'Malt Store No. 1,' may still be read on the old door which, though now dilapidated, must at one time have resembled the door of a strong-room with its wooden beam and two heavy locks. Into this room no man was permitted to pass unaccompanied, for the exciseman held one of the keys !

At one time the farmer at Borlick, an Alexander MacLean, was chief partner of the Pitilie Distillery business ; and that is why the malt kiln was at Borlick.

Just west of the distillery, on the site of yet another old clachan, is the farm of Pitilie—old spelling 'Pettaingle,' or 'Ingle's Piece' (of land), a spot where people were wont to light signal fires. At one time also it bore the Gaelic name 'Baile-na-Mòin' which means 'the town of peat.'

In a survey, dated 1862, Pitilie is marked as the site of a sawmill, but there is no sign of it now. In these days sawmills in this neighbourhood were permanent stone-built buildings ; to-day they are wooden erections and mainly mobile.

As already stated, the Rev. John MacLean was born here (in 1829). He was a recognised authority on the folk-lore and Natural History of the district, and also a great character possessed of a pawky sense of humour and with a fund of good stories which he told as he alone could tell them. Stories, too, gathered round his name, many of them no doubt apocryphal but some believed to be authentic ; here is one of the latter group : Once while waiting at Grantully Station for the Aberfeldy train he spied a porter about to kick on to the line the body of a dead bird. "No, no," he said to the man in his inimitable drawl, "No, no ; don't do that. Give me the bird and I'll take it home and give it a decent burial"—and the tiny body was duly consigned to the tail pocket of his long clerical coat. A week or ten days later he was again on the platform at Grantully, and was greeted by the porter, "Well, Mr MacLean, and did you give the bird a decent Christian burial ?" A look of puzzlement on the minister's face quickly gave place to one of horrified realisation, and his hand flew to his tail pocket, *"That's* where the awful smell's been coming from !"

* * * * * *

A hundred yards or so on from Pitilie a path strikes off to the right beside yet another old lime kiln, and, passing the Aberfeldy curling pond on the left, continues down along the line of General Wade's military road to the site of 'Tigh-na-leckan' or 'Tigh-na-leacain,' 'the house of the cheek or face of the brae' and then on to the Aberfeldy Cottage Hospital.

About seventy years ago the tenant farmer of Borlick was ill-advised enough to raise a stone wall across this road some 60 or 70 yards on from the old kiln. The outraged public tore it down the first night after its completion. Nothing was *said* by either party, but the wall was not re-erected ; instead, a gate, never locked, was set up ; this has been sufficient to prevent animals straying and at the same time does not interfere with the right-of-way.

180 yards from this gate, nearer Aberfeldy, almost exactly opposite the little entrance gate to the curling pond enclosure at its north-west corner there is an oldtime spring of very fine water the outflow of which, now much less than formerly, passes through a small culvert beneath the road. This culvert is surely one of the smallest of Wade's bridges—about 1 foot high by about $2\frac{1}{2}$ feet wide. An examination at either end shows that it is not built like other 'bridge-lets' over similar tiny streams round about—of flagstones laid flat—but is a properly built arch. The stones, owing to the smallness of the structure, look large for the job and the general impression derived is rather like that from the sight of a little boy dressed up in his father's clothes pretending to be a man !

There is now no trace of Tigh-na-leacain, bar possibly some signs of the old garden clearing, which is a pity for it was a picturesque old place, at one time an inn, and had semi-historic associations. It stood until about the beginning of the present

TIGH-NA-LEACAIN (*The barrow is of the type that was used for wheeling in Peats*).

century by the side of the path from the curling pond on a site exactly opposite that of the present Hawthorn Cottage. When it was demolished a rafter, black with age and smoke, was found bearing the date 1745. This relic is now in the Scottish National Museum of Antiquities in Edinburgh. A pretty story is told of one of its former occupants : During the Jacobite Rising in 1745 the wife of a soldier in Prince Charlie's ranks stood at her door to see the soldiers of the King (George II) go by. To one of the officers, fatigued by marching, she gave a glass of milk for which she refused payment of any kind, with the remark that some day her husband—an Adam Menzies— might be in sorer straits. Some time afterwards she learned that her husband was a prisoner in Carlisle, over 150 miles distant, and trudged all the way thither in the hope of being able to procure his release. Access to the prison was denied her and in her despair she was wandering round the walls, when she was recognised by the officer whom she had befriended in the Highlands. When he learned the facts of the case he used his influence successfully in her favour, and joyfully she led her husband homeward.

The old two-piece key of the inn is now in the possession of Mr Malcolm MacCallum, Dundee.

At this point a rough road strikes up the hill to join the main road to Crieff. Known very appropriately as the Stony Road, it was constructed long ago by the united labour of a number of Aberfeldy crofters as a means of getting their cows up to the Laichan grazing grounds in the neighbourhood of the Bulghan or Bulgan (pronounced 'Boolchan') quarries. These quarries, by the way, supplied most of the stone of which Aberfeldy was built before the now almost ubiquitous brick came into use in the district.

Alongside the Stony Road, to the east, stood for 35 years some of the steel trestles of an aerial ropeway for conveying road metal for the roads in the Highland District of the County from the basalt quarry above Gatehouse to Aberfeldy railway station ; the $\frac{7}{8}$ inch five miles long endless cable was one of the

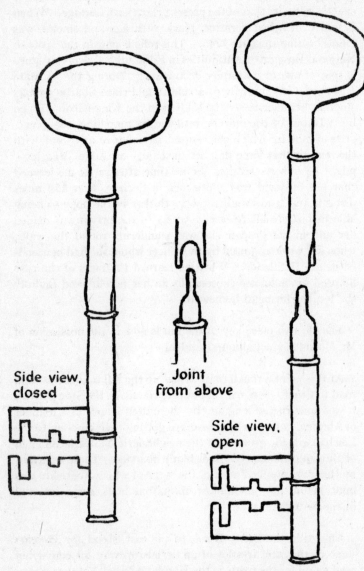

Side view, closed

Joint from above

Side view, open

TWO-PIECE KEY OF THE OLD INN AT TIGH-NA-LEACAIN.
(*Sketch by Mrs Malcolm MacCallum*).
LENGTH OF KEY CLOSED, 6.7 INCHES.

longest in the country.   The ropeway was set up in 1903 and operated till 1938 when it was found that the quarry was petering out and that the stone could be obtained more conveniently elsewhere.   It is now dismantled, though still shown on the Ordnance Survey map, and all that is left to mark its course is a series of concrete stumps on which the trestles once stood.   Gatehouse quarry was already in use for ten years before 1903.—(*B*)

*   *   *   *   *   *

The Cottage Hospital, now a well equipped and up-to-date institution, was not always so.   The history of its inception and growth has to be told in such an Account as this ; in fact no story of Aberfeldy would be complete without it.

In 1861 a few philanthropic ladies formed themselves into a society for visiting the sick and poor of the village and for the formation of a soup kitchen and of a Home for the Sick. The funds for the soup kitchen were partly raised by a work basket placed at the entrance to the Falls of Moness, where articles to the value of 6d. or 1/- were sold.   The Home for the Sick was opened in a house in Kenmore Street (No. 26) where facilities were almost non-existent, there not being even a bathroom ; the inmates were under the care of a woman paid for the purpose ; there was no trained staff.

As time passed it became apparent that something a little more elaborate was called for and, largely owing to the kindness and generosity of Mr and Mrs Douglas then of Killie-chassie, which made the move possible, the 'Home' was transferred to more commodious premises in a street then in the making and to which it gave its name 'Home Street.' This new building was of two stories, the lower one being originally intended for the treatment of medical and surgical patients and the upper for the care of infectious cases ; there was no direct inside communication between the two floors. Later, when fever cases ceased to be treated locally, the whole 'Home' became purely medical and surgical.

This new 'Home' in Home Street was opened in 1879 with, to begin with, a working matron and one maidservant. It was not until 1892 that a probationer was added to the staff ; this was a Miss MacLeod, who ultimately became matron and moved with the hospital to the present building where she continued for many years, finally retiring in 1921 on account of age.

The 'Home' gave good service within its limits and carried on until the end of the first decade of the present century— latterly, officially, the Aberfeldy & District Cottage Hospital but, popularly, still 'The Home.'

Again in time, however, the need for expansion and fuller facilities became urgent and the present hospital was erected in 1909/10 under the auspices of Sir Donald Currie of Garth on a site granted free by the Marquis of Breadalbane. It opened for work on 27th October, 1910.

From time to time additions have been made, and more accommodation rendered available in the middle 1940's by the removal of the staff's quarters to a villa (Beechfield), bought for the purpose, on the opposite side of the road a few yards nearer the town.

Under the recently inaugurated National Health Service there are three specialist clinics, each held monthly, at which attend consultants in medicine, surgery, etc. Further, Aberfeldy Hospital is now, under the National Health Service, the Maternity (lying-in) Centre for the Highland District of Perthshire ; the number of confinements attended in the past year was 120.

A comparison between the figures given in the 19th *Annual Report of the Home for the Sick*, 1892, and the returns for 1952 is illuminating :

	1952	1892
Number of cases admitted 243	} 363	30
add babies born 120		—
Number of Cases discharged	337	28
Number sent to other hospitals	4	0
Number died	22	1
Out-patients { No. of Patients	592	0
{ No. of Attendances ...	673	—

Staff in 1952 (when full strength) : Matron (working, maternity trained), 2 sisters (1 maternity trained), 4 probationers, 1 woman in kitchen (cook, etc.), 2 general domestics, and 1 porter.

(For the above figures for 1952 I am indebted to Dr. W. Mackie, Medical Superintendent, County and City Royal Infirmary, Perth, and Miss Jessie Cameron, Matron, Aberfeldy Hospital).

That even this, our modern and efficient Hospital should still often be referred to as 'The Home' goes to show how slow to change their ideas the people are and how they cling to old names and associations.

*   *   *   *   *   *

In the field opposite and half left from the hospital there is a knoll beside three good sized trees where once stood the hamlet of Dundai, or Dundaie. Within living memory there were four or five little cottages here, one of which in its latter days was occupied by a tailor, Alexander Cameron, generally known as 'Cut the Wind' on account of his extreme leanness, and another by a farmer who rejoiced in the very unusual name of Sandy Helipper. Access was by way of a track leading in from the Stony Road, crossing a little bridge over the burn which flows down on the field side of the wall. The bridge still stands but of the old hamlet itself nothing remains now but the memory.

The next house but one to the hospital, nearer the town and on the same side of the road, is the Free Church Manse ; it, like the hospital, dates from 1909/10. Before this the site was occupied by an old cottage called Tomchulan ('the whelp's mound'). This was the last of the many thatched cottages which in the old days existed in Aberfeldy. When the Black Street cottages were finally cleared away in the 1890's they were actually, at that time, the 'last thatched cottages' in Aberfeldy. Tomchulan was then outside the burgh and was included only when it was, so to speak, on its death-bed when the town boundary was extended to take in both it and the hospital.

The small stream which flows, sometimes a mere trickle, through the manse garden is the Tomchulan Burn, and it is on record that on 5th November, 1951, when 1.66 inches of rain fell, following a fall of 3.47 inches the preceding day, the burn came down as a torrent so considerable that it allowed the run upward from the river of salmon, one of which, about 7 or 8 lbs., was caught by a small boy a little way below the manse.

* * * * * *

Victoria Cottage, in turn the next house but one nearer the town (from the Free Church Manse), with its gable end to the road, was built as an auction mart and served this purpose for a short period. The present mart, with which during its existence the small one at Victoria Cottage was contemporary, stands at the corner of Home Street and Market Street. Outside Perth the Aberfeldy Auction Mart is now the most important in the county but, big as it is, it is none too big for the great sheep and cattle sales which are held in it from time to time and which attract dealers from all over the country. At the February sale of store cattle this year over 1,500 head changed hands at an average of £40 per head. At 2% commission the auctioneer would seem to have done very well at £1,200 for the day's work ! For comparison with these figures consider the following : At a displenishing sale in Glenlyon in the middle 1700's cows fetched £1 3 4 per head. Also

TOMCHULAN — THE LAST OF THE THATCHED COTTAGES IN ABERFELDY.

Open Air Auction Mart in Bank Street (*Discontinued in* 1883).

consider that in the early 1700's Daniel Defoe recorded that at the Highland Fair at Crieff on one occasion cattle were sold at £1 per head !

The mart at Victoria Cottage was never of much real account, but the markets and sales which are held in the premises in Market Street continue a series which began long before these premises existed. On 15th January, 1883 a letter was circularised by Robert McLaren, auctioneer and live stock salesman, to the effect that Lord Breadalbane had intimated his desire to have the Aberfeldy fortnightly sales removed from the site in Bank Street, where they had been held for upwards of fifteen years, to a new site behind 'The Home.' The site in Bank Street was an open air one in the space beside the Black Watch Inn—now occupied by a smithy.

At a still earlier date they were held, also in the open, in the field just west of Tomghiubhais— the same field, as has been noted, in which the original Free Church congregation met to celebrate communion, etc., while their church was being built. In these days the toll house at the end of Kenmore Street, now the Armoury, was still in operation and farmers from the west, to avoid the tax, were accustomed to divert their flocks and herds through the fields to the sale ground before coming to the gates.

* * * * * *

The road, known now as the Old Crieff Road but, when I was a boy, more often as the Tomchulan Road, from the hospital to The Square, continues in the line of General Wade's military road. Until the end of the first decade of the present century it was little more than a rough stony lane between bush-fringed banks and barely wide enough for the passage of an ordinary farm cart. On the east bank at that time a large boulder stood as it were overlooking and to some extent over-hanging the roadway down near The Square. This was known locally as 'Clach mhòr,' 'the big stone.' In *The Highland Tay* Dr Hugh MacMillan wrote : "On the high tree-covered hillock —" (no longer tree-covered) "—rising abruptly behind the centre of Aberfeldy called The Tullich—" (Gaelic, 'Tulach,' 'a knoll') "—there was once a Druidical Circle, one of the stones of which, called the Clachmore, forms part of a garden wall on the old military road passing along its base,"

Wade's roads were called Military because they were made by soldiers but, though their proposed object was the improvement of the means of communication for the benefit of the district through which they passed, military or strategic ends were certainly kept in view.   They proceeded in straight lines except where some great necessity compelled a deviation, not where a deviation would be for the good of a locality.   Small obstructions were simply removed.   The Clach mhòr bore curious indentations which received various explanations.   Dr Macmillan thought they were cup marks ; the late Rev. John MacLean believed they were made by the levers, jacks, etc., of Wade's men, and a third solution was given by the son of a one-time local strong man called Big Robert, "What a strong man my father was," he said, "he lifted that stone.   Don't you see the marks of his fingers on it ?"

This stone, much as the step was regretted, was blasted and and broken up in 1910 in the course of road widening operations but a considerable part of it was built into, and still forms the lower corner of, the garden boundary wall, nearest The Square, of the house which bears its name, 'Clachmhòr.'   Its present position is slightly east of the site it occupied when I first knew it and, unless Wade's men did actually move it, the site it occupied for centuries.

It is an interesting fact that the road from Crieff, through Aberfeldy, to Dalnacardoch was first used for military purposes not by Government troops or agents, as envisaged by its builder, but by Prince Charlie and part of his retreating army or their way to Culloden.

The section of this road from Pitilie to Aberfeldy fell into comparative disuse with the construction of the present main road to Crieff about the beginning of last century ; the bridge by which this newer road crosses the Moness Burn above the town is of the type erected between 1790 and 1810.

On top of the Tullich still stands the Anti-Aircraft Observation Post set up during the 1939/45 War. From this height a rather unusual view of Aberfeldy is afforded, and one which makes the little climb well worth while.

Between the Observation Post and Moness House the stackyard of Moness Farm is situated on a knoll beside which until recently there was a roughly circular arrangement of flagstones locally believed to have been the floor of a hut, or some such erection, used by General Wade and his staff as an office or orderly room while Taybridge was in process of construction. Little trace of it remains now.

It was round the base of the Tullich and a short way up the line of the old Crieff Road that long ago were clustered the cottages of the hamlet of Moness, the largest of a small group of neighbouring hamlets which were later to become joined to form what is now called Aberfeldy, the others being 'Aberfeldy east of the burn' (Aberfeldy proper), and, west of the burn, the Over and Nether Miltons of Aberfeldybeg.

As stated elsewhere Moness was bought from the Flemyngs by the fourth Earl, later first Marquis, of Breadalbane in 1787, and the hamlet became united with 'Aberfeldy east of the burn' to form what came to be known as Easter Aberfeldy.

In 1414 Grantully and 'Aberfeldy east of the burn' (excluding the hamlet of Moness) were granted by Archibald, Earl of Douglas, to his shield bearer and cousin, Alexander, fourth son of Sir John Steuart of Innermeath. This Alexander was the founder of the family of Steuarts of Grantully and among the lands included in his charter were the Strades, Dundai, and Brucecroft. Since that time 'Aberfeldy east of the burn' passed through various hands till in 1921 the superiority was purchased along with that of the rest of the town, by its present proprietor, ex-Provost J. D. Haggart, O.B.E., C.B.E., J.P., from the Breadalbanes who had been the owners since 1771 when the third Earl bought it from the Menzieses who in turn had bought it from the Steuarts.

West of the burn lay the Over and Nether Miltons of Aberfeldybeg, which ultimately became joined as Wester Aberfeldy The lands of Weem and 'Abyrfeallaidhbeg' were noted in a Charter dated 1301 as having been obtained by Sir Robert de Meynes (Menzies) from John de Strathbogie, Earl of Athole and grandson of MacDuff, sixth Earl of Fife, but, though this appears to be the oldest dated Charter in which Aberfeldybeg is mentioned, there is another, undated, which is presumably older as the names of the granter and witnesses are of the period of the Ragman Roll, 1296.—(C).

Wester Aberfeldy remained in the heritable possessions of the Menzieses until it was taken over by the third Earl of Breadalbane in the same year as 'Aberfeldy east of the burn,' 1771. In a marriage contract, dated 22nd and 25th June, 1622 between Duncan, son of the then Sir Alexander Menzies, and Lady Jean Leslie, Aberfeldy is referred to as a "seven pund land in the Barony of Bolfracks."

Though Aberfeldy east of the burn, Aberfeldy proper, is not mentioned in Charters prior to 1414, its existence at least a century earlier seems implicit in the fact that the hamlet to the west bore the distinguishing title of 'Little' Aberfeldy (Gaelic, 'beg' 'little').

As a matter of interest, the fact that Wester Aberfeldy at one time belonged to the Earl of Athole explains why it was included in the old Parish of Logierait. When parish boundaries were rearranged in 1891 it was transferred to Dull. (Parishes date from the reign of David I (1124-1153). In the old Columban Church the organisation was monastic, not parochial, and when the change over to Roman Catholicism came it was effected mainly by the establishment of Parishes and the Benedictine monastic Orders from abroad. The proprietor of a manor built a church or endowed one already existing for the use of himself and his people with the tithes of his land, and nominated a priest with the sanction of the Bishop to serve it. His manor came to be recognised as a parish, and this was the origin of Parishes, Tithes, and Patronage).

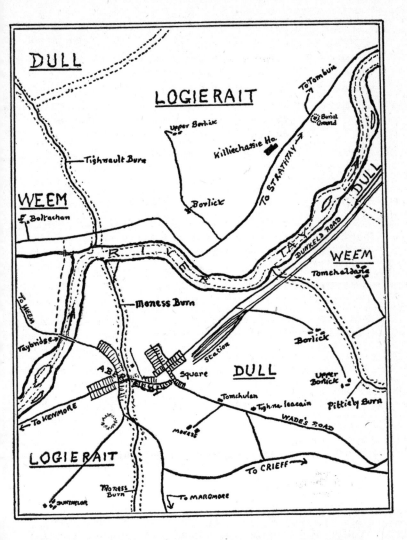

Chart, from an 1862 Survey, showing
old Parish Boundaries.

Scale: 3" to the Mile.

In 1906 Mr John Christie, clerk in the Breadalbane Estates Office, published a brochure entitled *The Antiquity of Aberfeldy* from which the following extract is quoted almost *verbatim* : "One feature which points to the antiquity of Aberfeldy as a centre of community is a system of agriculture which was pursued by the villagers in former days, a system it may be remarked not in vogue at any of the other villages in the vast Breadalbane estate, a territory stretching in a line, unbroken save by water, from the centre of Perthshire to the Firth of Lorn.

"It was somewhat akin to that of runrig, but it differed from it in respect that the cultivated lands did not lie in continuity, but were scattered broadcast as if by a huge dredging-box with holes of every conceivable shape. It would seem as if each of the inholders had, at a remote period, gone forth to a newly discovered land and there pegged out his claim according to the contour of the ground, and stuck to it in undisputed possession. Thus, isolated patches of old Duntaylor land ran close to where Wade's bridge is now.

"With Aberfeldybeg this did not much matter as there was but one landlord, east of the burn there were the Steuarts of Grantully and the Flemyngs of Moness, which led to complications.

"Northward Moness estate had as its boundary the Tay, extending about half a mile east of the Moness burn to Pirl-channel; southward it extended for a similar distance. The area embraced was intermingled with numerous portions of old 'Aberfeldy east of the burn' and its subordinate lands of Borlick, West Strade, and others. The Square, now, lies wholly in what were the lands of Moness, and Dunkeld Street partly in Moness and partly in West Strade, Brucecroft, and Borlick, the last named running to a point not many yards east of The Square, and portions of these lands were under cultivation up to the commencement of the 1800's." See Plan opposite.

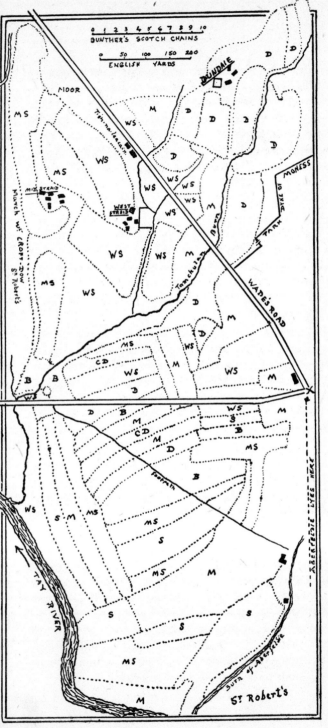

A PLAN OF THE
HAUGH OF
ABERFELDIE
ETC.
AS RAVELD IN
PROPERTY
BETWEEN
SR. ROBERT MEN-
ZIES AND THE
LAIRD OF MONESS.

———

A. WINTER *fecit*
1753.

LANDS :

B. - BORLIG
(as spelt on
the original
Plan).

C.D.-CROFT DOW

D. - DUNDAIE

M.S.-MID STRADE
(or Straid)

M. - MONESS

S. - MR SPALDING

W.S.-WEST STRADE

X————————X

This shows the line
of the old road to
the east from a
point corresponding
to what is now the
south-east corner
of THE SQUARE.

(Under the system of runrig or 'run-ridge' the possessors occupied their arable lands in alternate ridges like stripes of different colours in a web of cloth, without any bounding marks between them except a few twigs annually fixed in the ground or a bank of waste soil left at the side of each ridge, and, what was more absurd and a bar to all improvements, the tenants often exchanged ridges from year to year, either by agreement or by casting lots).

As regards Pirlchannel, though I have been unable to locate this site with absolute certainty it would seem legitimate to presume, from the fact that the Borlick (or Pitilie) Burn once formed the eastern march of the riverward extension of the Moness property, that the mouth of this burn, which is almost exactly half a mile east of the mouth of the Moness Burn, must indicate its position.

With reference to the Strades, or Straids, (Gaelic, 'sraid,' 'street') the origin of the name is uncertain. The Strades were small farm holdings on the hill slopes above the railway station, the buildings of West Strade being situated behind the site of the Cottage Hospital and 50 or 60 yards from the road, and those of Middle Strade about 150 yards still further east.

It was the bringing together of these various lands under one landlord (Breadalbane) that really marked the birth of Aberfeldy as a single community, though the names Wester and Easter Aberfeldy are still found in the County Valuation Roll.

Another big help forward was given in 1796 when the fourth Earl of Breadalbane framed terms upon which Building Leases of 99 years could be obtained, a further stimulus following when in the 1870's the then Laird started granting Feus. The safeguard of the feuars lies in the fact that there is now no one living who could point out the old boundaries, and the feu charters in defining the situation of each feu are so framed as to embrace the lands of both Moness and Aberfeldy.

The final tying up of loose ends, as it were, came about in 1887, when the village became a 'town', for in that year Aberfeldy was created a Police Burgh managing (or perhaps sometimes *mis*-managing !) its own affairs. though peculiarly enough, not those of its Police ! In July 1887 the Burgh Boundaries were fixed and on October 1st the nine newly elected Police Commissioners met and took office for the first time in a room thereafter known as the Commissioners' Room in the Old School Buildings in the Crieff Road, the meeting being presided over by John Grahame, Esq., Sheriff Substitute. Office bearers were elected—Chief Magistrate, two Bailies, six Commissioners, Town Clerk, etc.—and the newly constituted body at once set about many necessary improvements. Pavements had to replace the rough cobble-stones that did duty here and there in front of the houses. The flagstones which in the first instance were used to replace the cobbles were later removed to make way for concrete, a material now in use practically throughout the town. The last of the old cobbles may still be seen at the entrances to several of the closes in Chapel Street and Dunkeld Street ; the only flag-stones now left are those on the upper level of the pavement outside the chemist's shop in Bridgend. A scavenger was also appointed and no one was permitted to empty dirty water, etc., in the channels or 'strands' as they were called and the gullies were periodically flushed and cleaned. That such regulations to maintain cleanliness in the streets were found necessary is strong evidence that the using of the street gutters as open drains was a common practice.

In the East Park (that part of the golf course which lies east of the burn) a number of parallel grooves or shallow depressions set at 5 to 10 or more yards intervals are seen running from the direction of the town in that of the river. These are present day traces of ditches which used to take the outflow of surface drainage from the streets and which were still in service when Mr James A. MacGregor came to Aberfeldy in the early 1870's.

In the 1860's, and probably before that, sanitation was the concern of the village Sanitary Society. A sewage disposal scheme had already been completed in the middle 1870's, before which cesspools were used. All over the town fire-clay pipes were laid and had their outlets in the Tay. One of these outlets used to discharge behind where the clubhouse of the Golf Club now stands and another just below the mouth of the Tomchulan Burn east of the town. It is told how the late Sir Robert Menzies, never happy unless involved in some controversy, complained of this river pollution. To settle the dispute two samples of water were sent to the Public Analyst for examination. One sample was taken from the Tay above the town and the other below the lower effluent pipe to the east. The report came back to the effect that the sample taken from *below* the town was the purer!

This system, however, involved River Pollution as defined under the Act of 1877 and in due course was discontinued— though not for a number of years after 1877. Filter beds were then constructed in a field east of the town and continued to function till the increasing use of tar and bitumen in road repair work killed vegetable growth on the irrigation beds, thus destroying the means of disposal. In 1933 new sediment- ation works were formed on the same ground.

Under the Town Councils Act of 1900 the Commissioners became Councillors and the Town Council as we know it now, with Provost, two Bailies, and six Councillors, etc., came into being. Our Provost's very handsome Chain of Office was presented to the Council in February 1924 by Mr James Haggart Dewar, Glasgow, during the Provostship of his nephew ex-Provost James Dewar Haggart, and each link bears the name and dates of service of one of the Provosts of the past :— Messrs. C. W. L. Forbes (Agent, Commercial Bank), 1887-1893 : James Mackerchar (Agent, Bank of Scotland), April 1893-May 1896 : John Cameron (Master Joiner), May to November 1896 : Peter Campbell (Retired hotel-keeper), November 1896 - February 1914 : J. D. Haggart (Woollen manufacturer), March 1914-May 1949. Our present Provost, Mr Charles W. Murray (Independent) took office in May 1949.

ABERFELDY PROVOST'S CHAIN OF OFFICE.

The pendent medallion of the Chain is a coloured represent-ation of the 'Symbolic Stamp' of the Council (adopted by the Commissioners in 1893) which portrays the Black Watch Memorial with, in the background, General Wade's Taybridge and the ferry boat which used to ply to and fro for public hire before the bridge was built and at a point slightly upstream. The accompanying legend reads " 'S DLUTH TRIC BAT ABAIRPHEALLAIDH"—"Swift and often goes the boat of Aberfeldy."

*　　*　　*　　*　　*　　*

When General Wade came to Scotland and commenced his work of road construction in 1725 as part of the Government's scheme to enforce the Disarming Act in the Highlands no road had been made north of Stirling ; tracks there were but no proper roads.　Prior to this time pack horses and 'carns' or sledges were used ; wheeled vehicles and bridges were unknown in this part of the country.　It has been said that the vehicle in which he travelled when surveying the ground was a heavy coach the like of which had never been seen in these parts and was a source of wonder and even awe to the Highlanders. When it is recalled that the Romans reported that some of the Picts and Gaels fought in wheeled chariots (wheels of such chariots have since been dug up), it is strange to think that their use should appear to have been forgotten in the Highlands for centuries.

In the *Highland Roads and Bridges Reports*, 1828, it is stated that "the usual practice in roads constructed by Wade was to excavate all the earth and turf until gravel appeared, when the road-surface was then dressed and formed on it, and the excavation and rubbish being thrown on either side, the road (generally not more than twelve feet wide) was left in the form of a ditch.　No great inconvenience was occasioned by this mode of construction in summer but in winter it evidently formed a complete receptacle for snow."　A good specimen of one of these ditch-like roads is the old road (Wade's) from Loch na Craig to Gatehouse.

In passing it may be noted that the cost of the roads over his whole system averaged out at about £70 per mile and that when they were first constructed no bridges were built ; fords were used first ; these were followed by wooden bridges, then by stone.

Wade's road and the three bridges which come within the scope of this Account formed part of his great Crieff to Dalnacardoch road, some of which, from Pitilie to The Square, has already been noticed. From The Square it followed the line of the present main street and crossed the Paldie Burn, as the Moness Burn was called at that time, by a bridge, since widened by about 5 feet, which when examined from below still shows the original arch ; the newer part, downstream, is carried on metal girders. The road then continued a little way along the line of the present Bank Street, between the hamlets of Over and Nether Miltons of Aberfeldybeg, before turning northward to reach the river in a slightly more direct line than that of the road now in use.

In Nether Milton, as already stated, there was a meal mill on a site near that of the present one at the top of Mill Street, and close by there was a lint mill. Both these mills were driven by the same water supply, fed from a dam which lay to the south near the eight or ten houses constituting Over Milton.

* * * * * *

Wade was accustomed to consider Taybridge his masterpiece. In its erection he had the help of William Adam the architect, father of the famous Robert Adam, and the whole work, begun in April 1733, was completed in nine months (!) as noted on one of the now badly weathered marble tablets let into the stonework above the piers next the banks on the upstream aspect and also on the grey stone plaques on the lower, north-east, side. On the completion of the bridge it is said that Wade declared that he had fulfilled his intention of "setting the rapacious ferryman and his boats on dry land !"

The statement on the tablet to the effect that the bridge was completed in nine months is not strictly accurate for by October 1733 it was built up only to pavement level. Wade was accustomed to knock off all work on his roads and bridges each October and in the case of Taybridge the parapet, four feet high over the side arches, was not added till the following year.

It was hailed in those days as the finest bridge in Scotland and was at the time, 1733, the only one spanning the Tay, the the old Perth bridge which was swept away in 1661 not being rebuilt till 1772. Of peculiar design, described on the one hand by guidebooks as "graceful and elegant" and on the other by Dorothy Wordsworth, sister of the poet, who visited the district in 1803, as of "ambitious and ugly architecture," it may at least, and without fear of contradiction, be labelled "picturesque."

Robert Southey in his *Journal of a Tour in Scotland*, 1819, wrote : "Near Aberfeldy is a bridge over the Tay, built by General Wade, but creditable to neither the skill nor the taste of the architect. It resembles that at Blenheim, the middle arch being made the principal feature. At a distance it looks well but makes a wretched appearance upon close inspection. There are four unnecessary obelisks upon the central arch and the parapet is so high you cannot see over it. The foundations are very insecure, for we went into the bed of the river to examine them."

When he criticises the taste of the architect one is justified in assuming that he is merely expressing his own opinion, and this need not therefore be taken at more than its worth as such. As regards not being able to see over the parapet, this never applied to any part except that over the central arch ; if there is any fault now it is that with successive layings of road metal over a long period of years the wall over the other four arches is becoming almost dangerously *low*—at parts less than 2½ feet. Finally, one has only to think back over the floods and frosts, storms and stresses, that the bridge has weathered during the past two centuries and more to appreciate how utterly wrong he was with regard to the foundations, his statement being all the more remarkable when it is probable that by his use of the pronoun 'we' he included with his own opinion that of his fellow traveller, Thomas Telford, the famous bridge builder.

Spanning the river in five arches, the middle one of which covers 60 feet, Taybridge measures in all 370 feet in length. The four obelisks to which Southey took exception—12 feet above the parapet and about 18 above the roadway—which are so marked a feature of the design and which appear in Adam's plan were apparently added some time after the work was otherwise completed as in a contemporary picture of the General with the bridge in the background they are wanting.

In 1932, two tablets bearing copies of Wade's original inscriptions were let into the stonework of the plinths of two of the four obelisks, the one on the right as one nears the summit of the rise from the Aberfeldy side bearing the English inscription, and that on the right as one comes up from the further bank the Latin. On one occasion very recently as I crossed the bridge I noticed two women visitors studying this Latin inscription. As I drew abreast I overheard their conversation. First woman, "What does all that mean?" Second woman, "Can't say. I don't know Gaelic!" I can imagine the expression on the face of Dr Friend, Headmaster of Westminster School and composer of the inscription, had he been privileged to share this experience with me.

These tablets were unveiled by the late J. Stewart Robertson, Esq., of Edradynate at a public ceremony held on 17th August, 1932.—(D)

Over the keystone of the centre arch, upstream, is a bevelled panel in white marble with the Crown, Sceptre, and Sword ; this is repeated in grey stone on the downstream aspect. Above the small arches on both sides of the bridge, projecting some 2 feet, are beautifully formed small stone cannon of a circumference of about 3 feet and a bore of 7 or 8 inches diameter.

WADE'S TAYBRIDGE.

There are hanging iron rings on both piers of the centre arch, upstream one on each side of the two cutwaters, and downstream an equal number in corresponding positions— eight in all. What purpose they were intended to serve is obscure ; an enquiry directed to the staff of the Royal Commission on Ancient Monuments elicited the suggestion that they might have been connected with drop-gates, but the fact that they are on both the upstream and downstream sides seems against this. As a boy I heard it said that they were used in connection with the rafting down the river of timber, a practice which was in vogue as late as the middle of last century when local timber was mostly used (all of which, by the way, had to be hand dressed) ; this explanation of their presence is at least not improbable as men in charge of rafts with wood intended for use in Aberfeldy would find in them a convenient means of tying up fore and aft in comparatively deep water.

It may be of interest to some to know that the wood which was used in the building operations was given by Alexander Robertson of Struan who, oddly enough, was a bitter Jacobite, and who as such, still more oddly, attended the opening ceremony in 1735 at which General Wade himself was present and laid on the parapet a turgid and rather stupid poem eulogising the General entitled "Taybridge to the Passenger." A reporter of that time must have made a copy of the verse for it appeared in *The Edinburgh Courant* of December 12th of the same year, when Struan's generosity in supplying wood from Rannoch for Edinburgh Infirmary was also noticed. The 'Poem' is quoted in full in Appendix (*E*).

After the building of the bridge was completed, at a cost, it may be noted, of £4,095 5 10, the scaffolding, mainly of fir and larch, was dragged by horse labour to the Kirk of Amulree where it was utilised as joists, seats, etc.

The stone used in the construction is chlorite schist from a quarry above Bolfracks (old spelling 'Bufrac'—'spotted hut') from which, later, the stone used in the building of Taymouth was also taken ; it was supplied by the Laird of Bolfracks, one of the Menzieses who at that time held the Barony of Bolfracks, and has the advantage of being soft and easily worked when quarried and of hardening on exposure. Skilled workmen were employed for over two years at Bolfracks ; all the stones were hewn, marked and numbered and conveyed to the bridge where they were laid in their respective places, like the stones in King Solomon's Temple, without the sound of a single hammer. The principal stones of the arches appear to have been wrought by the Masonic Guild, who put their mark upon their work.

In the *House of Commons Journal*, 7th February, 1734, it is stated that "the starlings are of oak, and the piers and landbreasts founded on piles shod with iron." Below the bridge the river bed is causewayed from side to side to prevent attrition of the waterway and undermining of the arch abutments.

Steep slopes from both approaches lead to the centre of the bridge, where the roadway is very narrow. In December of last year temporary traffic lights similar to those used by road working gangs were given a try out and found so successful that permission to set up a permanent installation was sought ; the cost was estimated at £200 - £300 with maintenance charge of £30 annually, exclusive of lighting. A traffic census was taken by the County Council, but the matter was turned down by the Ministry of Transport and the Chief Constable. The danger continues.

Within the past year or so a scale has been marked out on which the rise and fall of the water may be read off in feet. It is on the cutwater of the pier furthest from but on the face that slants towards Aberfeldy. In low water this pier stands almost high and dry on a gravel bank ; spawning salmon sometimes use this bank in season and may be observed from the bridge.

Some twelve years after completion Taybridge was put to its first big test for in August 1745 Sir John Cope, in his expedition against Prince Charlie, with his forces, artillery, baggage waggons, and all, passed through Aberfeldy and camped on the north side of the river. It is more than probable that Wade in his building kept in mind the need for a bridge strong enough to stand up to the passage of such artillery and heavy vehicles as were used in his day, indeed it is said that the passing of a train of artillery was the test of strength of the forty or so bridges in his road system, but, were he to return in this mechanised age and see the traffic it had now to carry, far heavier than any artillery he could have visualised, I am sure he would feel tempted to say, "Truly, I builded better than I knew !"

It was in the 219th year of its existence that Taybridge sustained its first real casualty ; on 18th December, 1951, some huge metal castings that were being transported by road for use in the construction of a hydro-electric station further west, though too wide to pass, were forced through and, after scoring both parapets, hit the shoulder of the high parapet beyond the obelisk furthest from the town and downstream knocking away the flat coping stones and part of the wall beneath, effectually rounding off the angle ; at the same time the coping stones on the parapet opposite were loosened and considerably splintered.

In 1746 Prince Charlie, retiring northwards before the advance of the Duke of Cumberland, 'Butcher Cumberland,' crossed Taybridge. Cumberland, fearing that the Jacobite army might again strike south, sent 200 men to garrison Castle Menzies and a detachment of Hessians to guard the bridge, the latter being quartered in an inn near by. Sir Robert Menzies, though a staunch Hanoverian, was turned out at a moment's notice and was forced to find accommodation in a neighbouring cottage. Later, he put in a claim, indorsed 1750, for "1000 l" and "humbly hopes that his Majesty will be gratiously pleased to order remede—" against damage resulting from the occupation of the castle and furniture rendered useless by the "outbreak of an epidemical fever among the troops."

When it is recalled that the oldest house in Aberfeldy, Moness, was not built till 1753 it brings home to us the fact, surely worthy of thought, that of the various hamlets, etc., which stood here in Wade's time not one solitary house remains. The view westwards from the bridge however is still just as he must have seen it—the broad stream divided by the tree-clad island in the foreground, the hill slopes sweeping upwards on either hand, the bold cliffs of the Rock of Weem to the north-west, and in the distance the lofty mountains guarding the entrance to Glenlyon, and the still higher summits of the Ben Lawers spur of the Grampians culminating in Ben Lawers (3984 feet) itself—surely a vista of natural beauty calculated to stir the blasé and satisfy the fastidious.

More prosaically it may be noted that the Tay, 110 miles from its source 3,000 feet up on Ben Lui (Beinn Laoigh) to the sea is the longest river in Scotland, that it carries down with it more water than any other river in Britain, and that in its name we have preserved that of Celtic river goddess, in Gaelic 'Tatha,' 'the Silent One'—in Ptolemy's *Notes*, 'Tava,' in Devon the Tavy and the Taw, and in Wales the Tawe.

*   *   *   *   *   *

Everyone knows, or ought to know, that the name of Aberfeldy is associated now and forever with what is the oldest and perhaps the most famous of all our Highland Regiments, The Black Watch or Royal Highlanders, the 42nd of the Line. A summary of the early history of this Regiment, therefore, together with a description of the very striking Memorial erected immediately to the south-west of Taybridge to commemorate their first muster, is bound to be included here.

Perhaps it is not generally known that what may be called the 'historic succession' of the Black Watch dates back to 3rd August, 1667, when Charles II issued commissions under the Great Seal to John, second Duke of Atholl and other Chiefs of the Whig clans to raise and keep such numbers of men as they should think fit "to be a constant guard for securing the

peace in the Highlands" and "to watch upon the braes"—
i.e., Independent Companies raised by the influence of the
Chiefs, clad by them in the national dress but paid and nominated by the State.   The dark tartans which were worn by
the men of these Companies to distinguish them from the
Guardsmen, 'Saighdearan Dearg' or 'Red Soldiers' led, about
1678, to their becoming known as 'Freiceadan Dubh' or 'The
Black Watch.'   The original name was 'The Highland Watch'
or, simply, 'The Watch.'

It is said that, to begin with, the men of each of these
Companies wore the tartan of their Commanding Officer, who
was loath to give it up, and that the difficulty was finally
overcome by the elimination of the distinctive or heraldic lines
of the different clans, *e.g.*, the yellow stripes of the Breadalbane Campbells, etc.,   The resulting pattern came to be, and
still is, known as the Government pattern or 42nd.   The Black
Watch and the Argyll and Sutherland Highlanders both wear
this tartan, the slight difference in appearance when the kilt
is made up lying in the fact that the latter wear the green bar
out in the pleat and the former the blue.

What part these Independent Companies played at the time
of the Jacobite Rising of 1715 is not clear, but they were dis-
banded in 1717 because—as General Wade declared a few years
later—of corruption, and their being open to bribery from
those they were supposed to bring to justice.

The true history of the Black Watch, as we know it now,
dates from 1725 when four new Independent Companies were
enlisted for the same purpose of preserving order in the Highlands.   In 1729 two more Companies were formed and, in all,
they numbered about 740 men, all of good family and many of
them attended by their own gillies (Gaelic, 'gille,' a 'man-
servant'), who carried their baggage and firelocks.

The letters of service for the formation of these six Companies
into a Regiment were issued to John, Earl of Lindsay, on the
25th October, 1739.   The Regiment was to consist ultimately

of ten Companies, each of 100 effective men, besides officers. The commissions of the officers were dated in October 1739 and the following months. It is said that the signing on for service of recruits in this district in the first instance took place on the spot where the house known as Netherby (in Taybridge Road) now stands.

Up to 1749 The Black Watch was known as the 43rd Regiment but, on the reduction of the original 42nd in that year, they were gazetted as the 42nd Highlanders and, in 1788, as The Royal Highlanders, 42nd Regiment of the Line.

They first mustered, in May 1740, on the low ground on the left (north) bank of the Tay, opposite Aberfeldy, and there the regimenting of the Highland Companies was effected ; in other words The Black Watch was embodied as a Regiment. Properly speaking the Memorial should have been set up on the actual site of the muster ; owing to the low-lying nature of the ground there, however, and the fact that several times a year as a rule it is covered with flood water, the idea was impracticable and the Aberfeldy site, in spite of a certain amount of opposition from the other side of the valley, was selected as the nearest suitable.

After this muster they remained for about fifteen months in the district of the Tay and Lyon where under their commanding officer, Lieut.-Colonal Sir Robert Munro, they drilled and exercised. They were then marched northward, where they remained in the stations assigned to them till the spring of 1743. In March of that year they were ordered to assemble in Perth as a preliminary to a march into England. This came as a surprise, as they considered it contrary to an alleged understanding when regimented that they would not be called for service beyond the confines of their own country, but complied when they were told that the King (George II), who had never seen Highland soldiers, was curious to make their acquaintance and hold a review.

Three privates remarkable for their figures and good looks were chosen to go on ahead, while the others followed. One of these privates, John Grant of Strathspey, fell ill on the way and died in Aberfeldy ; the two others, Gregor McGregor, called Gregor the Beautiful, and John Campbell, son of Duncan Campbell of Duneaves near Fortingall, proceeded to London and, on their arrival were presented to the King by their Lieutenant-Colonel.

In a contemporary account (*Westminster Journal*) the visit is described thus : The two Highlanders "performed the broad-sword exercise and that of the Lochaber axe, or lance, before his Majesty, the Duke of Cumberland, Marshall Wade, and a number of General Officers assembled for the purpose in the Great Gallery at St. James's. They displayed so much dexterity and skill in the management of their weapons as to give perfect satisfaction to his Majesty. Each got a gratuity of one guinea which they gave to the porter at the Palace gate as they passed out." Apparently, as they said, the King was unaware that he was entertaining gentlemen ! In any case at that time the Highlanders, owing to tales repeated by the Lowlanders concerning them, were regarded in England as barbarous, and little better than savages.

The Black Watch marching down the length of England created no little sensation for hardly an Englishman in these days had ever seen a Highlander. The two divisions of the regiment reached London on the 29th and 30th April, respectively, 1743, and on 14th May were reviewed on Finchley Common by Marshall Wade who, having been Commander in Chief in Scotland, knew them well.

In the interval between their arrival and the review, rumours had reached them that it was not true that the King had wished to see them and that the real intention of the Government was to transport them for life to the American plantations and thus rid the Highlands of so many Jacobites. To lend colour to these rumours it was pointed out that the King, so far from wishing to see them, had actually sailed on the 30th April to join his army at that time campaigning in Flanders, and, further, that transportation to the American plantations was the penalty imposed upon the Highlanders who came out in the Rising of 1715.

Concealing their intentions even from their own officers, and before the review took place, the men secretly prepared themselves to return to their own country and one night a day or two after the review they assembled at Highgate and set forth upon their journey north, avoiding the main roads and keeping as far as possible among the woods.

When their flight was discovered orders were sent to the commanding officers of the various forces stationed on the way to Scotland that they should be stopped and arrested. They were finally found and surrounded in the Lady Wood near Oundle, Northamptonshire. After a certain amount of parleying, and faced with forces outnumbering their own, they agreed to surrender at discretion and to return to London where, on 8th June, they were tried as deserters by general court-martial, found guilty, and condemned to be shot. The death penalty was, however, remitted to all except Corporals Malcolm and Samuel McPherson (brothers) and Private Farquhar Shaw, who were shot upon the Parade within the Tower, the rest of the prisoners being drawn out to see the execution. Of the remainder of the regiment 200 were distributed among various corps serving abroad and, soon after, the others were sent to Flanders to take part in the campaign there.

After Fontenoy (1745) it was deemed unwise to return them to Scotland as about 300 of the men had brothers and relatives out with Prince Charlie and, instead, they were sent, after one or two short postings in England and Wales, to Ireland where they continued for about ten years. Had they been permitted in the first instance to remain in Scotland to fulfil the police duties for which they were enlisted it is possible that the Rising of The '45 might never have taken place.

When the erection of the Memorial was being decided on, a representation of Farquhar Shaw in the old uniform of the regiment, with his flintlock musket slung over his shoulder and in the act of drawing his sword, was chosen for reproduction as the dominating figure, and it must be conceded that the sculptor has done his work well, though it might seem perhaps that a more natural posture for a man to assume while drawing his sword would have been with the right foot forward instead of the left.

The unveiling ceremony was performed on the 14th of November, 1887, Jubilee year, by the Marquis of Breadalbane in the presence of between four and five thousand people, the greatest concourse of people the town has ever seen either before or since. The day was fine but cold and Aberfeldy was *en fête* ; it was a general holiday and flags fluttered from most of the houses, and bunting festooned the streets. From early morning visitors came pouring in by road and rail ; special trains arrived from Edinburgh, Glasgow, and Perth ; a procession formed up in and started from the Auction Mart and proceeded via the main streets to Dunolly at the west end and thence to the Monument.

After the unveiling ceremony and what seemed endless speechifying (I was there !) the procession reformed and, led by Pipe-Major Bain of the Dundee Highlanders, a Crimean veteran who on the 20th September, 1854, had piped the "42nd" up the Heights of Alma, the various bodies marched to the (then) new Public School where a public banquet took place— and more speeches ! The rank and file of the soldiery who took part in the ceremony were entertained in Weem Hotel.

(For details and order of the procession see Appendix)—(*F*).

On the north-west face of the cairn is a tablet bearing an inscription in Gaelic, and on the south-east another in English. By the observant a mistake in spelling may be noticed in the English inscription : in the words "Independent Companies" the word "Independent" is mis-spelt "Independant."

On the south-west face is carved in relief the bust profile of Queen Victoria, and the inscription :—"1887. The Year of the Jubilee of Queen Victoria. This Site has been kindly granted by the most Noble Gavin Marquis of Breadalbane."

On the north-east face, dwarfed somewhat, perhaps, by that of Farquhar Shaw above, is the finely executed figure of another Highlander in the parade uniform of the regiment, as it was in 1887, in the act of completing a list of the engagements in which the Black Watch had won renown. Were the list to be extended to include the names of the many battlefields on which the regiment has fought since 1887 the whole of the tablet, even were the Highlander removed, would scarce suffice to hold them.

(The full text of the inscriptions is given in Appendix)—(*G*).

Some time after the 1914/18 War five captured German guns were allotted as war trophies to Aberfeldy. They arrived on 2nd April, 1920, and for a few years were domiciled in the Monument grounds, four of them occupying each one corner of the grassy platform on which the cairn stands and the fifth a site facing across the river a few yards to the west. Besides being a defacement they were a constant reminder of the horrors of a nightmare still fresh in men's minds and I think the reaction to their removal was a general feeling of relief.

About two years ago, through the instrumentality of Mr John Reoch, an Aberfeldy native now for over fifty years resident in Canada, the Black Watch Association in Toronto presented to the town a seat to which is affixed a tablet bearing, in addition to the regimental Badge, the inscription : "Presented to the Burgh of Aberfeldy by the Black Watch Association, Toronto, in appreciation of kindness shown to Service Men during World War 1939/45." At a function in the Monument grounds, attended by various local civic dignitaries, a detachment of the Regiment from Perth and a large crowd of spectators, this seat was duly 'opened' for use and now occupies a prominent position at the foot of the cairn. (*L*)

From time to time parties of Black Watch men are brought from their regimental depot at Queen's Barracks, Perth, to see the Memorial and to hear something of their regiment's wonderful story, and it is not too much to believe that they go away proud of the great traditions they have inherited and are so much the better soldiers in consequence.

Unveiling of The Black Watch Memorial in 1887.

THE BLACK WATCH MEMORIAL.
SHOWING DAMAGE DONE BY LIGHTNING. 22/6/1910.

The initial cost of the Monument was about £500, raised by public subscription, many of the contributions coming from overseas. Collectors were appointed in Aberfeldy and district to go from house to house. The late Rev. John MacLean was one of these and in course of his round he called at Loch Kennard Lodge which at the time was occupied by the Conte de Paris, 'Pretender' to the French throne, who had the shooting for the season. Approached for a subscription the Comte asked, "And what did the Black Watch ever do for France?" Pat came the reply, "They helped to put your ancestor Louis Philippe, on the throne." He got £5 !

On 22nd June, 1910, during a thunderstorm a flash of lightning split the cairn from top to bottom, the tablet facing southwest being shattered ; the figure on the top was not damaged. The necessary repairs which included the installation of a lightning conductor—there had not been one before !—cost £200, which sum also was raised by public subscription.

To complete the tale : The sculpture is the work of Messrs. J. & W. S. Rhind of Edinburgh and the cairn was erected, under the personal supervision of Mr W. Birnie Rhind, R.S.A., by Messrs. Gow & Dewar, builders, Aberfeldy.

At the time of the Coronation of King Edward in 1903 a ceremony was held in the Monument grounds and the two oak trees near the little gate that opens on to the roadway at the end of the bridge were planted to commemorate the occasion.

* * * * * *

If the building of Taybridge marked the beginning of an era of prosperity in Aberfeldy the opening in 1789 of a Post Office marked another big step forward.

The earliest post office in the village of which I can obtain definite information was run by a Mrs McKerchar in a tiny cottage on the south side of Dunkeld Street twenty or thirty yards east of The Square, though this may not have been the first for Dunkeld Street was only coming into existence in 1800. Mrs McKerchar's name as postmistress in Aberfeldy first appeared in the 1803 issue of the *New Edinburgh Almanac* and continued to appear in successive issues until 1824.

After 1824 the postmaster was a man named Alexander Kippen, who was also Registrar, and the post office while in his charge was in a house since removed which stood on a site facing the milestone at the east end of the Breadalbane Hotel in Bridgend, where it continued until 1854.

By present day standards facilities for a long time were primitive in the extreme ; thus, the late Rev. John MacLean (born 1829) stated that he could remember when there was no daily post to Perth and letters went once a week, and to Fortingall, only nine miles away, also once a week.

To send by post then, from Aberfeldy, a single sheet of notepaper—envelopes were unknown—cost at least 4d., and Sir Robert Menzies (born 1817) when performing the opening ceremony at the present post office in March 1897 told that he remembered when it cost 7d. to send a letter to Perth and 1/3½d. to London.

According to money values to-day these amounts represented quite a tolerable sum, as may be realised when it is remembered that, in a school established in Aberfeldy in 1796 by the Scottish Society for the Propagation of Christian Knowledge at which 107 children at one time attended, the salary of the headmaster, a Mr Donald Cameron, was £10 per annum and that, in the recollection of a woman who died in the town in 1917 aged 91, female farm servants got £3 a year, and *saved* on it, while children whose work was at the beck and call of the Laird were paid 2d. a day, and with no eight hour limit on the day either !

To look at the present post office in Dunkeld Street, say, during the press of the late December season, and watch in the morning the departure of the great motor mail cars piled high with bags, parcels, etc., and the squad of postmen, rural and urban, regulars and specials, setting out on their rounds with bulging letter bags and hung around with parcels like so many Christmas trees, makes it difficult to realise that, from the time the premises in Bridgend were given up in 1854 until 1897, the needs of the town and district were served by the small shop that stands at the corner of The Square at the top of Chapel Street opposite the Birks Cinema where the postmaster, a Mr William Cowper, who with his daughter was in charge, sold cutlery, crockery, jewellery, etc., as well as stamps and postal orders ! In this office the 'sorting' of the country letters was done on a glass cutlery case on the counter.

It was, in the 1870's during the existence of this office that postal telegraphy was introduced into Aberfeldy, the first operator being the daughter of the postmaster who took up the duties after a term of training in Edinburgh. Later, this daughter became postmistress and carried on as such for a number of years after the transfer to the new building in Dunkeld Street in 1897. The public telephone service was extended to Aberfeldy in 1907.

An amusing story is told of Sir Robert Menzies at the opening of the new office. It appears that it was arranged that, during the ceremony, his daughter Miss Menzies of Menzies would post the first letter, but he found that she had made a mistake by posting it in the old office. They managed to get it out however and it was duly posted as planned. "This was a remarkable letter," he said in his opening speech, "as it was the last to be posted in the old office and the first in the new !"

The four deliveries daily which the town enjoyed then and for a good many years after were undertaken by one man, Mr James A. MacGregor (referred to in the Foreword of this Account) who, in addition bore on his shoulders the duties of sorting in the office and attending the arrivals and departures of the various trains to take delivery of, or to dispatch as the case might be, the baskets in which the mails made less 'destructive' journeys than they do, in bags, now.

Mr MacGregor, who entered the service in 1883, was the first male uniformed postman in Aberfeldy. Prior to this date deliveries were by non-uniformed but officially appointed post-women—'Letter Lassies' they were called—who carried the mails in their upturned skirts or aprons! Correspondence, though ever growing, was of course much lighter then than now and they did their one delivery a day in about an hour.

Before the introduction of motor mail cars for country deliveries outside the range of walking or cycling postmen—to Glenlyon in 1910, and Lawers in 1911—the work was under-taken by post-boys driving gigs. One of these was on the Lochtayside round daily, and two on the Glenlyon run, the drivers on this beat making the outward trip on alternate days and the return the day following.

About three years ago the local service was strengthened by the addition of three Royal Mail motor delivery vans, and the sight of postmen mounted on bicycles is less common. Two of these vans are in regular service, the other being kept in reserve.

No doubt the introduction of Universal Penny Postage in 1840 led to a big increase in the work handled by post offices all over the country. That Aberfeldy contributed its share of the increase is suggested by some particulars given in *Oliver & Boyd's New Edinburgh Almanac for 1858.*

According to this authority mails ran daily :—
Per Post Gig from Dunkeld to Kenmore and
    the North and South at ... ... 3.5 P.M.
From Killin, Kenmore, and Fortingall at ... 8.20 A.M.
Despatched to the North and South at   ... 8.45 A.M.
Despatched to Kenmore, Killin, and Fortingall at 3.30 P.M.

According to the same authority, for general passenger ser-vice there were coaches running daily to Perth during the winter months, at 7 A.M., and from Dunkeld Railway Station (Birnam)—(the then terminus of the Highland Railway)—

on the arrival of the 4 o'clock P.M. train from Perth ; and during the summer months there were stage coaches daily to and from Glasgow, Loch Lomond, Rannoch and Perth.

This was in 1858, but the late Rev. John MacLean told that as a boy in the 1830's he remembered the starting of the first passenger coach to Perth. Before this the only public service was by carrier's cart. This was a two-day trip and passengers had to spend the night at Bankfoot not because one day would not serve but because of the carrier's business. Most people preferred to go by private carriage or on foot. He himself taking a short way did the walk, 26 miles, in eight hours.

Actually before 1800 no public coach or other regular vehicle of conveyance existed anywhere in the Highlands and it was not until 1806 that coaches were regularly established on the Perth-Inverness run, being the first that ran on roads in the Highlands.

It was natural that the comings and goings of the stage coaches in these days, from the late 1830's to the 1860's, should be events of considerable importance in the daily lives of the local folk for they constituted the town's main, if not its only link with the outside world. At their hours of arrival The Square presented a busy and animated scene ; here it was a case of 'all passengers ashore' for travellers from east to west or west to east were obliged to sleep at least one night in the town before proceeding on their way. It was here too that through-going carriages changed horses, and it is on record that Queen Victoria and Prince Albert *en route* from Scone to Taymouth in 1842 halted for a little in front of Breadalbane Hotel while a fresh team was being yoked in.

Some of the old coach drivers were real worthies and well aware of their own consequence in the scheme of things, which is not to be wondered at in view not only of the importance of their jobs but the facts that as kings of their particular castles, as it were, they were responsible for the safety of and met and conversed with people in all walks of life and that, further, they were carriers of news as well as passengers at a time when, in Aberfeldy at all events, daily papers were practically unknown.

Such a man was Peter Rough (or Ruff, as I have seen it spelt) who drove the Perth coach for many years. So much a character was he, indeed, that there was generally keen competition among his passengers for the privilege of sitting on the box beside him. On one occasion Sir Robert Menzies as a young man on his way home from Oxford University, finding that this, his favourite seat, was taken, declared that rather than sit elsewhere he would complete his journey on foot. The sequel will stand telling here: He declared further that he would beat the coach to Aberfeldy. He set off across the hills—and did !

Numerous good stories are told of these drivers. Here are one or two :—

Once Peter Rough found himself running behind schedule and showed his irritation and impatience so obviously that a clergyman who was sitting beside him felt called upon to exhort him to practise patience, quoting Job as a shining example. The retort was instantaneous, "What coach did *he* drive ?"

A contemporary of Peter's was Alexander McLaggan on the Dalmally coach. A gentleman sitting beside him on one of his runs, thinking he was treating his horses harshly, was impelled to remonstrate. This was too much for McLaggan—he blew up ! When he got the chance of a word again the gentleman said, "I don't think you realise to whom you are talking. I am Lord Fortesque." "I don't care," thundered Mac., "I don't care if you are Lord Fiftyscue !"

One of his favourite 'cracks' was when passing the ruins of Corrycheroch ('the sheep corrie'), reputed birthplace of Rob Roy, some eight miles west of Killin. "That," he would say pointing with his whip, "That is one of the places where Rob Roy was born !"

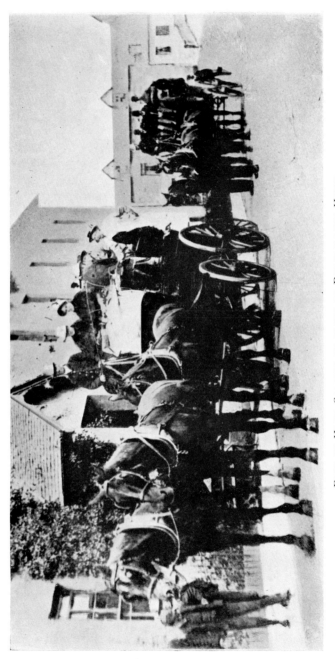

Four in Hand Coaches in front of Breadalbane Hotel.

With the gradual creep northward of the (then) Highland Railway the range of the Perth coach was shortened. When the line reached Birnam, Perth ceased to be the limit in that direction, and when the Aberfeldy branch was opened the coach was discontinued altogether. Coaching however continued for some time after this, to Loch Lomond, Callander, and other places in the west, till the inauguration of the Callander-Oban Railway cut off the outlying points beyond Killin ; later, in 1883 when the Loch Tay Steamboat Company started operations, Kenmore was the limit.

After the passing of the stage coaches, until the now ubiquitous motor car drove them finally into oblivion, one or two four-in-hands continued to ply for the benefit of visitors. Kinloch Rannoch was a favourite run, as was also the round of Drummond Hill via Fortingall, Fearnan, and Kenmore ; another was to Kenmore to connect with the pleasure steamers that used to complete the day trip to Killin and back, and to the minds of those who remember them I think there can be no doubt that the colourful spectacle of the coach on a fine morning, jingling and clattering, the trotting horses, the driver in grey top hat and red coat with silver buttons waving his whip, the passengers chattering in their high seats, (to reach which they had to use a ladder) and the brake boy or 'strapper,' at 2/6 a week, perched percariously down at the back, proud of his job and, with his halo of far horizons, the envy of his less fortunate friends, was one that had a glamour about it that no motor bus can ever hope to achieve.

* * * * * *

It was on 3rd July, 1865 that the Highland Railway came to Aberfeldy—surely a red letter day in the history of the village.

That an extension of the line to Aberfeldy would be a good thing for the town had already been decided some twenty years before by the local Debating Society at one of its meetings in "The Auld Smoky Ha' " referred to later, and there was a big turn out of the villagers to see the first train arrive. When it came puffing and clanking into the station and pulled up with a loud hiss of escaping steam many in the crowd were terrified. Not so old Carmichael, the lamp-lighter. "Waterloo" he was called, and a veteran who had faced the cannon of Napoleon in 1815 was not to be intimidated, "It's only the iron horse breathing!" was his comment.

One of the passengers on the train was the new station-master, Mr T. A. Fyfe—with all his goods and chattels in the luggage van—and it is said that the manner in which the engine-driver, accustomed to the long straights of the line further south, brought the train hurtling round the twists and windings on the way from Ballinluig, gave him the fright of his life!

The first station was a mere wooden shanty but it served to meet the needs of the case for a time. In December 1878 it was destroyed by fire and the people obtained what otherwise they might have had to wait for, a new stone-built station. This after fifty years of service was, like its predecessor, burned down (8th January, 1929), to be followed by the station as we see it now.

In the wall of the second station building was a niche in which stood a large hand-bell which used to be rung vigorous-ly by a porter to announce the approach of the train and again to herald its impending departure.

In my boyhood days 3rd class travel was a somewhat Spartan proceeding. The coaches were very much shorter than their successors of to-day, and everyone knows that the shorter the wheelbase the rougher the riding. At the same time, though there were no corridors, it was an easy matter to move from compartment to compartment, but not from coach to coach, by the simple expedient of climbing over the intervening seat backs. There was plenty of room for this pastime for, as children, we considered it a pastime on the rare occasions we had the opportunity to indulge. Add to this that the seats and the backs were of bare wood, polished certainly but bare

ABERFELDY'S FIRST RAILWAY STATION.

ABERFELDY IN 1868 FROM S.E. (*From a drawing*).

of padding or adornment, and the appropriateness of the word 'Spartan' is obvious, though, in comparison with still earlier types of trains which, with carriages open to the winds and rains of heaven, tore about the country at a speed of 12 to 15 miles an hour, scaring the wits out of people and animals alike, and of which naturally I cannot write from experience as I was not born then, they were, I suppose, the height of luxury, and only to be surpassed by that of the 1st and 2nd class compartments, the latter of which were still in use in my early days though I never aspired to anything above the level of 3rd.

Each compartment had a circular hole in the roof fitted with a removable lid which was fastened to the said roof ; after dark this lid was pulled aside and a paraffin lamp fitted into the hole by a man climbing along the top of the train from carriage to carriage catching the lamps for the successive compartments as they were thrown up, already lit, by a colleague with a barrow-load keeping pace with him along the platform.

Heating of the carriages was often more alleged than real and was by means of metal foot-warmers which, after being supposedly warmed up, were slung in, one per compartment, by the porter in charge—when he remembered !

For many years I am afraid the authorities were inclined to treat our branch as a 'poor relation' on whom to foist the cast-offs of the main line. This was bad enough but now that for a few years we have been favoured with carriages as good as the average elsewhere we live under the threat of discontinuance of our passenger service. Competition from the roads, say the powers that be, has made our little line an uneconomic proposition, and so it is that in the year of grace 1952, 87 years after the first train steamed proudly into Aberfeldy, while hoping for the best we fear the worst.

* * * * * *

Of course what people accepted as luxury when I was a youngster is far removed from what they accept as luxury now, and I rather fancy that the young people of to-day would take a very poor view indeed of what their parents and grand-parents were satisfied with, just as we older people tend to shudder at what *our* forebears accepted as part of the normal scheme of things.

Dr John Kennedy, in his *Old Highland Days*, draws a picture of life in Aberfeldy as it was when he was a boy in the second decade of the 19th century. I do not quote *verbatim* but, to avoid dubiety, set out in inverted commas the points made by him : "In those days people lived in very squalid conditions, many of the houses being little better than hovels. Lighting was by the aid of 'cruses' with wicks of the pith of rushes, or sometimes merely sticks of resinous firewood. Life was primitive and the belief in ghosts and fairies prevalent. Most of the people spoke Gaelic—the language that came out of the Garden of Eden !"

"Most of the girls and young women went bare-headed—" as they do now. The wheel has gone full circle ! "—while the older women wore mutches. When Kennedy's mother came to Aberfeldy in 1806 the only woman who wore a bonnet was the wife of the exciseman !"

"Most of the food was obtained locally but there was neither butcher nor baker in the place ; sheep at a certain season were bought by a group of people and killed in the ground behind the houses, the mutton being shared out and dried as ham is now. What wheaten loaves there were, were brought from Perth by carrier—" not in batches for retail in such shops as there were but in ones and twos purchased by the carrier on behalf of private individuals who could afford the cost. "Barley was grown in considerable amount in the district and, as high freights prevented its export to the Lowlands, private stills were common and smuggling was often done openly in every glen and on every hillside." In Perthshire turnips were first cultivated as a field crop in 1750, and potatoes ten years earlier. Before then potatoes were grown in some private gardens as a luxury. Salmon would appear to have been a glut in the market. In the *Statistical Account*, 1791, Tay salmon is reported as being sold at 6d. per lb. in spring, and 3d. per lb. in summer.

"Coal was too expensive to buy and peat was the fuel used. Each family had its bit of peat-bog or 'moss' and the cutting and drying of the winter's supply was a matter of much time and labour. One morning in May or June of each year the whole available population, led by the bagpipes, set out for the peat-cutting and the peats cut in the spring or early summer were dried and brought in in August, and during the winter each boy brought a peat to the school to help to keep the school warm."

"The school holidays depended on the harvest and, shortly before Kennedy's time, the end of the session was celebrated by a cock-fight, the owner of the winning bird being the 'king' or 'queen' of the school. This practice was stopped by Kennedy's father, Rev. James Kennedy, who was Independent minister."

"Practically every householder had a croft, and many of them cows. Every morning the herd boy blew his horn in The Square and the cows trooped out as he passed, to proceed under his guardianship to the cow parks. In the evening he conducted them back again, each cow turning aside to find its own home *en route* ; the herd would then leave his 'ox-horn' at the house where he was to get his supper the following evening, the owners of the cows entertaining him in turn. On Beltane Day he had the right of exacting an egg or, failing that, a halfpenny from each owner and then set out with his friends to the moor to boil a pot of 'Brochan Buidhe' (yellow porridge—milk, meal, and eggs)."

Beltane Day was observed in Scotland on May Day, Old Style. A fire used to be kindled on the hills and the young people danced round it and feasted on a cake made of milk and eggs. The custom at one time was supposed to be a relic of the worship of Baal, the chief male diety of the ancient Phœnicians. The word was believed to mean Bel's Fire (Celtic, 'teine,' 'fire'). Though this derivation has long been popularly accepted, modern scientific philologists are of the opinion that Beltane was a survival of a Druidic festival and that another derivation must be sought. In Gaelic 'Bealtuinn' means simply 'May Day,' which in ancient Scotland was one of the four quarter days, the others being Candlemas, Lammas, and Martinmas. I shall have more to say about Beltane later on.

"Hallowe'en was observed on 11th November (Old Hallowe'en) ; bonfires were numerous and there was always a great blaze on the Tulloch."

Hallowe'en is of course Scotland's own particular variety, with its own particular observances, of the harvest festivals which have been held in most countries from far back in pagan times.

The dipping for apples, roasting of nuts, etc., indulged in by children nowadays are survivals of rites symbolic of the laying in of a store of fruit for the coming winter. These are understandable from the nature of the festival as it used to be observed, as was also the now extinct practice of keeping the last sheaf of the harvest till Christmas and dividing it among the cattle to make them thrive during the ensuing twelve months. (If this sheaf was cut before Hallowe'en it was called the 'maiden,' if after 'cailleach'—'old woman').

The bonfires were associated with the ghosts, witches, imps, fairies, devils, and so on, who on this night of all nights of the year were most active. Long ago it was the practice to lay a ring of stones on the ground where the fire was to be built, each stone representing one person among those present ; if, after the fire had burned itself out, any stone was found to have moved from its place in the ring it was believed that the person or persons represented would die within the year.

* * * * * *

Soup Kitchen Group.

Some of the customs, etc., referred to by Dr Kennedy persisted long after his day, thus : 'An Old Black School Pupil' writing in *The People's Journal* of 7th January, 1928, tells that when she herself in the 1860's attended this school—one of the old thatched cottages in what is now Burnside—it was still the practice of children in winter to bring a peat or a log for the school fire daily ; she adds that the fire was in the middle of the floor of the schoolroom and that her teacher, Charlie Hollack, an old lame man who must have been a character, was in the habit of keeping his top hat on during lessons and of smoking his pipe between times.

When I, the present writer, first attended school in the new school, now Breadalbane Academy, transferred some months before from what is now part of the Town Hall Buildings, in the late eighties of last century, the practice of bringing peat had stopped but I recollect that at times 'coal money' had to be taken and handed over to the teacher. Likewise in my time had the practice died out of giving 'Hansel' or New Year's gifts to the teacher on Hansel Monday (Old Style), a practice which was followed in the Black Street school at all events, as late as 1860.

When Mr Donald MacCallum was a schoolboy in the 1860's Gaelic was still the main language of the people, and all the children spoke it.

Mutches, too survived long after the dates covered by Dr Kennedy's reminiscences, as is shown in the accompanying photograph of a 'soup kitchen' group. As the soup kitchen was not established till 1861 at the earliest it is obvious that the wearing of this head-dress was still almost universal among the older women, at least of the poorer class, half a century after his time. They were worn, however, much later even than that, in fact well on into the 1890's, less commonly certainly than earlier and then only among the very old women, yet not so rarely as to be curious.

So also with Hallowe'en which we as children always observed on 11th November (Old Hallowe'en) with bonfires, turnip lanterns, dipping for apples, and so on—all essential parts of the proceedings. The observance of Hallowe'en seems to be dying out in this district, and probably elsewhere as well, young people having many other diversions which were not available to their parents and grandparents, though oddly enough Guy Fawkes Day within recent years would appear to be coming in for more attention. In my young days we never heard of it ; possibly the usually associated squibs, rockets, crackers, etc., may have something to do with it.

Though there were butchers and bakers in Aberfeldy as far back as my memory goes, the practice of buying a sheep and having it killed in the back garden, as described by Dr Kennedy had not entirely died out and I well remember one such occasion at which I as a youngster was present, and a hideously gruesome and brutal business it was, the bloody details of which haunted me for many a day and are better forgotten.

As I remember it, each of the butchers had his own slaughterhouse and one of these was in Mill Street in a small building that still stands by the roadside at the foot of the steep slope down from Bank Street and is now used as a garage. When in 1895 or 1896 the town abattoir was erected just east of the railway station the various butchers did their slaughtering there, though to begin with the authorities had difficulty in persuading one or two of them to use the new premises ; prosecution even was contemplated but fortunately did not prove necessary. Now the work is in the hands of one man appointed to do such killing as has to be done, for them all.

I remember, too, when many of the town's folk kept pigs ; and when the time came for a pig to go the way of all pigs the local pig killer was called in, after which the carcase was steeped in a tub of boiling water and then strung up on a ladder to have the hair scraped off with a pot lid.

The pig sticker in my young days was a highly popular old worthy named Donald McLeish (born 1822, died 1897) who lived in a small white-washed cottage which was removed to make way for the new post office in the late 1890's, and who, as well as pig sticker, was one of the last of the old cottage weavers. Other 'trades' he followed with equal facility and cheerfulness were those of bill poster, bell-man, hair cutter (he cut mine many times), church beadle, bowling club green-keeper, grave digger, and so on—a real jack-of-all-trades.

What Dr Kennedy wrote about the herd boy still held with little change in the 1870's for Mr Donald MacCallum has put it on record that when he left school in 1871 'to earn his living' as he said at the age of nine he acted for three years as herd boy. In his day the herd had two horns—one of tin for blowing and the other a real cow's horn for leaving at the cow-owners' houses to warn them that he would be their guest the following day or days according to whether his prospective host owned one or more cows, not only for his supper but for all his meals. His money was hard earned for what he received from 1st April to 11th November was only £1 (*i.e.* 7½d. per week) plus his food, his day commencing at 5.30 A.M. and ending at 8 P.M.

The custom was still in vogue when I was at school in the late 1880's and the 1890's except that the nightly supper at the expense of the cow owners was a thing of the past, as was also the 'egg or halfpenny' fee on Beltane Day. Practically every close or pend in Kenmore Street had one or two byres—later converted for human habitation, the resulting dwellings being such was would not be tolerated under any present day Housing Scheme, yet some of which are still in use.

*　　*　　*　　*　　*　　*

When I was a youngster one of the great occasions was the annual Feeing Market held in late October. Farmers from all around gathered in to engage employees for the ensuing year, 1/- arles or earnest money to seal the contract being given to each person so engaged. Prospective employees, male and female, paraded the streets in their best attire, the girls gradually accumulating, as the day wore on, armfuls of sweets, etc., 'fairings' from their male admirers. The Square was filled with booths of travelling showmen ready and eager to relieve all and sundry of their spare cash, cheap-jacks, try-your-strength merchants, etc., vying with the rest in creating a scene noisy as well as colourful, especially after dark under under the naked lights of paraffin flares. Often these booths overflowed from The Square down into Dunkeld Street and up Bridgend into Bank Street.

I remember particularly one of them in which was housed an amazing new invention—a phonograph ! The instrument was inside a large sound-proof glass box from which were led a number of rubber tubes each ending in a binaural earpiece not unlike that of the stethoscope used by doctors nowadays, and for the fee of one penny one was privileged to listen in to such music as a well worn cylindrical record and an equally well worn needle between them could scrape out. But it was a wonderful and unheard of experience at the time—in the middle 1890's—and the enterprising showman reaped a rich harvest.

In *Morison's Perth and Perthshire Register, Supplement to Oliver & Boyd's Edinburgh Almanac or Universal Scots and Imperial Register for 1830*, under 'Aberfeldy,' five annual Fairs were listed :—

January — First Thursday, Old Style.

March — Tuesday before Kenmore Market.

April — Last Thursday, Old Style.

July — Last Friday, Old Style.

October — Last Friday, Old Style.

In *Oliver & Boyd's Almanac for 1899* only this last Fair is mentioned and the date given for it is 'The Thursday in October before the Doune Tryst.'

Not one of these Fairs survives to-day. The July, or Groset Fair (Gooseberry Fair), was still held in the 1860's, and the October Fair, in the form of the Feeing Market, up till about the beginning of this century.

'Old Style' though superseded by 'New Style' in 1752 was adhered to for many annual functions long after that date, thus, the Hogmanay feast and treat for the inmates of the Poorhouse at Logierait was given annually an 11th January— Old Hogmanay—as lately as the early 1930's, and Hallowe'en, as already stated, is observed by some even to the present day on 11th November. Prior to 1752 the corresponding dates of course, December 31st and October 31st.

Though the Almanacs do not appear to list any Fairs as having been held in Aberfeldy in the 1700's there is no doubt that such gatherings took place. They cannot have been of any great antiquity, however, as they were not named after Saints but were usually known by the time of year at which they were held or by the commodity sold on the occasion, as linseed or 'grosets,' etc. One was called the 'Race Fair' and at it there were races—for women as well as men.

As time went on the obstruction to traffic in The Square caused by the October Feeing Market came to be a problem and the 'shows' were removed to an open space at the east end of the town ; short term engagements between farmer and employee made the yearly gatherings meaningless, and the Fair, like many an old custom before it, died out.

One can scarcely label 'German Bands,' as they were called an old custom but, like the Feeing Market and many other things, they were one of the features of our irrecoverable pre-1914 world the like of which we shall probably never see again. Whether they were truly 'German' or not was not always certain ; enough it was that the men talked some foreign language and, dressed in (usually) blue suits with caps like railway porters, dispensed somewhat blaring (usually though not always brass) music, one of their number at intervals detaching himself from the group at each stance to go cap in hand to the doors of all houses within reasonable earshot.

Other 'foreigners' who moved about the country in those
days for our entertainment and their own profit included the
mid-European with his dancing bear and the Italian organ-
grinder with his miserable little monkey. Many years have
gone since these were seen in Aberfeldy.

* * * * * *

To come now to the subject of Education :   The real pioneer
bearers of the torch of knowledge in the Highlands were, of
course the 'Saints' and the monks attached to the various
primitive monasteries, including that at Dull, set up in the
country chiefly during the period of unrest of the 5th and 6th
centuries which followed the fall of Rome.   During this time
learned men tended to retire to safe retreats where they could
converse and study those high problems which exercised their
minds.   Secular to begin with, these societies in time became
converted into monasteries seeking the protection of the Church
of which the barbarians, many of them already Christians,
stood in considerable awe.   Young men who were admitted
as members of these establishments had passed on to them such
learning as the monks possessed, and others, in exchange for
work done, were accepted as part time students, while the
people in the surrounding district were taught to clear and
cultivate the land and instructed in the useful arts and crafts.

With the coming of St. Columba in A.D. 563 this development of monastic life found a centre in Iona and, though
there is nothing to suggest that St. Columba himself ever visited
Central Perthshire, there is not lacking evidence in the way of
tradition, place-names, etc., in our countryside of the presence
in the past of members of the Columban and other clergy
attached to the Christianisation movement.   The story of St.
Cuthbert's association with Weem will be told later and the
problematical association of St. Palladius with Aberfeldy has
already been referred to.

After the Norman Conquest, with its influx of Roman Catholic clergy, and the marriage in 1068 of Malcolm III of
Scotland (Malcolm Canmore) with the English Princess Margaret,

an ardent Catholic, Roman Catholicism which had for long been in conflict with the doctrines of the old Celtic Church was declared the Established religion of the country. The monasteries, etc., of the Columban Church came under the sway of the Church of Rome and the work of the monks was carried on by the priests who voluntarily took in hand young people who showed a desire to learn and taught them to read and write.

After the Reformation in the 16th century, brought about by the increasing laxity of discipline in the monasteries, the hoarding up of riches, the well-stocked cellars, the acquiring of property contrary to the rules of Benedict, etc., the Highlands lapsed back into a state bordering on complete illiteracy, some of the lairds and chiefs being unable even to sign their own names, and it was not until 1646, when the Scottish Parliament passed and Act calling upon every parish to set up a school within its bounds that the light began to shine again.

Even before 1646, however, young men even of the humblest class occasionally managed not only to obtain an elementary education but to push forward to college and become pupil teachers.

In this district parochial schools were set up in Kenmore (1651), Dull (1654), and Weem (1665). Though a school is reported to have been conducted in Aberfeldy in 1682 by a man named Donald Bruce it would appear not to have been in the same class as the new parish schools and many parents in the town who wished their children to have the benefits of 'book learning' sent them to where they felt such could best be obtained—mainly to Dull and Weem.

In 1796, as has been told, a school was established in Aberfeldy through the efforts of the Society for the Propagation of Christian Knowledge in Scotland as part of their campaign to fill in gaps left open by the Act of 1646, and it was still functionong under the auspices of this Society in 1842. Where it was housed is not now clear but it is probable that, in one form or another, it carried on until, as Breadalbane Academy, it began work in the late 1840's under the auspices of the Free Church in a new building in the Crieff Road.   This school was sometimes referred to as the Free Church School.

Of Breadalbane Academy in its early days Dr Macmillan (*The Highland Tay, 1901*) writes :   "The present Town Hall is an extension and adaption of the old Breadalbane Academy —" (called Breadalbane Seminary in *Oliver & Boyd, 1885*) "— which, fifty years ago, was one of the best schools in the country.   Under a succession of admirable masters it attracted boarders from many parts of England and Scotland and the Colonies, and the education imparted was more varied and of a higher character than could at the time be obtained in any village in Scotland."   Dr Macmillan himself (born 1833) was educated in the Academy under a Mr Johnstone, of whom he wrote very highly.

In 1872 the struggle for control of education in Scotland which had been going on for a considerable time between the various Churches, other religious bodies, etc., and the laity was finally resolved by the passing of the Education Act of that year and the appointment of School Boards which relieved all other bodies of responsibility,   The Head-master of the Aberfeldy school at that time was a Mr William Smith, who was followed in 1881 by a Mr James Allan who continued in office until 1885, when he was followed in turn by Messrs. A. Grieve (1885-1922), E. J. Balfour (1922-1942), and Doctors R. S. Brydon (1942-1952), and A. Goldie (1952) the present Rector.

Even throughout the 19th century, but in gradually diminishing numbers, children from Aberfeldy continued to tramp daily to and from the school at Weem, latterly mainly those whose parents rightly or wrongly had fallen foul of the Education Authorities in Aberfeldy.   When, about fifty years ago the school at Weem was closed these parents felt they had a real grievance !

While these changes and developments were proceeding a number of so-called 'dame-schools' and 'adventure schools' came and went.   The old school in Black Street and that at

Tominellow have already been mentioned—both now vanished without trace—and the late Mr J. C. Campbell (referred to in the Foreword) in his notes tells of others that functioned in his young days from about the middle sixties to the middle eighties of last century.   There were three in Kenmore Street, all in the second close on the right (No. 14) as one goes west : on the left an Infants' School run by a Miss Malloch who had removed there from her former premises in a house which stood on the site of the present Commercial Bank, on the right Miss Smith's Young Ladies' Institute and, also on the right, facing the street, Alexander Gow's Secondary School.   Three boys educated in Gow's school subsequently attained profess-orial rank—John Harrower, Glasgow (Latin) and, later, Aberdeen (Greek) :   John Macnaughton, Kingston, Ontario (Classics) : and Duncan MacGregor, Dunedin, New Zealand (Mental and Moral Philosophy).   Reference to Mr Gow is made in the Foreword to this Account.

In Breadalbane Villas, now Taybridge Road, in the house known as St. Margaret's—then Lucknow Villa—(third from the end going towards Taybridge, on the right) a Miss Scott conducted her Young Ladies' Institute.   This school contin-ued well into my own early days.

Mr Campbell also refers to the old school in Black Street, in his time run by a Dominie McLean, and to one conducted by a Miss Macdonald in Dunkeld Street, in the western part of a block which once stood just east of No. 34.

The Black Street School must have been discontinued in the middle 1870's as the effects of Dominie McLean, who was the last teacher in this school, were sold off in 1876.

When the school at Tominellow went out of existence is not clear, but the gradual disappearance of the scattered hamlets and small 'farm towns' which in the old days dotted the country round about and from which its pupils were drawn was already in progress in the 1840's.

Breadalbane Academy, as we know it now, started work in the east block of the present buildings on 11th April, 1887, the old Academy (as just quoted from Dr Macmillan) becoming part of the Town Hall Buildings. When the School Board took over from the Free Church in 1873 the name was changed to Aberfeldy Public School, and the School Log Books dating back to that year are preserved in the school. Fees for compulsory standards, which were still charged when I first attended, were done away with in 1889. On the abolition of School Boards in 1919 the name Breadalbane Academy was resumed and control passed into the hands of the Education Committee of the Perth County Council, with a Sub-Committee and Clerk stationed locally.

The work of the old Academy in the Crieff Road was conducted in what is now known as 'The Library,' the small room opening off it, and what is now called the Commissioners' Room. This was generally known as 'The Big School' to distinguish it from the Infants' School which was carried on in what is now the back or Lesser Town Hall. At the time of the move in 1887, and for a dozen or more years before and a good time after, the Infants' Department was in the charge of a Miss Christina Clark, who was the first certificated schoolmistress in Aberfeldy.

Since 1886 the school has gone on from strength to strength, expanding and spreading its wings. Behind and to the west of the original block has grown up what now resembles a small village and, when the additions at present in hand and contemplated are completed, it is proposed that the original block shall be devoted entirely to the purposes of the Primary Department. It is also envisaged that the present playing fields behind the gardens of the houses in Kenmore Street and the Crieff Road will ultimately be required for additional new buildings and the field to the west of Tomghiubhais acquired in its place.

A number of years ago two villas in the town were taken over by the Authority and are now used as hostels for country pupils whose homes are too distant to be reached oftener than at weekends ; these are Dunolly at the extreme west end of Kenmore Street (north side), and Craigthuil, the last house but one from the foot of Taybridge Road (north-east side). The former of these, Dunolly, was inaugurated in January 1930 and has sleeping accommodation for 24 girls. Craigthuil with similar accommodation for 18 boys, was taken into service in April 1936. In 1922 the house known as Edengrove, in Taybridge Road was acquired as the official residence of the Rector.

The following figures give some indication of the work now undertaken in the Academy and, for comparison, the figures for 1876 and 1886 are appended :

1952 :—7 Honours Graduates, 8 ordinary Graduates, 1 Art (D.A.) Teacher, 4 Teachers fully Qualified in special subjects, and 4 non-graduates—24 in all. In addition there are 3 peripatetic or visiting part-time Teachers. There are no Pupil Teachers. The number of children attending is 477—Primary Department 229, Secondary Department 248.

1876 :—2 Teachers, 1 presumably a Graduate though I have been unable to verify this, and 1 Certificated Teacher. There were several unqualified and uncertificated Teachers and 183 children—boys 100, girls 83.

1886 :—3 Teachers, 1 Graduate. Several unqualified and uncertificated, and 219 children—boys 112, girls 107.

I am indebted to Dr Goldie, Rector of the Academy, for the above figures and also for the following notes from the School Log Books :— At 2.30 P.M. on 31st August, 1939 the school was closed to prepare for the arrival of War evacuees from Glasgow and, by order of the Education Committee, remained closed for teaching purposes until 15th September, 1939. The evacuee children, though not all of them, continued as pupils in the Academy until the date of their return to Glasgow, 16th October, 1943. For the term of their stay in Aberfeldy the local staff had the help of 5 Teachers lent by the Glasgow Education Authority.

For a considerable time prior to 1935 Breadalbane Academy and Pitlochry High School were both Senior Secondary Schools but in that year, owing to the degrading of the school at Pitlochry to a Junior Secondary School, Breadalbane Academy became *the* Senior Secondary School for the whole Highland Area of the County.

*   *   *   *   *   *

The main or large hall of the Town Hall Buildings in the Crieff Road stands in part of what was the playground of what we as children used to call 'the old school.' This hall, together with the various rooms of the old school behind, form the Town Hall Buildings as they are to-day. The unbuilt-on part of the old playground now functions usefully as a car park, etc., on occasion as required.

On this spot, away back in the past, is supposed to have stood The Black House, mansion of 'Aberfeldy west of the burn,' where, it is said, the Menzieses of Weem lived when they first came to these parts from Nithsdale nearly seven hundred years ago. It is also told how, in the 17th century, one of the MacGregors, at that time under the ban of the Government, took refuge here and the dog that tracked him, the last of its breed, was killed.

Within the precincts of the Town Hall Buildings are the Aberfeldy Fire Station, the Club Room of the Comrades of the Great War, the Societies' Room, the Commissioners' Room, and the now extinct Public Library and Reading Room.

Though this last has not functioned as a library for many years it is still known as 'the Library'; on its outer wall, by the side entrance to the hall from the yard, there is a tablet bearing the inscription : "This site and the original buildings were presented to the town of Aberfeldy by the Most Honourable Gavin 3rd Marquis of Breadalbane. Anno Domini 1887." and on the west front of the main hall, towards the Crieff Road and to the left of the entrance, there is another which states that "The Foundation Stone of this Hall was laid on September 21st, 1889 by Sir Donald Currie, M.P."

The local Fire Brigade, formed in 1903, is now part of the National Fire Service. Their original fire engine was a manual the operation of which was no work for weaklings. This was followed about 1922 by a 'steamer' which came from Taymouth where it had formed part of the anti-fire defences maintained by the Marquis. The present motor engine, acquired in 1940, is more in keeping with the times. At strategic points in the streets there are hydrants which deliver water at a pressure high enough to send a jet over the tallest building in the town. Members of the brigade are equipped with telephones in their houses by which they may be summoned during the night; by day they receive notice by a siren fixed to the wall of the Town Hall.

The Commissioners' Room of course serves the purpose implied in its name but in addition it has, as has also the Societies' Room, been the meeting place of some of the Societies which exist now or have existed in the past in Aberfeldy.

For a time the Freemasons met here in secret conclave. They now have their own Temple, erected at a cost of £400, in Moness Terrace where the Brethren of the Craft (Lodge Breadalbane 657) assemble once weekly and the Companions of the Royal Arch Chapter (Breadalbane 181) once monthly to practise their mystic rites.

Prior to 1881 though there was no Masonic Lodge in Aberfeldy there was another Lodge which had embraced the surrounding district for the preceding sixty-two years, the Tay and Lyon Lodge (No. 276), Kenmore, which extended its work to Killin and Rannoch as well as Aberfeldy.

Oddly enough, though there was no Lodge in Aberfeldy at that time, the Royal Arch Chapter was already in existence, but only just, for it came into being in 1880.

Before the present Temple was consecrated in 1905 Lodge Breadalbane passed through many vicissitudes and for over twenty years had a hard struggle for life ; with no fixed abode and a lamentably small membership often its days seemed to be numbered and doubtless, but for the keenness and determination of the few Brethren then on the roll, the Craft would have vanished from Aberfeldy. Indeed this actually happened so far as the Royal Arch Chapter was concerned for it perished of sheer inanition early in its history, only to arise, however, phœnix-like from its ashes in 1911.

The following notes bear witness to the pioneer efforts of the Craft in the 'eighties and 'nineties :—

5/2/1881 : Lodge opened in one of the upper rooms in the Breadalbane Hotel.

2/11/1888 : Meeting place transferred to a private room over the old school in the Crieff Road.

18/7/1892 : Meetings removed to the Commissioners' Room in the Town Hall Buildings.

6/9/1899 : Meetings again removed, this time to Breadalbane Terrace (the ground floor rooms nearest the Palace Hotel—now used as a dwelling house).

2/12/1905 : Present Temple consecrated.

On occasion, prior to 1899, meetings were held elsewhere— e.g., The Crown Hotel in Bank Street, Weem Hotel, Reid's Temperance Hotel, etc.—when the Commissioners' Room, etc., were otherwise required. (Reid's Hotel is no longer in existence. It was on the east side of The Square, in the building which is now linked to the stores next door by an upstairs covered way and serves as a confectionery shop, tea-rooms, dance hall, etc.).

Lodge Breadalbane 657 is the only Lodge in Britain the Brethren of which wear tartan shoulder sashes and tartan edging to their aprons and, I believe, with the exception of a Lodge in Australia, the only one in the world. This tartan edging, etc., Breadalbane Campbell, was adopted in 1886.

The Ancient Order of Foresters (Court Breadalbane 6774) once strong in the town is now practically extinct ; one or two of the old members remain but, the functions of the Society having been more or less usurped by the State, first under the National Health Insurance Acts of 1912 and after, and further under the National Health Service inaugurated in 1948, there is little inducement for new members to come in. I remember them though, as an imposing body of men who made a brave show when they turned out in procession in their best attire set off with green shoulder sashes, quaint plumed hats and white gloves, and with their great two-handed banner and all the pomp and panoply of state that they kept laid by against big occasions.

* * * * * *

Behind Breadalbane Academy rises a mound which has been identified as 'Dùn-eas' (the fort of the den or waterfall), one of the nine ancient 'forts' in the district.

Though now planted with oaks it was evidently at one time covered with firs, the Gaelic name by which it is known locally, 'Tomghiubhais' (pronounced 'Tom-i-uish'), meaning 'the fir mound.' In one or two large scale maps of the district of half a century ago I have seen it marked as 'Torr Hill' ; it is never so referred to by the people of Aberfeldy. It is a terraced rectangular fort and traces of trenches on the ascending slopes of its southern aspect and of walls or ramparts enclosing the broad flat top may still be seen. The fort is remarkable for its rectangular form and almost unique in that earthen forts are very rare in Scotland. Whether the mound is wholly artificial or whether the earthworks, as is more probable, have been thrown up around a natural mound it is impossible to determine without excavating. There is a large flat topped boulder on the top which is supposed to mark a grave.

Memory of the others is preserved in place-names in the neighbourhood :

Duntaylor	Dùn-an-tailear	Tailor's Fort.
Dunskeig	Dùn-sgitheag	Fort of the Thorn.
Duntuim	Dùn-tuim	Fort of the Mound
Dunacree	Dùn-na-craoibhe	The Tree Fort.
Duntaggart	Dùn-an-t'sagairt	Priest's Fort.
Dundavie	Dùn-Daidh	David's Fort.
Dundai	—	do.
The Dùn	Dùn	Fort.

In his book *In Famed Breadalbane* the late Rev. W. A. Gillies, D.D., writes : "Several place names beginning with the Gaelic 'Dun,' 'fort,' suggest the existence here of round forts similar to those in Glenlyon.   There are hardly any traces of these ancient structures now remaining, but the names are still attached to farms."

The list given by Dr Gillies is that given above, except that it does not include Dundavie.   Whether one is justified in accepting all these as forts or not is open to question ; 'Dùn,' in Gaelic, may be translated not only as 'fort' but as 'heap'— the late Rev. John MacLean preferred the latter interpretation —and the traces referred to by Dr Gillies are not very obvious.

This uncertainty does not apply to the last of the nine listed. It is set to the south of the town on the summit of a prominent hill to which it has given its name, The Dùn (pronounced Doon).   It is definitely one of a chain of hill forts that extended right across Central Scotland from Killin to Stonehaven. Access to it is difficult at present as the approaches are densely wooded, but the strength of a fort placed as it is on the summit of a bold and rocky eminence commanding extensive views of the valley and surrounding district is easy to see.   The structure has been erected in an almost complete circle with an inside diameter of 110 feet ; the walls vary in thickness from 14 to 15 feet.   To the south-west, its most vulnerable side, three trenches or earthworks run from east to west for a distance of about 50 yards.   There is a tradition that, somewhere in the neighbourhood, there is a treasure so ill-concealed that the sun shines upon it every day at noon, which is destined to be found by a red-haired woman looking for a horse !

Dundavie and Dunacree lie more than a mile from Aberfeldy and so fall outwith the scope of this Account ; Duntaggart and Dundai have already been noted ; there is nothing noteworthy about Dunskeig, but Duntaylor and Duntuim call for a word or two in passing.

Until the early part of the present century the site of Duntaylor was occupied by a hamlet of quite a number of cottages, and a lime kiln.   One by one these cottages became vacant, fell into disrepair, and were cleared away ; in the meantime a new farm-house was erected and now no trace either of the old hamlet or of the kiln remains.

On 18th February, 1878 an old man named Peter Fegan or Feggan died in Duntaylor at the advanced age of 107 years and 9 months.   Peter, or Figgins as most people called him, was an Irish peddler who had been in the district for a long time.   In his Glengarry bonnet, sleeved waistcoat, coarse trousers and clogs, and with a sack over his shoulder, he went about the country selling handkerchiefs.   Latterly, when he became too old to travel the roads, Mr Thomas A. Fyfe, Aberfeldy's first stationmaster, gave him facilities at the station for selling his goods to people coming and going by train.   He had a card printed and hung up :   "Peter Fegan, aged 107 years.   Please buy."

Fantastically, it was whispered in the district that poor old Figgins was none other than that atrocious monster William Hare who, to save his own neck, turned King's Evidence in the Burke and Hare or 'West Port Murders' Trial in Edinburgh in 1828.   Peter was said to have declared that his extreme old age was a visitation on him as a punishment for the sins of his youth but, as he was nearer sixty than fifty at the time of the Burke and Hare murders, he could scarcely have been referring to these ; besides, it is generally accepted that Hare died a blind beggar in the streets of London.

Good as Peter's record is it was beaten by a resident tinker or tinsmith in Aberfeldy, John Stewart by name, who was born in the 17th century, lived through the 18th and married in the 19th—dying at the age of 112 ! Though 'The Colonel', as he was styled, was married in the 19th century he was married in the 18th also for, in 1751, according to the Parish Register of Weem, John Stewart, tinker in Aberfeldy, and his wife had there a son baptised and called Charles.

In the field above the Duntaylor Road and about 150 yards to the east of the site of the old hamlet there is a small knoll, rocky and tree-covered, in the north-east corner of which may be traced the grass-grown foundations of what must have been a building of some kind. They lie in the form of a square with sides of about 15 feet, that to the east being absent. As to when and why this building existed nothing seems to be known now, but what is left of it certainly does not appear to conform to the usual 'oblong' of the ruined cottage.

Duntuim, like Duntaylor, stands on the site of a vanished hamlet in which in the early 1800's dwelt eight families ; the ruins of the old cottages could still be seen well on into the second half of the century. The clearances here, like those on the lands of Borlick, Mains of Murthly, and elsewhere on the Breadalbane Estates, were carried out by the second Marquis who came into possession in 1834 (died 1862), on the advice of his factor, James F. Wyllie.

Harsh though these clearances may have appeared at the time they were at the worst merely a forestalling of the inevitable, for there is no doubt that, with more settled conditions in the country generally and people beginning to feel that they were no longer obliged to live in hamlets and clusters for security, the hamlet system was doomed. Young men too, seeking wider range of choice of employment in the towns and greater scope in the Colonies, were drifting away. It was also becoming obvious that the old system of runrig, which meant the breaking up of fields into small patches, was not only absurd but wasteful, and that great improvement of food production would follow the placing of larger tracts of land in the hands of one man.

PETER FEGAN, 107 YEARS OLD.

DUNTAYLOR FROM THE EAST.

DUNTAYLOR FROM S.W.   (ABERFELDY IN BACKGROUND).

Mr Thomas A. Fyfe.
Aberfeldy's first and most imposing Station Master.

Some 25 years earlier James Robertson, *Survey of Perthshire, 1813*, had advocated improvement more or less along these lines and remarked on the possibility of new taxes being necessary to help to meet the costs. One of his suggestions, quaint though it seems now, was that watches and clocks, already bearing a limited and selective tax, should be taxed up to the hilt and *without exception* as luxuries !

(As an aside here one may quote a rather illuminating note on the Parish of Logierait in the *Statistical Account, 1791*, "Many of the young men wear watches, and several of the farmers now have clocks in their houses" !)

* * * * * *

The field to the immediate west of Duntaylor, running down from the lower boundary of what was the Heart Wood to the Kenmore Road, was once one of the town's cow parks—the West Cow Park. Right at the top of this park, and reached by the Dunskeig Road, is the town refuse dump. It was removed here not many years ago from its former location at the east end of Breadalbane Terrace where, before it was filled in, there used to be a small pond well known to the children as 'the Lochan,' a favourite playground when ice-bound in the winter.

A little lower down (in the cow park) are traces of old flax retting beds and, down near the foot and visible from the Kenmore Road, is a glacially straited rock similar to that at Duntaggart. This stone from time immemorial has been known as 'The Sliding Stone,' not from any inherent power of loco-motion but from the use put to it by generations of children past and present, to the detriment of trouser-seats and boots (when worn) !

(The glaciated stone already mentioned at the Mains of Murthly, too, has seen service of this kind at the hands or, rather, the feet, etc. of the children of the vanished clachan of Tominella in the past, and still sees it from time to time in the present when there are children living about the farm. The field in which the Murthly stone lies goes under the name of 'the sliding stone field' to this day. Marks of 'sliding' are also to be seen on the Duntaggart stone and, when one recalls that there was once a hamlet here, the cause would appear to be not far to seek).

Westwards from Aberfeldy the road to Kenmore runs under the shadow of an avenue of oaks. These trees owe their planting to a suggestion made by Queen Victoria to Lord Breadalbane at the time of her state visit with the Prince Consort to Taymouth in 1842. Just outside the rim of our 'circle of one mile radius' stand 'The Twin Trees'—oaks also but of a very much earlier date. Sometimes known as 'Lord and Lady Breadalbane' they are endowed with mystic powers, for it is held that the unfortunate (or fortunate ?) individual who cannot pass between their gnarled old trunks must remain forever unwed !

* * * * * *

From the eastern boundary of the Heart Wood to the Den of Moness extends the hillface known locally as 'the Torr' (Gaelic, 'torr,' a 'hillock'), the summit of which before it became so thickly overgrown with young trees was Aberfeldy's favourite site for bonfires on special occasions after the Tulloch ceased to be so used. (Another favourite site within our 'circle,' and a better one would be difficult to find, was—and still is, for it is clear of obstruction—that used by the people on the far side of the valley on the prominent cliff-top towards the eastern end of the Rock of Weem).

The Torr was another of the town's old Cow Parks.

Near the boundary of the Den of Moness and running to a certain extent parallel with it up and down the steep face of the Torr are trenches having the appearance of ancient earthworks. They are very well marked, but nothing is known of their origin or purpose. Marshall, in his *Historic Scenes in Perthshire, 1879,* writes, "In the neighbourhood to the south (of Aberfeldy) are vestiges of some old entrenchments which are supposed to mark the site of a Roman Camp." It is presumed that he refers to those under mention as there are no others anywhere near, but the likelihood of their being of Roman origin is, I imagine, extremely remote.

* * * * * *

About a quarter of a mile beyond the summit of the first steep pull up the Torr, at an altitude of about 850 feet above sea-level and about 500 feet above most of the town—there is a 320-feet Ordnance Survey bench mark on Breadalbane Parish Church—and on the right of the road to Urlar (Gaelic, 'an t-urlar,' 'the floor') is the Clear Water Basin or reservoir of the Aberfeldy Water Supply. Strictly speaking this is outside our 'one mile circle' but as it forms the last stage so far in the development of the town's water supply it has to be mentioned.

It is not clear when a water service was first introduced but it is known that a few gentlemen residents in the West End of the town were the first to undertake the laying of a service main. This main was of mostly of wood and was for use west of the burn. Subsequently this was extended to the east of the burn, but only surface water was allowed, the branch being taken off the top of the first pipe, thus giving water to the East End only when the pipe was full.

Later a new system was introduced for the whole of the town, with a reservoir to hold 12,000 gallons. This reservoir was, and still is, just inside the entrance to the Den of Moness from the Crieff Road, and the dam on the burn which maintained a steady flow lies a short way further up. Metal mains were laid in the streets with stand pipes at convenient spots, house-holders who did not have supplies brought into their houses having keys to boxes containing mechanism for turning on and off the water as required. Before this there were wells, some of them with hand pumps, at various points in the town giving so excellent a supply that inhabitants were slow to give them up for the new supply.

One of these pumps was at what was called 'Stewart the plasterer's corner' at the foot of the Strulach, a footpath which branched off about the middle of Dunkeld Street and ran southwards to join the Tomchulan (now Old Crieff) Road at Victoria Cottage. This pump was cleared away when the Strulach was widened to form Moness Terrace at the time of the building of the warehouse of Messrs. P. & J. Haggart (Breadalbane Woollen Mills) in 1899.

Another, which I remember well, was 'Cooper's Pump' which stood at the top of Chapel Street beside the old post office. The owner of the property and post-master at the time was a man called Cowper—'Cooper' in the local vernacular—hence the name. In its day, I should think, this pump must have come very near the picture one has of the Parish Pump of fiction for here, according to 'An Old Aberfeldy Boy' writing in *The People's Journal* (30/8/1930) of fifty years before, the village fathers, keen politicians all, were wont to forgather to debate and decide the questions of the hour, local and general, and hither the wives—Pen Hamish, Pen Iain, Pen Pharic, and so on as they were called (meaning Mrs James, Mrs John, Mrs Peter, etc., as the case might be)—used to come in their mutches, their home-made petticoats and short gowns, to fill their stoups and pitchers and exchange gossip. Nor was it unusual to see them with their skirts turned up and draped over their heads and shoulders to act as combined hoods and capes should the weather be cold or inclement. Of course they wore layers of heavy voluminous petticoats in those days !

There was a well (without a pump) at the foot of the Tulloch on the south side of The Square in the close between the taller modern building and the lower and older block to the west which had a fame that extended beyond the bounds of the town. It was known in my young days as McLeish's Well as it was situated just outside the bakehouse of one of Aberfeldy's first bakers, a man named McLeish. This well had the reputation of being one of the best wells in the town and was regarded as particularly excellent for butter making ; it was said that good butter-making wives used to come in with their flagons for supplies even from Camserney and Dull. The late Mr William Robertson, of Messrs. W. & A. Robertson who built the large premises on the east side of The Square, was so impressed with the qualities of this well that he had it properly enclosed ; it is practically forgotten now.

Other wells in regular use at one time were :—

(a) Behind a shop in Bank Street which bears the date 1838, and reached via the close opening southward directly opposite the top of Mill Street. At present this close gives access to a motor garage.

(b) A little way up the Strulach, near where the Masonic Temple now is. Before this well was eventually covered up the outflow was piped off into one of the town drains.

(c) At the foot of Burnside, on the east side of the road. This well was so completely forgotten that about 25 years ago a motor lorry driver who knew nothing of its existence, when swinging well out to take the left turn on to Alma Bridge, sent one of his offside wheels through the cover.

(d) Another old well, of which no memory persisted whatsoever, was found by chance comparatively recently under the platform of the railway station some yards west of the main buildings. It is now fitted with a metal cover.

(e) A well which is still as it used to be and may still be sampled lies below the little swing gate at the south-western entrance to the grounds of the Black Watch Memorial, at the river bank and led down to by a short flight of stone steps. This spring rarely runs dry but it becomes submerged when the river is above its normal level.

The gathering ground of the present supply, which was opened on 7th October, 1910, is in the hills above Urlar ; the intake from the Urlar Burn (as the Moness Burn is called in its upper reaches) is below Urlar farmhouse and the water is conveyed about 1100 yards in a 6-inch pipe to the clear water basin already referred to. This basin has a storage capacity of over 1,500,000 gallons, about 13 or 14 days supply for 2,000 persons at 60 gallons per head per day ; the average daily consumption is 19,200 gallons. Between the reservoir and the town are two break-water cisterns to give two heads, one for the upper and one for the lower part of the town ; the upper of these is beside the road that ascends the face of the Torr just where it swings to the right to slant westwards towards the upper end of the eastern boundary of the Heart Wood ; the other is lower down, on the east side of the road, quite near Torrhill (house). * * * * * *

Across the head of the Den of Moness from the clear water basin is Margmore—'The great merk (land)'. Here are the ruins of another of the many deserted clachans of the district, at one time a busy market place. It is now represented by a single house and some semi-derelict out-buildings ; close to the lowest of these lies a curiously marked stone concerning which tradition has it that when the Devil jumped over the hills from Glenquaich he alighted upon it, leaving his prints

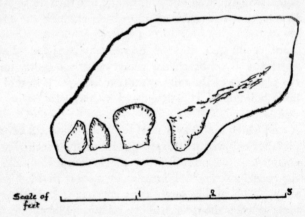

Scale of feet

indelible thereon forever. There are three markings called respectively 'The Cow's Foot,' 'The Horse's Hoof.' and 'The Pig's Foot.' (The accompanying sketch is from *The Proceedings of the Society of Antiquaries of Scotland*, Vol. XLV., p. 395). Nothing is known of the origin of these markings.

The deserted and ruined hamlet of Tomnago lies, almost on the 1,000 ft. contour, about 500 yards slightly north of east along the hillface from Margmore. It was known also as Tomnagoi and Tomnagui (Gaelic,'Tom-na-gaoithe,' 'the mound of wind'—a name thoroughly justified by its exposed situation). It is told that on one occasion, when the press-gang was reported to be in the district, a simple-minded youth went missing ; he was ultimately found up one of the chimneys, where he had remained hidden all day ! The village ceased to be occupied about a century ago.

At one time there were two other old hamlets on the hill near here, one at Urlar, and the other at Coilleaichur ⅞ mile almost due south-west of Margmore, but both fall outside the range of the present Account. A stone circle stands near the Coilleaichur site, less complete than it was, many of the stones having been removed.

The road from Margmore to Aberfeldy runs down the eastern rim of the Den of Moness and, passing through the farm steading of Croftness (the croft of the den or waterfall), shortly turns sharp left and continues straight down to reach the main road to Crieff near the entrance to Moness House. About a hundred yards back up the road above Croftness and on the west side of it lie the recognisable ruins of another of the seven old lime kilns noticed in this Account.

Overlooking the angle where the road takes the left turn is a knoll on the top of which is the long range butt of the old shooting range ; the targets were well up the slope alongside the wood which clothes the hill on which stands 'The Dùn,' with the shorter range butts between. This range is no longer in use, having been replaced by the miniature range behind the Armoury.

To the right of the entrance gateway to Moness House the old skating pond will be looked for in vain for when the eastern part of the Breadalbane estates came into other hands in 1921 the site was drained and planted with trees. Skaters are now even less well served than they were prior to (about) 1880 when the pond was constructed by a club got up by the youth of the town. Before 1880 a mill dam on the hill above the Heart Wood was used by those who practised the art and also, before the pond at Pitilie came into being, by local curlers. This dam, which was for the purpose of supplying water power for the farm mill at Duntuim, is now derelict but the old channel from it may still be traced.

(Note : Not many of the old farm mills that used to abound in the district remain operative, either of the water wheel driven kind or of the circular type worked by horses; the travelling mills which move from place to place and the oil driven mills owned by some of the farmers have almost completely ousted them).

At one time there was a mineral spring at Moness farm the disappearance of which, it was said, deprived Aberfeldy of becoming one of the most famous spas in the country. The source was under the farm steading and the water was piped down to a spot in the Den of Moness near the entrance from Bridgend where a small primitive pump room was erected. An eminent analyst reported in September 1845 that the qualities of the water were very rare, the quantity of iron being as great as in the water at Tunbridge Wells and little less than that at Harrogate. He went on : "The water at Moness can be regarded as a valuable mineral spring ; the only drawback is the organic matter contained in the well. ....It may be expected that, almost to a certainty, the organic matter is conveyed to the well by surface waters and that the mineral spring itself rising in a more vertical direction from below is not charged with such matter." He then went on to advise ways and means of removing the difficulty, and concluded : "The fine situation of the village of Aberfeldy recommends itself strongly as a place of public resort and a Highland spa ; the pure air of the country will enhance the healing power of the iron waters."

All seemed set for the financial advancement of Aberfeldy when, for no discoverable reason, the water suddenly ceased to flow in the pipe leading down to the 'pump room,' but it was not until about 1900 that an explanation of the phenomenon was offered. It appeared that Lord Breadalbane's masons had been carrying out repairs to the farm buildings at Moness and during these operations they diverted the flow from the well into the Tomchulan Burn which runs down the hill just east of the steading. (This story was given to my informant by one of the masons engaged on the job, but as to whether or not it is the true reason I can only comment that there is no trace of iron discolouration anywhere on the bed or banks of the Tomchulan Burn).

The restoring of the well was under consideration about fifty years ago but the matter never got beyond the talking stage.

As regards further evidence of the presence of iron in the soil of this neighbourhood, there was in my young days a spring of highly impregnated water down near the Crieff Road bridge across the Moness Burn, close to and on the same side of the road as the small swing gate that gives on to a path to Moness House, and only a few yards from the roadway. This well no longer exists ; for some reason or other the water, diverted from the source of its iron content, now finds egress elsewhere, perfectly clear.

Though this piece of evidence has gone the way of that of the spring at Moness farm there are not lacking signs in the district that long ago efforts were made to turn the various minerals found there to account.

At Lochs, in Glenlyon, there are slag heaps which show that bog iron was worked there at some period in the past, and near Woodend, in the Black Wood of Glenlyon, there is an iron well similar to the one I used to know near the small gate to Moness. Copper, lead, silver, and even gold have been dug from the hills of Glenlyon and Lochtayside ; copper and lead were once worked commercially, but the difficulties of transport and the cost of labour ultimately brought the endeavours to a close. Silver and gold were extracted in small amounts in the copper and lead workings, and the second Marquis of Breadalbane, who mined copper on the hillface at Tomnadasun near Ardtalnaig, had in his possession several trinkets of gold derived from this source.

Immediately downstream from the road bridge over the Moness Burn, on the right bank of the burn, near what are obviously the ruins of some old building, a large tree was blown down about ten years ago. Among the roots were found entangled two old mill-stones. Over 200 years ago, before the road and bridge were made, a meal mill stood here and the line of its lade may still be traced.

*   *   *   *   *   *

Coming now to the Den of Moness—not the least of the 'lions' of Aberfeldy : As this is not a guidebook singing its praises for the benefit of the stranger within the gates rhapsodies are not called for. If any resident has failed to see for himself a beauty spot practically on his doorstep, then the loss is his own. No description is adequate and photographs are a poor substitute for, as with all the wonderful works of Nature, the Den of Moness has to be seen and 'experienced' if it is to give birth to a living memory ; even the carping Robert Southey (1819) was constrained to concede that "there are some falls upon this burn which, when the streams are full, should be among the *videnda* of this part of the country," while John Stoddart, in referring to the Middle Fall in his *Local Scenery and Manners in Scotland, 1799-1800*, described it as "one of the completest specimens of the secluded waterfall that I have ever seen," and Pennant in his *Tour of Scotland, 1772*, more quaintly, wrote "An epitome of everything that can be admired in the curiosity of waterfalls."

Beyond this in the way of description I do not propose to go ; the Falls are there for all to see, and in flood time when their roar is audible throughout the town, for all to hear ; but there is some information that can be conveyed by writing and which, though possibly prosaic, may be of interest.

In 1914 the Den of Moness was gifted to the town by the Marquis of Breadalbane, at the nominal rate of 1/- a year conditional on the proper care and maintenance of the paths and bridges, and, since then, entrance has been free.   Prior to 1914 admission was on payment of a small charge—6d.— to the caretaker or 'guide' who lived in the cottage at the Bridgend entrance, and spent his day ranging up and down the Den or sitting at the receipt of customs in a little hut just inside the Crieff Road gateway.   In these days Aberfeldy householders could secure admission for themselves and families by paying 2/6 per year for a key which served, as it were, as a season ticket.

Entering, then, from the Crieff Road one sees on the right remains of small trenches or fox-holes, dug when the fear of a German invasion in the early 1940's was very real in men's minds, and, a few yards away, the hut covering the reservoir of the old Aberfeldy water supply ; a short distance upstream, though not visible from the path, is the old intake dam.   The dam on the further side of the burn here is for the maintenance of a steady flow of water as power supply to the Breadalbane Woollen Mills, and is fed by means of pipes which were laid on from the intake dam of the town's old supply system after the discontinuance of its original function when the present supply took over in 1910.   The old reservoir, by the way, is still maintained in proper order as an additional supply in case of need for the mills.

Still a little way further on the path to the Falls forks to the left and crosses the burn by an iron and concrete bridge built not many years ago to replace its somewhat rickety, if more picturesque, rustic predecessor.   Before this rustic bridge was built, access to the Den was by way of a path which joined the present path at this point and led in from the Crieff Road where the road to Croftness forks off, almost opposite the main gateway to Moness House.

About 430 paces beyond this bridge, on a steep little rise, lie, almost edging the path on the right, the foundations of a small building. Possibly, a hundred or two years hence when their origin has been forgotten, they may be pointed out as some antiquarian relic of obscure significance, but the explanation of their presence is simple enough ; they are all that remains of a rounded summerhouse which stood here in the latter years of last and the early years of the present century. It was called 'the Heather House' from the fact that its walls were, so to speak, thatched with heather.

Mr James A. MacGregor informs me that in his younger days there were what seemed to be the ruined foundations of a small building on the flat piece of ground on the side of the path distant from the burn at the foot of the rise that leads to the site of the Heather House. There appears to be no sign of it now and concerning it, beyond what can be surmised, nothing seems to be known.

Still further on one crosses the Margmore Burn (a tributary stream) between the two lowest cascades of the Lower Fall and soon comes to a seat-like rock tucked in under the overhanging bank. This is sometimes spoken of as 'Burns's Seat' and as often as not the speaker goes on to state that it was here that the poet sat when, on the occasion of his visit to the Den of Moness on 30th August, 1787, in the company of his friend William Nicol, of the High School, Edinburgh, he composed the song "The Birks o' Aberfeldy" (first published in *Johnson's Musical Museum*). For words and music, see Appendix (*H*).

For years a controversy has raged regarding the presence or absence of birks (birches) in the neighbourhood of the Falls of Moness in Burns's time, the supporters of the 'absence' contention holding that "The Birks o' Aberfeldy" should really be "The Birks o' Abergeldie." I have even seen it stated in print that it is strange to think that Aberfeldy should be best known for what it never had, at all events at the time of the poet's visit, birch trees in The Birks. This delusion would seem to owe its origin to a statement in the *Ordnance Survey*

Gazetteer and the testimony of Miss Dorothy Wordsworth who visited Aberfeldy in 1803 and apparently failed to see these trees. On the other hand we have such evidence as the following : In his *Journey from Edinburgh, 1803*, Alexander Campbell reports on the Den of Moness, "—a deep wooded glen along the course of a mountain streamlet, which bounds in fantastic wildness among chasms and impending rocks overhung with brushwood and birch trees." In 1811, in his *Observations on a Tour through the Highlands of Scotland*, Dr T. Garnett writes, "—a deep glen, wooded to the top with hazel and birch," and a picture by W. H. Watts, who accompanied him, of the Middle Fall shows unmistakable birch trees. Lastly, C. Lessingham Smith wrote thus of the Middle Fall, "From the crevices of the rocks, hang pendant birch and ash whose colours are rendered vividly green by the perpetual spray" (*Excursions through the Highlands and Isles of Scotland in 1835 and 1836*).

For a time these trees were cut down ruthlessly to supply mementoes of the place, but it would seem that the controversy need never have arisen if the testimony of so close an observer of Nature as Robert Burns himself had been considered. He put it on record : "I composed these stanzas standing under the Falls of Moness at or near Aberfeldy." These few words would seem to dispose of the whole thing, and at the same time of the fiction that he wrote them while sitting on the so-called 'Burns's Seat' lower down, a fiction which, though it might be lapped up eagerly by visitors, might in time come to be accepted as fact, which would be regrettable.

There is supposed to be a hollow or cave once used by smugglers in the neighbourhood of either the Middle or Upper Fall. This notion appears to be based on the following story : At one time a private or illicit still was believed to be in operation in the hills above Bolfracks and one of the men suspected of working it, on being challenged by a gentleman of Aberfeldy, replied that if his questioner would consent to be blind-folded and led he would take him to it. To this the gentleman agreed and one night, with his conductor, set out from Bolfracks and ascended the hill. After much walking and scrambling up and down banks and over rocks, and changing direction frequently, he had the bandage removed and found himself at the bottom of a ravine beside a waterfall. There are no other waterfalls in the immediate neighbourhood (except one or two small but pretty falls on the Margmore Burn above the Lower Fall of Moness) and the Bolfracks moor runs right across the hill to Urlar, not far above the Upper Fall.

From the geologist's point of view the Moness Falls owe their origin to an outcrop of hard 'green beds' among the softer mica schists. Other outcrops of these occur in the Rocks of Weem and Cluny. The inclination of the strata is slightly downwards from east to west, whereby landslides and rockfalls occasionally occur on the east (right) bank, particularly when the binding of ice which has expanded the cracks in the rock during winter is lost in the spring thaw. Two quite considerable falls have occurred within recent years near the Upper Fall, one no longer ago than 1950. About the middle of the latter half of last century there was a rockfall near the Middle Fall that swept two visitors (brother and sister) down into the stream. One was killed and the other crippled for life, and only six or seven years ago a large and heavy mass of ice, crashing down on two others, injured both, one seriously.

Down near the Bridgend entrance to 'The Birks' is the Craignish Bridge. It bears an inscribed metal plate : "Craignish Bridge. Erected through the Generosity of Miss Jessie Campbell, Ericht House, Aberfeldy. July 1914." It replaced a more rustic looking wooden structure which was known as the 'black bridge,' presumably from its dark colour for there is no story attached.

On the rising ground of the right (east) bank of the burn here, and looking almost straight along the 'black bridge,' there stood for a number of years the primitive 'pump room' of the iron well at Moness Farm. The bank shows traces of the old wall, and the path leading up to the shelf-like ledge on which the building stood is still there. Mr J. A. MacGregor tells me that he remembers this shed, for it was little more, and also that on one occasion, while investigating the source of some jets of water which he found bubbling to the surface in the field above, he lit upon the small bore lead pipe that brought down the water for the use of those who wished to benefit from its healing properties.

* * * * * *

Actually spanning the entrance to the Den is the Aberfeldy War Memorial Arch (unveiled 3/6/22). On it are two tablets bearing the names of those who went forth with the colours when the call came, and did not return, and here on Remembrance Sunday each November parade the local service and ex-service men and the general public to pay homage to the dead. There are other reminders of the nightmare years of 1914-18 and 1939-45 in the shape of inscribed panels in the schools and churches around.

(Dr John Kennedy tells that in his boyhood days a blacksmith's workshop was in operation at the entrance to the Den of Moness near the site now occupied by the Memorial Arch.)

As one comes up the slope to the level of the main street in Bridgend and looks down the slope on the further side to Burnside one realises that at some time or other the street here must have been raised. This raising was undertaken to ease the approach to the steep-sided hump-backed bridge built by Wade across the Moness Burn at this point ; it achieved its object but, in so doing, it had the effect of converting what had been the ground floor of the Breadalbane Hotel into a semi-basement, making necessary the opening of a new main door into the floor above. The old door, now built up, is under the present one.

A certain amount of road raising was done also on the west side of the bridge in Bank Street as evidenced by the fact that under the shops facing the Bank of Scotland and to some extent under the Crown Hotel there are flats sunk completely towards the street but opening on the ground level behind. Before the shop premises opposite the Bank of Scotland were built in 1910 the street here was flanked by a wall continuous with the present parapet of the bridge and with, on the off side, a drop of 10 or 12 feet to the garden, as it was then, below.

An examination of the Breadalbane Hotel, which was built obviously before these alterations in the street level were carried out, shows, both externally and internally, that it was originally composed of two seperate buildings. The eastern part, white-washed and with a milestone tucked in at its base and with its entrance from The Square, was known then as the Caledonian Hotel, the memory of which until about the end of the second decade of this century lived on in the pet name of the public bar—'the Caley' or 'Callie'—which for many years after the hotel fusion found its home just inside the door in The Square. This door now gives access to the offices of the motor garage which occupies the old hotel yard (now roofed over) and stables behind ; the name is almost forgotten to-day and another link, or memory of a link with the past seems likely to be broken.

The Breadalbane and Caledonian Hotels were still separate buildings up to the late 1850's, the gap between them giving access to the old Breadalbane stables. The stables of the Caledonian Hotel, which at one time accommodated from 15 to 20 horses, were up the Tomchulan Road on the site now occupied by Atholl House.

It is interesting to note that in the old coaching days Breadalbane Hotel took the coach passengers while 'the Caley' catered more for the local traffic. It was almost certainly the Breadalbane to which, as a coach traveller, C. H. Townshend referred when he wrote in his *Descriptive Tour in Scotland, 1840*, that in Aberfeldy he "rested for the night in a very tolerable Christian-like inn !"

Opposite the Breadalbane Hotel, and standing below the present street level, there were formerly several small cottages. When they were finally cleared away in 1892 the builder of the premises which now occupy the site had some difficulty before he was permitted to go on with the work as, when the then Laird of Breadalbane granted the land for the erection of the Breadalbane Hotel, an unobstructed view into the lower part of the Den of Moness was part of the agreement.

Nearer the burn, where the block containing a chemist's house and dispensary now stands, there was formerly a similar small cottage, also dating from before the time of the raising of the street. An old Aberfeldy resident who died in 1947 aged 85 once told me that in his early days the cottage was still in existence and that he and some of his young contemporaries when passing used to practise tossing stones, etc., down the chimneys, which were just about level with the road. It is interesting to me, if to no one else, that it was in the house over the dispensary that I first saw the light, for it was from it, 'the doctor's house,' that my father, not then long in the town, carried on for four or five years the work of his practice—work in which some twenty-two years later (1904) I was to be privileged to join him.

Facing this site there stood, until it was burned down on 14th March, 1907, (with the loss of two lives), a building, on the street level of which there were two small shops. Of these the one nearer the burn was occupied by a butcher's business run by two brothers named MacGregor, one of whom was deaf and dumb. The sloping road that runs down here beside the Breadalbane Hotel is still occasionally, even now, referred to as 'The Dummy's Brae.'

Incidentally, the only other fatal fire in Aberfeldy within my recollection occurred in a close in Kenmore Street— No. 22— on 27/10/1911. Here again two people lost their lives, an elderly woman and her son.

The blocked-in doorway which, from a height of some three feet or so up the west wall of the Breadalbane Hotel, overlooks the Dummy's Brae, at one time gave access to a large room within. This room used to be in considerable demand as a ball-room and was approached by a gallery running horizontally along the face of the wall from Bridgend.

* * * * * *

However much one may regret the passing of old buildings with their associations and reminders of days when life was very different from what it is now,sentiment in this utilitarian age is rarely allowed to interfere with what we are pleased to call 'Progress' and in the last quarter of last century many of the old houses in Aberfeldy, picturesque possibly, squalid frequently, were razed to make way for the new.

When one looks at our present day houses, even the meanest of them, it is almost impossible to realise the conditions under which our ancestors lived. According to the reports of various travellers who visited Scotland between the 14th and 18th centuries housing conditions of the humbler folk in 'la sauvage Ecosse,' as Jean Froissart, a French visitor in the days of David Bruce (about 1430), labelled the Highlands, were appalling, and, it would seem, little removed from those of the old Pictish dwellings of over 1,000 years ago.

The walls were of turf, or rough stones jumbled together without mortar or cement and roofed with pieces of wood supporting an outer covering of slabs of turf about an inch thick, laid on like tiles and fixed down with wooden pegs. In most cases there were no chimneys, a small vent in the roof sufficing to take the smoke away ; the doors were of hides of oxen, and the windows small holes unglazed. Inside was a single room, too low to stand up in, with a central fire round which the occupants sat, in the language of a Cromwellian soldier in Scotland in 1650, amid "smoke and noysome smells." This accommodation was often shared with cattle and other animals.

Even so late as 1754, when the Rev. Duncan Macara, writer of the *Statistical Account of Fortingall, 1791*, came to the district some of the people in the remoter parts of the parish were still living in similar hovels under similar conditions, without beds, sleeping on the ground with heather or ferns below them, and with no covering but their body clothes and one blanket. Pennant in 1769 called the houses of the poorer class on Lochtayside "the disgrace of North Britain" and, of those on Deeside, wrote "—shocking to humanity ; formed of loose stones and covered with clods which they call 'devots,' or with heath, broom, or fir. They look, at a distance, like so many black molehills." —Little wonder, then, that the inhabitants thought more of their crops, poor as these were, than of their homes, "for," as Froissart noted, "with six or eight stakes they would soon have new houses."

When the building material was turf, in due course it became dry enough to burn. It then served as fuel and another house was built. As Thomas Morer in 1689 remarked, "it does not cost much more time to erect a house than to pull it down." Coal, of course, was unknown in these early days and, though not apropos of the Highlands, a note made by Aeneas Sylvius de' Piccolomini, later Pope Pius II, who visited Edinburgh in the middle of the first half of the 15th century, is very interesting : He tells how, in the Lothians, almost naked beggars at church doors departed with joy on receiving stones as alms. "This stone," he goes on, "whether by reason of sulphurous or some fatter matter which it contains, is burned instead of wood, of which the country is destitute."

Even the better class houses did not escape the notice of our early visitors. According to Piccolomini, "the towns have no walls and the town houses are constructed without lime." Two hundred years later, in 1650, the Cromwellian soldier mentioned above wrote, "The houses of the lairds are large and spacious and built of stone,"—"few or no glasse windows and then they have wooden shuts below and the glasse above," and, in 1661, John Ray in his *Itineraries*, confirmed and extended this by noting that even in the king's palace the windows were so fitted, with the addition, "the lower parts have two shuts to open at pleasure to admit the fresh air,"

Probably the writer of the following, in 1617, believed to have been Sir Anthony Weldon but in any case obviously a cross-grained Sassenach, would have suggested that the windows might just as profitably have been kept closed : "The air might be wholesome but for the stinking people that inhabit it. The ground might be fruitful had they the wit to manure it. Their beasts are generally small, women only excepted, of which there are none greater in the world. There is great store of fowl too, as foul houses, foul sheets, foul linen, foul dishes and pots—" etc., etc., in the same strain. Regarding women : "Pride is a thing bred in their bones and their flesh naturally abhors cleanliness ; their body smells of sweat and their splay feet never offend in socks. To be chained in marriage with one of them were to be tied to a dead carcase and cast into a stinking ditch.......I do wonder that so brave a Prince should be borne into so stinking a town as Edinburgh in lousy Scotland." Sir Anthony Weldon must have been a charming man to meet !

From a letter written in 1672 by an ex-Capuchin monk named Denis de Repas it would appear that he too had a low opinion of our country, particularly the Highlands ; "I never saw a nation in general more nasty, lazy, and less ingenious in matter of manufacture.......Amongst the Highlanders they live like savages and go half naked.......Was I to give a whole description of their nasty, sloving (? slovenly), and scabby way of living I should have matter enough for a dozen of copious letters."

All our visitors of course have not been quite so scathing and critical. Two writers in 1498 have left accounts each of which might be complementary to the other ; (1) Don Pedro de Ayala, —"The King (James IV) speaks many languages including the language of the savages who live in some parts of Scotland....... The Scotch are not industrious. They spend all their time in wars and when there is no war they fight with one another.

They do not know what danger is." (2) Writer unknown, but of about the same date as de Ayala : "The inhabitants of the country—" as distinct from the towns "—are called the wild or savage Scots, not however from the rudeness of their manners, which are extremely courteous.......These savages are great soldiers and go to the help of the king against England, the natural enemy, at their own expense for thirty days, after which they are relieved by others who do likewise."

By 1551, on the report of another French writer, Etienne Perlin, a move in the right direction would seem to have set in. "It is to be noted that there are some savages in some of the counties of Scotland, but that from day to day the country strengthens and amends and is in a daily state of improvement"

Real improvement, however, could not take place in the Highlands while the housing and living conditions of the poorer classes continued as described, and it was not until after the two Jacobite Risings in the 18th century had been overcome and the country opened up by the construction of proper roads that real improvement began to be apparent, or even possible.

Of course it must not be concluded from all this that the population of the Highlands was a population of savages living in utter squalor. Far from it : Castle Menzies (1571) in our own district is a refutation of any such idea, and notes left by travellers of various dates through the centuries confirm that Chiefs, Feudal Barons, and many others of the upper classes lived in a state, in view of the nature of the times and despite the extremely primitive notions of sanitation and ordinary body cleanliness then holding, of considerable opulence and, in some cases, splendour. Thus, the anonymous writer of 1498 already quoted put it on record that "the nobles have excellent houses of hewn stone or brick and magnificently appointed ;" and, to get rid of all doubts on the matter, one has only to read, in the *Black Book of Taymouth*, the "COMP of the graith quhilk Patrik McAwyre, porter of Balloch, has within the platt thairof, maid at Balloch the XI day of Februar 1600"—in other words, the account of the plenishings, etc.

During the 1700's the more primitive of the houses in Aberfeldy began to give way to better built stone-walled thatched cottages, small and primitive themselves no doubt and more or less hovels by present day standards, but a great advance on their predecessors. Slating came later for though, traditionally, credit is given to General Wade (1733) for having erected the first slated house in the town—an inn which is said to have stood on the site of the present Bank of Scotland—many years had still to pass before the older practice was given up, and, as already stated, it was not until the end of the first decade of this century that Tomchulan, the last of the real old thatched cottages in Aberfeldy disappeared.

Dr John Kennedy, writing of the early years of last century, described many of the houses then in the village as little better than hovels, and Robert Southey in 1819 wrote : "Aberfeldy is a place which might properly be called Aberfilthy, for marvellously foul it is. You enter thro' a beggarly street, and arrive at a dirty inn—," and even Dr Macmillan, a native, writing of some twenty years later but with a less acid pen, could only report that in his younger days "Aberfeldy was truly a primitive village with streets of thatched cottages covered with moss and only two or three old-fashioned shops, principally in The Square."

In view of all this it is perhaps not surprising that in 1832 the town was struck by a epidemic of what was labelled 'cholera,' with a deathrate of 54 in the first 13 days—truly a harsh visitation on a village which some fifteen or twenty years before had, as reported by Dr Kennedy, a population of only about 800.

In what part of Aberfeldy the "dirty inn" referred to by Southey was situated is not clear—he gives no indication—but even in Wade's day three-quarters of a century earlier there were several inns of a sort in the village. One of these, called Inver, was said to be the oldest erection at the time, early 1700's, in the several hamlets now included in Aberfeldy. It stood not far from the junction of the Moness Burn with the

Tay on the site now occupied by the first block of houses in Tayside Place riverward of the Factory and on the same side of the road, and was frequented by drovers coming down from the north ; there was a ford near by which, when the river permitted, they used to cross, hanging on to the tails of their cattle !

As regards other old time inns reference has already been made to the one near Taybridge where a detachment of Duke of Cumberland's Hessians were quartered in 1746, and it is also recorded that in 1788 "a post-house was erected for the convenience of travellers who previously had to be content with what accommodation the then existing change house offered." (According to Lord Oxford who travelled in Scotland in 1725, inns and public houses were called 'change houses').

It was well on in the 1800's before the town began to assume its present appearance, but even in 1847 it was the reproach of the Brothers Anderson in their valuable guidebook that the houses were "cold and comfortless," and a considerable part of Aberfeldy as we see it now dates no further back than 1870.

* * * * * *

In tracing the gradual development over the years it may be best to take things, as it were, street by street, beginning with THE SQUARE which, in the middle of last century, in the words of an old inhabitant who died some years ago, "was the centre of life in the town, the place where everything of interest took place ; it was the meeting place of young and old, the playground of the children, and the place where the stage coaches changed horses." Now it serves as a convenient parking place for cars, and sometimes on the day of a big sheep or cattle sale every available inch is taken up.

About 1770 there were some fifty houses east of the burn ; a number of these were congregated round the base of the Tulloch (*i.e.*, along the line of what is now the south side of THE

SQUARE) and along General Wade's military road to the bridge across the Paldy, as the Moness Burn was then called. At that time THE SQUARE as such did not exist, but Dr Kennedy noted that in 1806 it was in process of formation and, later, Southey (1819) continued his remarks (v. above) "—a sort of Square or market place has been lately built so that, mean as the village or townlet is, it appears to be thriving."

THE SQUARE, as we see it now, has little of the 'old' about it, a considerable part dating no further back than the last quarter of last century. The Caledonian Hotel and the corner block which housed the post office up till 1897 are older, as are also the block at the southern end of the east side where Reid's Temperance Hotel once functioned, and the lower building to the west end of the south side where Bridgend branches off. It was in the western section of this last mentioned block that the Rev. Hugh Macmillan, D.D., LL.D., F.R.S.E., F.S.A.Scot., author of *The Highland Tay*, etc., etc., was born in 1833. In this building his father carried on business in a shop which, up till the 1860's, was fitted with a door of the old-fashioned barn-door type which could open either at the top or at the bottom.

The Rev. John Kennedy, D.D., also was born in THE SQUARE (1813), in the old Independent manse which, before its removal to make way for the Congregational Church, stood on the north side, directly facing Dr Macmillan's birthplace. As already noted, the Commercial Bank of Scotland Buildings date from 1886. When the Aberfeldy Branch was first opened on 24th August, 1868, business was conducted in a house(Auchrannie) in what is now known as TAYBRIDGE ROAD part of which was occupied by the Branch Manager, Mr C. W. L. Forbes who had been formerly employed in the local Branch of the Bank of Scotland and who, in 1887, became the town's first Chief Magistrate.

* * * * * *

Before THE SQUARE was built up the road to Dunkeld diverged to the east from the line of General Wade's road at the foot of the Tulloch.   Until about the end of the 1700's there was no DUNKELD STREET as now, but we know that it was in process of construction in its present line in 1800 and the two accompanying photographs taken in the 1860's or 1870's and 1896 respectively, will serve as a text for what I have to record concerning the changes which occurred in the intervening years and as an introduction to certain other matters not yet touched on or already mentioned but merely in passing.   In each the view is of the street as one looks westward towards THE SQUARE from a stance opposite what is now the entrance to the station yard.

No one will deny that eighty or ninety years ago DUNKELD STREET presented a picture dreary and dismal in the extreme. As seen in the older photograph the houses make no pretentions to architectural elegance and show little variety ; pavements are conspicious by their absence ; the road surface looks dirty and, if we except the attentions of the two hens in the foreground, uncared for !   Altogether the appearance is one of shoddiness and neglect ; indeed the late Mr Donald MacCallum was wont to tell how, in his early days in the 1860's, pigs and ducks used to wallow all the way up DUNKELD STREET and how there were no proper drains in the town, the streets being surface cleaned—mostly when the rain came ! He also told how at that time the rubbish dump for KENMORE STREET and the west end of the town was by the mill lade behind the shop at the corner of MILL STREET and BANK STREET.   Lighting in those days was both scanty and primitive ; only two lamps are to be seen, both of the house-wall type which was in use in Aberfeldy in those days.

In the second photograph are to be noted the marked changes for the better which took place with the passing of a half or, more accurately, a quarter of a century, for most of these changes date from about 1870 and after.   There is over all an appearance of brightness and cleanness absent from the older picture ; for one thing the town scavenger with his barrow, etc., has taken the place of the hens !   New buildings have replaced many of the old ; pavements have been constructed ;

lamp-posts have ousted the wall lamps; the Commercial Bank Buildings have replaced the earlier white cottage which looked down the street from THE SQUARE, and altogether the picture is not unlike that of the DUNKELD STREET we know to-day.

At the time the older photograph was taken three blocks of houses occupied the ground extending from the present entrance to the station yard to where Moness Terrace branches off to the south. In the centre block, which was removed to make way for the motor garage which now fills the stance of part of it (the other part stood in the open space in front of the present row of petrol pumps) there were three dwelling houses, the most easterly of which, before my time but still within living memory, was the town's 'Pie Shop.' Here pies and lemonade were dispensed by a Mrs Carmichael at prices which make those of to-day look foolish. Mrs Carmichael must have been an enterprising old lady with a keen eye to business in other directions too, for, as the proud possessor of a mangle, not a common article in the town in those days, she added to her income by allowing neighbours, less favourably placed, to bring in their washing and turn the handle themselves at a charge of a 1d. or 2d. a time.

Next door to Mrs Carmichael (same block) in the middle of last century lived a remarkable character—Alexander Mc-Donald, better known as Laird McDonald. Bombastic and highfalutin in his speech, he never used a short word if he could find a long one. On one occasion, on arriving at Amulree, he is said to have addressed the ostler who came forward more or less as follows : "Extricate the quadruped from the vehicle ; stable him and give him an adequate supply of nutritious elements, and when the sunbeams shall illuminate the oriental horizon in the morning I shall award thee a pecuniary recompense equivalent to the hospitality rendered !" No doubt this story is entirely apocryphal but, as smoke generally means fire, it probably gives a good idea of his style.

Laird McDonald followed no trade but lived with (and, no doubt, partly on) his sister who had a small croft ; he seemed

DUNKELD STREET 80 OR 90 YEARS AGO.

Dunkeld Street in 1896.

satisfied with doing odd jobs from time to time—occasionally acting as boatman for visitors fishing the Breadalbane Hotel water. In his regular costume, tile hat and frock coat, he was a terror to the youngsters around. He died about 1890, aged close upon eighty.

In the same house, but at an earlier date, there lived a doctor, and the ring in the wall by his door to which he used to tie his horse was still there when the house was pulled down.

An odd feature of this block was the unusual method of indicating the year of erection adopted by its builder; on one end of it was a stone bearing the figures '18,' and, on the other, another stone completing the date with '11'—*i.e.*, '1811.'

The next block nearer THE SQUARE, on the same side of the street, was made up of two houses ; one of these still stands but the more easterly of the two, after standing semi-derelict and supported from the outside by wooden props for some years, was, in the interests of safety, pulled down. The plot is still vacant but during the 1939-45 War it was found a convenient site for a brick air-raid shelter.

In the eastern half of this house, last century, lived yet another of Aberfeldy's 'characters'. This was Duncan Dewar, known to everyone as 'Clangan'—officially village bellman but, unofficially after dark, a shebeener in a quiet way. In his official capacity he had a method of delivery peculiarly his own ; In a high-pitched voice he 'cried' his message to the people, then, after a short pause, gave vent to an explosive "Quick ! Dam' quick !" and sped off to his next halting place to repeat the performance.

Unofficially he attended to his customers through the kitchen window which faced to the back. There would come a stealthy 'tap, tap'; Clangan would then cautiously open the window and, if all was well, pass out the bottle—no glass. In the darkness it was impossible for him to see what was going on, but he could *hear*, and as the fiery liquid went 'glug, glug,

glug' down the invisible customer's throat he counted the 'glugs,' and the charge was at the rate of so much per 'glug' ! Sometimes he was his own best customer to the extent of finding himself in the Court at Perth next morning. On his return home however he put right the matter of the fine imposed by going round with a subscription card among the inhabitants who made up the amount ungrudgingly !

Clangan (1814-1888) died before I was old enough to remember him but I recall another town crier, who was also the husband of the female caretaker of the Town Hall, and who, in the 1890's was sometimes a source of amusement. This was Charles Baird. Though he could not read and though everyone knew this he persisted in trying to conceal the fact by carrying round with him a written copy of the announcement he was to make and which he pretended to consult but the contents of which with the help of his wife, a better scholar than himself, he had already committed to memory. On one occasion, after a dram too many I am afraid, he set out, complete with bell and notice, to inform the public of the forthcoming arrival in the town of a travelling show, mainly of performing animals. At his first halt he pealed his bell lustily —"Notice ! Notice ! Notice !" he shouted—and there he stuck. It was no good ; he had forgotten what he had to say. Lustily he gave another peal—"Notice ! Notice ! Notice !" —while the world held its breath to listen. Manfully he struggled with his memory and the paper ; it was still no good, but he did his best—"Well—" pause, "Well—" another pause, "Well—" and then desperately, "Anyway there's a canary !" and he turned on his heel and stumped off, unsteadily, homewards !

The sole remaining house of the three blocks under description is No. 34. It stands at the corner of DUNKELD STREET and MONESS TERRACE with, tucked in behind and facing MONESS TERRACE, a tiny cottage where, in 1909, at the good age of ninety-two, died one John McPherson, or 'MacVurich.' He was a familiar figure in the streets for many years and was rarely seen without his donkey. He was a tall remarkable looking man and to see him perched up in his little home-made cart or sitting astride his tiny mount with feet dangling an inch or two from the ground was a sight not easily forgotten. A mason to trade, he had his sidelines among which were town bellman and bill-poster. He hated being photographed !

In the picture of DUNKELD STREET in 1896, near the top on the right is seen a small white house ; this, with its low roofed neighbour, was removed shortly after the photograph was taken to make way for the new (present) post office. On the site next nearer THE SQUARE, before the building now standing there was erected, there used to be another small house (partly shown in the older photograph) in which, last century, dwelt one of Aberfeldy's local 'celebrities.' This was William McLeish, born 1808, died 1890, an accomplished musician whose services as a violinist were always in demand at functions where music formed part of the proceedings. He was known as 'the Second Paganini' and at one time had officiated as leader in one of London's orchestras. I do not remember him, but as a boy I often heard his name mentioned. He was a cousin of Donald McLeish, pig-sticker, etc., already referred to, who lived next door.

At present, just across the street from the site of 'Paganini's' house, stands the burnt out ruin of No. 12—one of the oldest buildings in the street. It has been stated that at the time of its erection this house was the biggest in DUNKELD STREET ; at the time of its burning it was the smallest. The last inhabitants were an old woman, a Mrs McKerchar and her daughter. In January 1950 the old lady died, aged 94. She had lived all her married life in the house and it survived her less than a year. (L)

Back then to the foot of DUNKELD STREET of eighty or ninety years ago. For whom the archway of lanterns, etc., was set up is now only a matter for conjecture, but no doubt it was part of Aberfeldy's welcome to some notable visitor, for even Royalty have from time to time graced the town with their presence. In September 1842 Queen Victoria and Prince

Albert passed through on their way to Taymouth *en route* from Scone where they had broken their journey from Dalkeith Palace, and in 1866, five years after the death of the Prince, she passed through again—this time incog.

Other notable people, too, at one time and another have passed through and sometimes tarried for a little in our district, thus : Tradition has it that Sir William Wallace after his defeat at Falkirk in 1298 sought and found refuge in these parts ; and there is evidence that Charles II after his Coronation at Scone in 1661 came to Castle Menzies to visit the Chief of the Menzieses.

The fact that in 1746 Prince Charlie with part of his retreating army trod our streets on his way to Culloden is a matter of history, but that he spent some days at Castle Menzies as the honoured guest of Sir Robert Menzies, reputedly a staunch Hanoverian, and gave his name to what is still pointed out as Prince Charlie's Room, is an unlikely story— almost as unlikely, indeed, as that which tells of a visit and sojourn there of Mary Queen of Scots in 1561, *ten years before the Castle was built*!

To come back, however to more recent times : Prince Leopold, Duke of Albany, in 1877—followed after ten days by his brother Prince Arthur, Duke of Connaught — passed through *en route* for Taymouth, being greeted in Aberfeldy by five triumphal arches a pipe band, and the Fechney Industrial School (brass) band from Perth.

In 1884 Oscar, King of Sweden, passed through, also on his way to Taymouth, followed a week or so later by his son, Crown Prince Gustav.

Other royal visitors to Taymouth who passed through Aberfeldy were :

Frederick, Grand Duke of Baden, in 1879.
Prince George, Duke of Cambridge, in 1881, and
H.R.H. Fredrica, of Hanover, in 1885.
In the days of the Breadalbanes brass plates on the main stair at Taymouth commemorated these visits.

The Conte de Paris, Pretender to the French throne, round about 1887 spent some time in our district as tenant of the Loch Kennard shooting, and in Kenmore Churchyard a stone over the grave of his little one-day old son records that the Maharajah Duleep Sing once sojourned in our countryside. The stone bears the date 1865.

In 1925 the Duke and Duchess of York, later King George VI and his Queen, spent a short time at Grantully Castle as guests of Earl and Countess Beattie who had a ten years lease of the castle and shooting round about then, and, in 1950, the then Queen Elizabeth, now the Queen Mother, motored through on her way from Balmoral to open the new hydro-electric station at Loch Sloy.

Though not royalty the late Mr W. E. Gladstone was accorded an almost royal welcome by the people in Aberfeldy, then strongly Liberal in their sympathies, when in 1878 or 1879 he passed through to visit Lord Breadalbane, one of the Liberal Peers of that time. He arrived at the station at 6.30 one winter night and received a great ovation. An awning lit by hanging lights had been erected across the platform to where his carriage was waiting, and from a rostrum set up outside the station buildings an address of welcome was read. Gladstone made a suitable reply and, as he drove away, was escorted through the town by a torchlight procession and a band. In the General Election shortly after, when his party was returned to power, when the first results began to come through carnival was held in THE SQUARE, and when the local result arrived to announce the victory of Sir Donald Currie, at that time a member of the Liberal Party, enthusiasm knew no bounds and crowds assembled at the Lochan where a huge bonfire that had been laid on was lit. The windows of some of the leading Tories were smashed and known members of the Party were wise who remained indoors !

* * * * * *

CHAPEL STREET, or FACTORY STREET as it once was, like DUNKELD STREET has undergone great changes but, unlike it, it owes these changes mainly to the present century.

Looking down its length from THE SQUARE, an ex-resident returning now to Aberfeldy after an absence of fifty years would have some difficulty in recognising it or picking out familiar features.

At the top on the right, but with its entrance in DUNKELD STREET, is the Birks Cinema built in 1939 and opened less than a month before the outbreak of the 1939-45 War. As one of a group of Picture Houses the Birks is able to offer its patrons a much better selection of films and more frequent changes of programme—three per week—than a small town cinema like our's, but operating independently, could normally afford to provide.

Our ex-resident would miss the quaint little Fancy Bazaar, to enter which one had to go down one or two steps, which used to stand at this corner, and also the row of little cottages that extended from it northward past the site of the newer Free Church almost to the old Independent Chapel.

In the next cottage but one from the bazaar, a cottage which stood, latterly in a semi-ruinous condition, into the later 1930's, was born John Anderson the son of a carter. An old native of the town, reminiscing of the 1860's in a newspaper article in the 1920's, recalls how Anderson carried on a small business venture here before burning his boats and striking out into the greater world. She tells also how as a young man he, with his wife, set off for Glasgow without enough money to pay their fares, and how, by walking part of the way and 'hitch-hiking' as it is called now, they reached their destination and set up a small business which, from necessarily humble beginnings, prospered and grew into the biggest of its kind in the city. This business, which he had called "The Polytechnic," later became merged with the large Manchester firm of Lewis Ltd., which, in turn, this year was taken over by the big combine known as the House of Fraser.

It was Anderson, it will be remembered, who was the means of bringing Spurgeon to preach in Aberfeldy.

McVurich and his Donkey Cart.

The Old Fancy Bazaar which once stood where the Birks Cinema now stands.

Chapel Street towards the end of Last Century.

Lower End of Chapel Street as it was till about 1930.

On the opposite (west) side of the street our ex-resident would look in vain for the row of hovels which disgraced this part of the town even so recently as twenty-five years ago—twenty years as a matter of fact in the case of those which stood where the furthest down block of new houses is. Of the three new blocks, with gardens in front, the two nearest THE SQUARE are Council houses, first occupied in 1925. It was about five years later that the third block (non-Council) came into being.

The two photographs shown may, to-day, be labelled 'OLD CHAPEL STREET' though in one sense, as just told, not so very old. In the first of these the house on the left with the street lamp attached was, until its removal in the middle 1920's, a so-called Model Lodging House mostly frequented by people of the vagrant class, and run at about 6d. a night, by the wife, later widow, of an Irishman named William McAllister, an expert tinsmith and bell-hanger who first came to the district to 'bell-hang' Taymouth Castle and who, finding that he liked the place, stayed on. When he began business in Aberfeldy he was a remarkable figure ; a big burly man, with a beard of the 'imperial' type, he wore to his work a tile hat, tail coat, and white moleskin trousers and vest ! When I knew him first he had discarded the tile hat and tail coat. He died in 1911, aged 67.

Behind the house next door to but in the same block as McAllister's another of the town's many characters of last century had his home. This was John Ross—"Rossie"—a plumber, born in 1843, who died of a burning accident in 1894. Many good stories are told of him and there was general regret at his untimely end for he was a jovial soul in spite of, or perhaps because of, an insatiable thirst. On one occasion a gentleman of the town, thinking to take a rise out of him, remarked, "What's this, Rossie ? I hear you have joined the Good Templars ?" "It's a downright slander !" was the outraged reply.

In the house occupied by Rossie, but before his day, there lived an old character with an unspellable Gaelic name who worked an illicit still. For a time all was well and everyone was happy, but in due course it came to his ears that the suspicious eye of the exciseman was beginning to turn in his direction, so, fearing trouble, he packed all his paraphernalia and a couple of barrels of 'whisky' on a farm cart and set out for Callwood Cottage, near Coshieville. There he hid the tools of his trade, but the barrels he dumped in the river. He was supposed never to have recovered the latter so that, for all that is known to the contrary, they may be there still ! It is said that his merchandise was sometimes sold in the town at 1/6 per *gallon*.

In the next block northward, but before McAllister's time, there was another lodging house, and certainly not a 'Model' one in any sense of the term ; it was run in the ground floor of the house nearest the camera in the second photograph of 'OLD CHAPEL STREET.' Dirty and ill-kept, it was little more than a low-class howff for any and every tramp and vagabond who cared to lay out 2d. or 3d. for the privilege of spending a night under its roof.

The lane which runs west to Burnside beside the block of Council houses which stand where the Model Lodging House used to stand was known in my young days as McAllister's Lane. On the opposite side of the street, almost in line with McAllister's is another lane which leads east to the yards of the auction mart through what might be termed a miniature "Square" lying behind the houses which front the main roadway. The first house on the left (north) side of this "Square" was where Aberfeldy's first bakery was established by a man named Peter Carmichael while, almost facing it from the south side, are the premises in which a firm of spool and bobbin makers, John Stewart & Son, once carried on business. This business was closed down about 1874/5 but part of the old square tower-like chimney of their workshop, now resembling some relic of the Middle Ages, still stands.

Further down CHAPEL STREET, just beyond the old Independent Chapel, is the now about-to-be disused Police Station which dates from about 1872/73. Prior to the erection of this building the site was occupied by a pool into which the surface waters of the street were drained. (*L*)

At the foot of the street, and in the angle which it makes with MARKET STREET, is the local Gasworks. It was in 1856 that a Building Lease was entered into between the Marquis of Breadalbane and the Aberfeldy Gaslight Company whose Directors were: James Ferguson Wyllie (factor to Lord Breadalbane): George Rankin, Bank Agent (the Perth Banking Company): Robert Peter, Bank Agent (the Central Bank): William Stewart, Saddler: Alexander Macdonald, Dyer: James Drummond, Miller: Alexander Macmillan, Merchant (father of Rev. Hugh Macmillan, D.D., LL.D.).

* * * * * *

To come now to BANK STREET (Bridgend and the old Crieff Road have already been dealt with): With the exception of the centre block of shops, the eastern end of which bears the date 1838, and the Bank of Scotland, the south side was rebuilt during the last quarter of last century. The Bank of Scotland Buildings, were taken over in 1868 when the Bank of Scotland, a Branch of which was opened in Aberfeldy in 1867, absorbed the Central Bank which had its offices there. The note in the *New Statistical Account, 1845*, which states that "There is a Savings Bank in Aberfeldy ; it was instituted in 1833," refers to this old Central Bank, the records of which, now in the hands of the Bank of Scotland, go back to 1834. The Building Lease bears the date 1837.

As already stated, the site at an earlier period was occupied by an inn believed to have been erected under the orders of General Wade, and also believed to have been the first slated house in Aberfeldy.

The present Union Bank and the premises next door date from no further back than 1905, having been rebuilt in that year after a disastrous fire which, in 1904, destroyed both buildings. In the case of the premises next door it was really the second rebuild as this fire was the second in ten years; on this former occasion it was with considerable difficulty that the Bank was saved. While the Bank was being rebuilt business was carried on in a shop between where the motor garage now is and the railway station entrance at the foot of DUNKELD STREET.

The Bank site was originally built upon in 1837 when a Patrick McDonald, merchant, erected a house on a 99 years Lease from the second Marquis of Breadalbane. In 1853 the Perth Banking Company opened in Aberfeldy ; in 1855 they bought McDonald's house, demolished it and erected a subs-tantial Bank building on the site. The Perth business was taken over by the Union Bank of Scotland as from 31st May, 1857 and business was conducted under the name of the Union Bank from 27th February 1858. The occupant of the Bank House, as had other holders of Building Leases in the town, had the right to cut peats on the hill for the use of the premises but not to sell until the Feu Charter was substituted for the Lease in 1878, but it is not recorded that advantage was taken of the right. The first Agent was Mr George Rankin, father of Mr A. Scott Rankin illustrator of Dr Hugh Macmillan's charmingly written but not always accurate book, *The High-land Tay*. As Mr Rankin is mentioned as George Rankin, Bank Agent, in a list of Directors of the Aberfeldy Gaslight Company in 1856 it would seem probable that he was Agent for the Perth Banking Company before it was taken over in 1857.

The local Branch of the Savings Bank of the County and City of Perth, next door to the Union Bank, has occupied its present office since the end of last year, having removed there from less suitable accommodation on the other side of the street. At a still earlier date its office was a tiny room at the back of an ironmonger's shop next door to the present post office and nearer THE SQUARE. In 1915 a Branch of the Clydesdale Bank was opened in THE SQUARE, in the shop once occupied by Dr Hugh Macmillan's father—already referred to —and in this bank office the Savings Bank commenced its life in Aberfeldy. With the death of the Agent in 1928 the Clydesdale side of the business was closed down and the Savings Bank transferred to the ironmonger's shop in DUNKELD STREET where it continued to function till 1938, when it was moved to BANK STREET for the first time under full-time officials.

On the north side of Bank Street the large business premises facing the Bank of Scotland were erected, as already stated, in 1910. The houses west of this to the top of Mill Street, and the Black Watch Inn, were rebuilt between 1875 and 1900. The eastern portion of the block just west of the top of Mill Street was reconstructed in 1951, and what was the last of the old house-wall street lamps (shown in the Bank Street 'shipwreck' photograph) was removed.

This lamp functioned in its 'gas-lamp' capacity almost to the end but a year or two before it went, the electrification of the street lighting had begun. The change over from gas to electricity for street lighting was slow to follow the introduction of the latter to the town in 1930, and took about four years (1948-1952) to complete.

In the early days of gas lighting in the streets, before the introduction of incandescent mantles, by-passes, and time clocks, it was necessary for a man to go round from post to post armed with a long rod fitted with a small projection for turning on and off the gas. At the end of this rod he had a small naked (caged) light, to apply which, having turned on the gas, he had to push the end of the rod up through a hole at the foot of the globe to reach the burner, which was a 'fish-tail.' Of course when the time came for 'lights out' he had to do the round again. Further back into the past, but still within my recollection, the operation was even more laborious, the lamplighter having to carry round with him a ladder and a box of matches.

It was in 1853 that the townsfolk woke up to the need of better lighting than that afforded by candles and oil lamps, or at all events to the fact that it was time something was done about it. Other towns had gas—Pitlochry, Dunkeld—so why not Aberfeldy? A number of the leading men met in the Breadalbane Hotel on 28th December, 1853 to discuss and consider the question, with the result that the Aberfeldy Gas-light Company came into being. Wheels were set in motion. Lord Breadalbane acceded to a request for a site; building was pressed on and the necessary plant installed, and by September 1855 everything was in order, the mains laid, a gas manager appointed at a salary of £28 per annum plus free house garden, gas, and fuel (valued at £20), and the Company ready to deliver the goods !

To begin with it would seem that the new facilities were taken advantage of only by householders, business men, hotels, etc., for, in the Minutes of the Company, 12th May, 1864, it is written : "The Meeting resolved that the Company should supply lamps in the street with Gas gratis in the event of lamps and posts being erected by the public." Later, this resolution was cancelled !

There is an intriguing entry under the date 10th January, 1854. It was at the first proper Meeting of the newly con-stituted Company : With a view to canvassing the village "for the subscription of shares and to ascertain the number of burners and hours of consumption of light" Messrs Cameron and Macmillan were alloted "the South Side of Square and Dunkeld Street," Messrs. Peter and Macdonald "the North Side of Square and Scott Street," and Messrs. Stewart and Drum-mond "the Rest of the Village."

The name 'Scott Street,' almost but not completely forgotten in Aberfeldy to-day, was at one time applied, popularly if not officially, to Chapel Street because of the number of families named Scott who lived there. It is curious that an unofficial name should find its way into an official publication but in the Valuation Roll for the Parish of Dull for 1872/73 there is an

entry referring to 'A House in Scott Street, Aberfeldy.' There
is no indication as to its location and in the following year
(1873/74) this entry is omitted, but there is another which
strongly suggests that Scott Street and Chapel Street were one
and the same. What is still more curious however, is that,
with one exception, none of the several 'oldest inhabitants' to
whom I applied for information, including one now aged 82
who was born and brought up in Chapel Street, can recall
ever having heard of Scott Street.

*　*　*　*　*　*

Dr John Kennedy, in his *Memoir of the Reverend James
Kennedy*, states that when his father came in 1806 the western
part of Aberfeldy (*i.e.*, west of the burn) consisted (in addition,
one assumes, to the already existing Over and Nether Miltons)
in one long row of miserable thatched cottages where KENMORE
STREET now is. Presumably these were the cottages already
referred to as having been built in 1775 to accommodate some
of the numerous flax spinners who had gathered in from the
surrounding parts during the years of increased prosperity
enjoyed by their craft after General Wade's roads opened up
to them the markets of the south. By this time, indeed, Aberfeldy was beginning to assume the appearance of a busy
manufacturing village for it had also acquired and was main-
taining a reputation for its smith work. In the old days the
smiths were swordmakers and armourers and men of importance in the Clan communities, figuring high in the order of
clan rank. A poem in Gaelic entitled 'The Smiths of Aberfeldy'
was composed by John Campbell or Macglasselrig, also called
'The Glasenach,' a weaver poet of Morenish, Lochtayside. A
few verses of an exceedingly crude English translation are
given in Appendix.—(*J*).

Present day Kenmore Street, *i.e.*, most of the actual
'Street' part of it, standing where the row of cottages referred
to by Dr Kennedy once stood, is of comparatively recent date,
from about the middle of last century for the most part ;

Until the beginning of this century many of the lanes or closes between the blocks led to cow byres which, when no longer so used, were converted for use as dwelling houses.

The first house of what one might call a 'new look' Kenmore Street is the new Police Station now almost ready for occupation. (*L*) Oddly enough it stands practically next door to a building used once for the same purpose—No. 23—where the cells were in the room to the left as one enters from the street and had iron-clamped doors and barred windows. The police officer who was on duty here in the 1860's and after was a Sergeant Allan, possibly the best known in his day of all the policemen who have at one time or another been stationed in the town, though now perhaps his name is liable to be forgotten.

When Sergeant Allan left No. 23 and before the new station, then being erected in Chapel Street, was ready for occupation he lived for a short time in a tiny house at the back of No. 12 Dunkeld Street, the burned out ruin of which still stands. There were no cells in this house and when there was an 'arrest' waiting to be taken to the Perth Court next morning the sergeant, who had no constable to help him, though he was the first Aberfeldy sergeant, later, to have such help, was obliged to sit up all night with his charge. Sergeant Allan, whom I can just remember, died in 1889.

Of the villas which stand beyond the western end of Kenmore Street proper, most of those on the north side date from the period 1875-1900 ; those on the south side, with the exception of the Armoury, are newer. The most westerly house on the north side, Dunolly, has served (as already told) for a number of years now as a Hostel for girls from the country attending Breadalbane Academy ; the most westerly on the south side, standing well above the road and approached by a winding drive, Eilean Riabhach ('brindled island'), was in use as a War Hospital in 1914-18, and again during Hitler's War and for two years after. In the early part of the First Great War the patients treated here were Belgian soldiers and in the Second, except for a short time at the beginning, Polish soldiers and airmen convalescent after discharge from Taymouth Castle, then Polish Base Hospital No. 1 in Britain, the staff being housed in Dunaluinn, the house on the hill just south of the hospital.

Incidentally, for some time during the term of the 'Polish Occupation' of Aberfeldy and district, the Crown Hotel in Bank Street served as a Hostel for Polish women employed on the domestic staff at Taymouth.

Eilean Riabhach is the residence of J. D. Haggart, Esq., O.B.E., (later C.B.E.), J.P., and Mrs Haggart, O.B.E., J.P. From 1913 to 1949 Mr Haggart was Provost of the Burgh— 36 consecutive years (37 if an extra year of duty as acting Provost before his term started be included). This constitutes a record for Scotland, and is one which will not easily be broken.

Ex-Provost Haggart has to his credit what must surely be another record. This year he attended his 68th Royal Highland and Agricultural Show, without a single break in the series.

Of the most easterly block on the south side of Kenmore Street the western section is a rebuild after a fire which gutted its predecessor on 22/3/1907. In part of this new building is housed the local branch of the County Council Library.

* * * * * *

CRIEFF ROAD : Prior to 1875 the only buildings here were the old school, now part of the Town Hall Buildings, and the original Free Church Manse, now the manse of the united Parish Churches—St. Andrew's and Breadalbane. The actual year of the building of the old school I have not been able to ascertain but the facts that Dr Macmillan, born 1833, records that he was a pupil here, and that it was under the auspices of the Free Church, would appear to date it to some extent. The manse, as already indicated, was built by Breadalbane soon after the Disruption in 1843.

The other streets, roads, etc., not yet specifically referred to can be quickly disposed of. With few exceptions they all date from 1875 and after.

TAYBRIDGE ROAD : The houses on the west side before 1875 were unbuilt. Those on the east side, except that one nearest the river, are older and, as told, used to be known as Breadalbane Villas, a name by which they are known even to this day by some of the older people. A number of these houses are dated from the fact that the 99-year leases on which they were built are expiring at the present time. Auchrannie, the second house down from Breadalbane Church, at one time was the Commercial Bank, the agent living in the older northern part while the office was in the newer part nearer the church. It ceased to function in this role when the present bank was erected in The Square in 1886, but the old hand-operated bolt of the safe, worked from an upstairs room, is still *in situ*.

TAYBRIDGE DRIVE : The houses here, with the exception of the two most westerly and that one nearest Taybridge Road which were erected during the 1875-1900 period, are productions of this century. In my young days there was no through road here, the two ends being connected merely by a footpath the line of which the present road follows. Taybridge Drive is now quite built up, except where the Putting Green run by the Merchants' Association occupies the plot where the Drive meets Taybridge Road.

TAYBRIDGE TERRACE : All the houses at the western end were built since about the beginning of this century ; several at the eastern end are from the 1875-1900 period. As with Taybridge Drive, in my boyhood days, there was no through road, but there was a footpath which ran along the line of the present road, from which forked off another path via the north side of the woollen mill to the Dyer's Bridge ; this branch is still in use though the Dyer's Bridge no longer exists.

MILL STREET has already been dealt with and there is nothing to add.

MARKET STREET, HOME STREET, BREADALBANE TERRACE :
Prior to 1875 there were no houses in these streets. The
buildings on the south side of Market Street date from between
that year and 1900, as do most of those in Home Street, and
the two western blocks of Breadalbane Terrace popularly known
as 'The Happy Land!' The Steam Laundry at the foot of Home
Street dates from 2nd February, 1900, when Sir Robert Menzies
performed the opening ceremony and set the machinery in motion. To begin with it employed a manageress, two girls, and
one man, and goods were collected and delivered in a small hand-
cart drawn by a donkey. Since then it has greatly expanded
in every direction, employs 40 women and 10 men, and operates
far beyond the bounds of the burgh and even the county—
during Hitler's War collecting and delivering in its own vans
as far afield as Oban and Invergordon. It has a branch office
in Perth, and does an extensive postal business with the Western Isles ; and 4 motor vans have replaced the donkey cart.

BURNSIDE has already been described but some further notes
are called for, for here it was, in what was then called Black
Street, that in October 1843 was started 'The Aberfeldy Debating Society' popularly known as 'The Auld Smoky Ha'.'
The Minute Book of this Society covering the period 1843 to
1849 is still in existence (in the possession of Mr J. C. Menzies,
Culdares, Aberfeldy) and the following notes and extracts may
be of interest :—

The meeting place of the Society was the schoolroom of
the Black Street school and the first of the Rules and
Regulations laid down "That this Society shall meet on
Thursday nights at 8½ o'clock and adjourn at 10," and at
the first meeting "It was agreed to pay Mr Stewart 3d.
per night for fire and the use of the schoolroom." At the
seventh meeting this sum was raised to 4d. at which it
remained.

In the Treasurer's Statement of Outlays for the year
1843/4, apart from the weekly 3d. and 4d., the only items
which appear are : "October 26th—paid for Minute Book

1/-," "November 2nd.—two yards cotton at 3½d. per yard, 7d.," and on "November 1st.—1 lb. candles, 7½d.," "December 2nd.—1 lb. candles, 6½d.," "January 24th.— 1 lb. candles, 6½d.," and "March 5th.—1 lb. candles, 6d.". The whole year's expenditure totalled £1 1/- !

The accounts were kept most meticulously, thus : At the second meeting a collection of 2/10 was made, of which 1/- was paid for the Minute Book. At the third meeting 'A collection of 2d. from each member present was made which amounted to 3/-.' Other entries at different dates show the same thing : 'The sum of one shilling and two pence collected. Paid Mr Stewart 4d. Arrears 1½d. Balance in hand 4½d. and, at the next meeting, 'Balance in hand 4½d.', and, at the next, 'Balance in hand 2d.'—and so on.

The two following extracts give an idea of the nature of some of the Proceedings :

(1) On May 6th, 1847, 'The question "Should there be a National Scheme of Education ?" was argued very eloquently, philosophically and logically, and as the members were entering still more and more enthusiastically into the vivid flames of eloquence and more and more keenly and valiantly into the literary contest, when the late hour of the night admonished them to dismiss the question until the next meeting.' (Even Laird McDonald could scarcely have improved on this !). At the next meeting it was decided by a large majority that there should be such a Scheme.

(2) On July 1st of the same year Mr C. Stewart, a schoolteacher member, read an Essay labelled simply 'Education.' The entry in the Minutes reads : "It was tattered to pieces and utterly condemned in its composition, as alike void of system and elegance, and in the ideas which it conveyed as unphilosophic, as a ludicrous huddle of trumpery ; yet Mr Stewart's essay was valuable in truth

in some parts, provided that some alterations would be made so as to limit the ideas ; but in the abstract as advanced by Mr Stewart, there was hardly a single truth from one end of the essay to the other."—not much of the velvet glove here !

The next two extracts are of interest, though not from a 'debating' point of view :

October 7th, 1847 : "This being the great and memorable night of the mighty Flood only seven members were present and only five of them gave any money, but these gave between them 11s½."

October 19th, 1848 : "Owing to the great snowstorm very few were present."

How the name 'The Auld Smoky Ha' ' originated is not far to seek ; the clouds of eloquence, candle smoke, smoke from the fire, and, doubtless, tobacco smoke, would seem to afford ample explanation !

* * * * * *

Through the early years of the present century Aberfeldy continued to grow. In addition to what has been written one has to note the completion of roads begun before 1900 but still unfinished, the widening of pre-existing roads or tracks, and the construction of entirely new roads. In 1900 the two ends of Taybridge Drive were linked only by a footpath through the fields ; Taybridge Terrace up till a short time before this date existed as a made road only at its eastern end. Both are now completed roads. Moness Terrace replaced the Strulach at its lower end ; Tomchulan Road was widened and became the Old Crieff Road ; Alma Avenue, a new road, was constructed—and so on.

After the First World War Council Houses were erected on the north side of Market Street, in Tayside Place and Tayside Crescent (two entirely new roads), and at the east end of Breadalbane Terrace. Those erected on the west side of the Chapel Street have already been noticed.

After the Second World War a small colony of 'pre-fabs' was set up between Tayside Crescent and the golf course, the road of access being made by German prisoners, and a new 'town' of Council houses of the Swedish, Cruden, and three -and four-roomed traditional types on new roads, MONESS CRESCENT and MONESS AVENUE, on the fields below Moness House off the Old Crieff Road and behind the Tulloch—a housing scheme not yet completed.

Concerning Aberfeldy's 'pre-fab town' a good story is told, for the truth of which I can vouch : A small girl aged about four, after being 'missing' for some hours, turned up at her home. On being asked where she had been she replied, "I've been down to see the new houses." "And did you see them ?" she was asked. "No," was the reply "They haven't started them yet—but the sheds are all up !" Out of the mouths of babes and sucklings—!

* * * * * *

But houses imply inhabitants, population, living space, and so on ; in this connection, and before considering the present, it may be well to look back a little.

In 1770 there were some fifty houses east of the burn, eight or ten in Over Milton and probably about as many in Nether Milton—seventy in all. If, in the absence of census returns to which to refer, one allows an average of, say, five persons to each house it would seem that the number of people in the combined hamlets in 1770 was in the neighbourhood of 350. It is unlikely that it exceeded this to any extent for even fifty years later, according to Dr John Kennedy, many of the houses were "little better than hovels," so that anything over an average of five persons to each would seem improbable.

Dr Kennedy also stated that in his young days the population of Aberfeldy was about 800 ; this would mean a rise of over 100% on the 1770 figures if his estimate was accurate, but in any case it is obvious that an increase was in progress ; this increase, negligible up to 1841, was continued, rapidly at first, then after 1861 at a slower pace right on through the remainder of last century and the first decade of this. 1911, however, marked the peak, for since then there has been a tendency to recession, with the result that the census of last year found us back to the figures of between forty and fifty years ago.

As since 1911 the town has increased very considerably in size and twice extended its boundaries it is clear that the living space of the inhabitants must also have increased by just this amount, for, with 453 occupied dwellings, as there are now, and a population of 1528, the average density works out at about 3.4 inhabitants per dwelling. According to the 1951 returns Aberfeldy, with 0.70 persons per room, shows almost the lightest concentration of any town in Perthshire. The excess of females over males is given as 152.

Census Returns

Year	Returns
1841 —	823
1851 —	—
1861 —	1145
1871 —	1159
1881 —	1260
1891 —	1469
1901 —	1508
1911 —	1592
1921 —	1560
1931 —	1504
1941 —	(War Year)
1951 —	1528

As for living conditions one has only to look at the photographs of old Dunkeld Street, Black Street, and Chapel Street, to realise the enormous improvements that have been effected in the past eighty or ninety years.

In spite of all this the waiting list for houses under construction is long and the waiting time for those on it disheartening, while small houses when they come on the market fetch prices which a few years ago would have been considered fantastic. Large houses are in less demand, in the main probably because of the 'domestic help' problem ; young women of to-day have many more outlets for their energies and ambitions than had their mothers and grandmothers, but it seems a pity that they should appear to shun the one occupation which on the face of it should be just that one best calculated to qualify them to run the homes that, I imagine, most of them hope some day to own.   *   *   *   *   *   *

Before leaving the subject of 'living conditions' it is necessary to include a survey of the living conditions and habits of the tinkers for, though not residents in the strict sense, a number of tinker families—the Campbells, Townsleys, Reids, McPhees, and so on—are sufficiently persistent as recurring phenomena in our district as to be almost considered so.

To begin with I may state that the following notes are based on first hand knowledge born of personal experience ofttimes repeated, for many and many a time have I enjoyed the questionable pleasure of meeting and dealing with the tinker at close quarters in his 'home' surroundings and not infrequently of being obliged to pass frosty winter nights in the comparative warmth of his tent with eyes and nose and throat smarting in an atmosphere fouled with the smell of dirt and the reek of a wood fire, and unbreathable at a level of over three feet from the ground.

Some of the words of Macara, when he described the living conditions of some of his remoter parishioners in 1754, may be applied to most of these people, 'tinklers' they call themselves, for they "sleep on the ground with heather or ferns below them, and with no covering but their body clothes and possibly a dirty blanket or two ;" and some of the words of Pennant too when he wrote of the dwellings of the humbler folk on Deeside and Lochtayside in 1769, but applying them to tents instead of houses, as "shocking to humanity" and "the disgrace of North Britain."

The tinker is a curious study, both genealogically and psychologically. His origin is doubtful, and it is a question whether the mists which enshroud it will ever be dispelled. His fate is equally uncertain in spite of the various committees elected or appointed to enquire into his affairs and to solve the riddle of his reclamation. Squalid and vicious as is his lot, he seems quite satisfied ; he does not want to be reclaimed ; what he wants is enough money to get drunk on as often and as thoroughly as possible. Compared with the tramp,whose habits are full of guile, he is a simple country gentleman. No

A Tinker Family at Home.

doubt he has his faults (but, then, who has not ?) ; when he gets drunk he shouts and makes a noise, and frequently even beats his wife, but, though he often disturbs people who live in stone houses and pay taxes, he rarely molests them. He may not profess politics but, for all that, he is an intense liberal so far as liberty of the individual is concerned ; he contributes little towards the upkeep of the State which protects him ; he comes and goes as he pleases, and the sky under which he pitches his tent belongs as much to him as to anyone else. In other things he is equally intensely conservative ; even with the tramp who shares the open road with him he rarely fraternises ; occasionally, true, it is told in a whisper that someone, generally a low class female, has 'run off to join the tinks,' but how often does one hear of a tinker changing his nomadic life for a more settled one ?   Not often, I am sure of that.

The wanderlust is in their blood.   In the 1870's or '80's a police sergeant in Aberfeldy—Sergeant Allan—adopted a tinker baby.   He brought her up as his daughter.   She enjoyed all the comforts a clean and comfortable home could give and lived the life of a normal village girl ; she played with the other children, went to school with them, and grew up to early womanhood ; but 'the call of the wild' was there, not to be denied, and, when the time came, she turned her back on all that she had known, married a tinker and took to the road— the road trodden in the past by un-numbered generations of her forebears and to-day by her children, grandchildren, and great-grandchildren.   Once a tinker, always a tinker.

To those of us who think about such things it must appear that the tinker's apparent love of filth, discomfort, and vice is unnatural, almost pathological, and that his ideas and mentality, like his mode of existence, cannot be as our's.   Typically he is possessed of a peculiarly twisted child-like mind, controlling or, rather, failing to control his emotions like a child, and appearing to view life at an oblique angle which disturbs his mental perspective and renders it quite different from that of ordinary people.   That alcohol is the chief besetting evil and curse of his race need occasion no surprise ; pre-natally he gets it in the maternal blood ; later he imbibes it at the breast ; he grows up with the craving in his soul and gratifies that craving whenever opportunity offers. I once asked a tinker, as an expert, to give his opinion on the drink question as it affected him and his like. "I don't know," he replied, "but I do know that, if I saw a bottle of whisky on the other side of a wall of fire, I'd go through the fire to get it."

All his money, however, does not go on drink. Despite the costs involved, not to mention bicycles, sewing-machines, gramophones, wireless sets, etc., quite a number of his fraternity run cars or motor lorries, not infrequently with trailer caravans attached. Rarely, now, does one see the sight, familiar enough twenty or thirty years ago, of the tinker family trudging along on foot with the sheaf of curved saplings which formed the framework of their wagon-roofed patchwork tents and all their worldly belongings in dirty bundles on their shoulders or piled high on a barrow knocked up out of an old packing case and a pair of discarded perambulator wheels, with babies slung in plaids on their mother's backs, and a swarm of ragged and dirty children trailing along behind. Quite often too they included in their outfit a semi-derelict light spring cart drawn by a half-starved horse or pony and with a mongrel dog trotting alongside or running underneath, tied to the axle. Cars and bicycles have largely altered all that.

Speaking generally the tinker, in the matter of his attire, is not swayed by the dictates of fashion. This, I may say, is absolutely true with regard to the male of the species ; anything is good enough and he is usually to be seen in clothes in the last stages of dilapidation and decrepitude. With the female it is not possible to be so dogmatic. In their youth which is short-lived, for their manner of life tends to age them rapidly, many of the girls possess real gipsy-like beauty, of which fact they would appear to be aware for flesh coloured stockings and high heels are common, and lipstick and rouge extravagances well within the range of their purses.

On the whole, however the fashion of 'dirt and rags' predominates, whatever their age or sex, for they are inveterate beggars, the women and children particularly being detailed off for this branch of their industry, and it is very obvious that any appearance of prosperity, such as might be given by cleanliness and 'well-dressedness,' would tend to dry at their sources the springs of charity which rise in the hearts of people who, often with less ready cash than the tinkers themselves, may be so misguided as to feel inclined to encourage them in their thriftlessness.

I conclude this rather long digression with two stories, two of the many I could tell, which convey more than pages of descriptive writing. This is the first : A tinker of my acquaintance had just got his discharge from Logierait Poorhouse, in the days when it was a Poorhouse. At the gate he was met by another who, some time before, had spent a few days in the same institution. Said the second to the first, anxiously, "Did they gi'e ye a *bath* ?" "Aye," answered his friend with a shudder. "Gosh !" exclaimed number two in an awestruck whisper, "an' whit did ye think o't ?" "Man," was the earnest reply, "A'd often heard tell o' a bath, but, dod ! A never kent it wis sic a bluidy awfu' ordeal !"

The second story is a very terrible one. It was told me by the wife of a gamekeeper, an old woman long since dead. I was visiting her husband at their lonely house on the edge of a wide moorland and, close by, from a disused sheep fank, I saw rising the smoke of a tinker's fire. I asked her if she did not object to such undesirable neighbours in such an isolated spot. "Oh no," she answered, "they don't trouble us. Sometimes they come begging, and we often hear them fighting." Then she told me this story : A year or two previously there was a camp in the fank and a little girl used to come to the house daily for a flagon of milk "for the baby," Day by day she came, and then, one morning, she did not come, nor did she come again. About a week later the old woman met the little girl and said to her, "Why do you never come for the baby's milk any more?" "There's no' a baby noo ; m' feyther slewed it !" was the terrible reply—terrible in its expression of a child's innocent acceptance of the tragedy as being in the ordinary nature of things. It is easy to picture the scene : the squalid surroundings, a puling brat, a drunken father, an oath, a blow, a furtive burial by night, and a little unmarked grave on the hill-side. The outside world knew nothing of the mite's arrival and, but for the word of a child, would have known nothing of its departure. The problem of the tinker is indeed a big and difficult one.

* * * * * *

Like many other small towns and villages in country districts Aberfeldy until the beginning of the present century was a more or less self-contained community. Certainly the coming of the railway in 1865 was a long step towards breaking down this 'insularity' but even in the 1890's and early 1900's, apart from the annual influx of visitors in the holiday season, there was comparatively little coming and going between our population and the outside world. We were, so to speak, all regular inhabitants, everyone knowing everyone else, all about them, their forebears, their traditions, and their business— often more about the last named indeed than the people concerned themselves ! The same families had lived and intermarried in the town and district for generations and newcomers, one might almost have thought, had to go through a period of probation before being finally accepted or refused admission into the family circle.

Things are changed nowadays ; our folk are citizens of the World in a far greater degree than of old. Life is more hectic than it was ; people move about more ; the First and Second Great Wars took our young men and women into the far corners of the earth, whence they returned with new ideas and new outlooks ; the cinema, wireless, and now television have contributed to a wider horizon, but, with it all, there is no gainsaying that life in Aberfeldy to-day lacks much of the peacefulness and picturesqueness that characterised it fifty and more years ago.

No doubt we have gained in many directions but I, for one, as I look back over my seventy years, cannot help but feel, well, a little nostalgic for what the rising generation seems sometimes tempted to call, sarcastically I am afraid, "The Good Old Days." Good or bad, however, they are gone and, whether we like it or not, we are living in the present—which brings us to Aberfeldy as we see it to-day, in the words of one guidebook "An exceedingly pleasant Highland town," for in spite of what it has lost it *is* a pleasant town.

The road traveller passing through at speed from east to west or from west to east may take with him merely the impression of 'just another small town' and let it go at that, and I shouldn't blame him, but at the same time he cannot fail to see that there are more than a few shops which would not disgrace or be out of place in the 'shopping quarter' of many a larger town, in fact the number of shops big and little may set him wondering whether this is not another case of a community the members of which exist by taking in each other's washing!

Aberfeldy, however, it has to be remembered is a railway terminus and the market town and emporium of a wide agricultural district, and also the residence of a considerable population of the 'villa' class. The evidence of this last is not to be obtained by the mere passer-through but by the traveller who pauses and takes time to inspect that part of the town which lies mainly to the west of the Moness Burn and towards the Tay overlooking the golf course and the haugh lands of Weem and Appin ; here he will find, unless he be hard to please, that the guidebook has not lied.

And now, what of the future ? What, in this Age of 'Planning,' have the 'Planners' in store for us ? In 1950 the East Central (Scotland) Regional Planning and Advisory Committee published a report by Gordon Payne, Town Planning Consultant, entitled *The Tay Valley Plan—A Physical, Social, and Economic Survey and Plan for the Development of East Central Scotland*. In this work recommendations are set out with regard to the anticipated expansion of Aberfeldy in days to come under a programme of long term planning designed to replace the more or less haphazard methods of the past.

As a Regional Centre Aberfeldy will be recognised not only as the metropolis and shopping centre of a wide countryside but as an industrial centre which will serve the upper reaches of the Tay and Tummel and the Highland Area of the County. The site chosen as the most suitable for a small industrial estate lies to the north-east of the Burgh adjacent to the railway station, or on the reclaimed land between the main road and the river in the same area.

It is recommended further that an increase of the population to 3,000 be aimed at and that the majority of the new housing should be carried out in the south-east and south-west of the existing town, with an additional Junior School to the east of the Crieff Road and an extension westward of the present Academy should the proposed development take place. The extension westward of the Academy with the necessary removal of the playing fields to the south-west has already been referred to.

The Report goes on : 'Additional Public Open Space should be provided in the new housing areas south of the town. A wedge of open space should also be reserved along the Moness Den linking up with the recreation ground adjoining the (new) playing fields,' and, in general, that a minimum reservation of Public Open Space of 10 acres per 1,000 of population should be adopted in all towns such as Aberfeldy which are holiday or residential resorts, and should provide for the inter-linkage of green spaces between use zones and separating major roads from housing areas. 'Use' zones are zones devoted to industries and to shopping and business extensions, which latter, in the case of Aberfeldy, should be provided in the present shopping and business centres in Bank Street, The Square, and Dunkeld Street.

The Report deals also with the improvement of transport in the area under survey but has little on this subject to suggest with regard to Aberfeldy, only advising the construction of a traffic roundabout at the crossing of the main east-west and north-south roads, and envisaging the possibility of a time coming when the provision of a landing ground for aeroplanes may have to be considered.

Now, after this short excursion into the future and with the knowledge that everything is comfortably mapped out for us and pigeon-holed for reference, it is time to continue the story of our town as we who live in it find it to-day.

* * * * * *

As regards recreation : Aberfeldy residents know that they have a lovely stretch of the Tay semi-circling them, and it is this fringe of their territory that they have wisely chosen as their playground, with tennis, bowling, football, cricket, curling putting, and golf, all laid on in season and within easy reach.

The TENNIS courts—two, red blaes—opened in 1905, were immediately popular among the younger folk and are well patronised. In the past year or two Sunday play has been permitted in non-church hours.

The present BOWLING green also was opened in 1905 when the devotees of the game moved in from the somewhat cramped and fly-infested quarters up till then at their disposal just inside the entrance to the Den of Moness at the War Memorial. The old green is still there but disused. When the Breadalbane Hotel was built the ground inside the entrance to the Den was granted by the then Laird of Breadalbane as an amenity for the guests in the hotel and the old bowling green was constructed in the first instance for their benefit. On May 27th, 1889, a meeting was held in the hotel with a view to putting the game in Aberfeldy on a proper footing and local players submitted proposals to Lord Breadalbane for his approval, one of these being that a club be formed which would have control of and be responsible for the green, and another that one rink should be available as required to visitors in the Breadalbane Hotel and strangers residing in the district. Election of new members was by ballot box and one black ball in three meant rejection.

CRICKET has its following in the burgh and enthusiasts play in the Victoria Park where the club has a prepared pitch and also two concrete strips for practice at the nets. These strips were laid down, in 1950, by members in their spare time. Breadalbane Cricket Club was formed in 1869 and played on a piece of ground, in the East Park (now the eastern section of the golf course), granted by the Earl of Breadalbane who was patron and supplied all the requirements for the game.

In 1880 an extraordinary one-innings match was played in this field against a mixed team of Perth clubs. Breadalbane batted first and, with a team in which most of the players were aged twenty or under, scored 254 runs ; they then proceeded to dismiss their opponents for 4, 2 of which were extras and the other 2 scored by a substitute supplied by the home team ! The Aberfeldy bowlers who performed this seemingly impossible feat were John Harrower (later Professor of Greek in Aberdeen University) with 5 wickets for 2 runs, and J. C. Campbell (referred to in the 'Foreword,') who added the remaining scalps to his belt for no runs.

In the same year (1880) an unusual one-wicket match was played in which five Harrower brothers—John (see above), Alexander, Peter, William (who, fourteen years later, became my uncle-by-marriage), and James—played five other members of that year's team. The brothers were beaten.

* * * * * *

VICTORIA PARK was leased to the town by the Marquis of Breadalbane in 1897 (Jubilee Year) at the nominal rate of 1/- per year ; the trees in it were planted in 1908.

In addition to serving as a cricket field, the Park is the arena in which various functions have been and are held from time to time, e.g., The Breadalbane Highland Gathering, the Annual Agricultural and Flower Show, etc.

The Breadalbane Highland Gathering owed its inception to the efforts of several private gentlemen and began its existence in Kenmore, the first assembly being on 9th

September, 1843, the first anniversary of Queen Victoria's visit to Taymouth, and during the years it was held in Kenmore proceedings were opened with a procession from Taymouth to the field, accompanied by the firing of guns and the hoisting of the Scottish Standard.

Later it was run in conjunction with the local 5th Volunteer Battalion Royal Highlanders, being held at the conclusion of the Company's annual rifle shooting competition, and, still later, by a Games Committee. When first removed from Kenmore to Aberfeldy the meetings for some years were held in a field in front of Moness House, then after that in the field where the distillery now stands and for a number of years in the field west of Tomghuibhais—in both these latter places within my personal recollection.

The Highland Gathering was discontinued a number of years ago after a run of bad gates, partly owing to adverse weather conditions, had made it financially impossible for the Games Committee to carry on. Its revival has been spoken of recently but nothing definite done up to the time of writing.

The Agricultural Show came into being about 1945/6 through the efforts of the Farmers' Association and was immediately successful. After a year or two those responsible for the Annual Flower Show—which used to be held in the Town Hall but had been in abeyance during the war years—joined forces with the farmers, and now the double show is one of the events of Aberfeldy's season.

In the Victoria Park in July 1951, in almost unbelievably fine weather, were held the first Pageant of Aberfeldy, and the first Pipe Band Contest open to the County for the Macpherson Shield, a trophy presented by a local business man, in which the Aberfeldy pipers secured 4th place in a field of eight.

The Aberfeldy Pipe Band was first formed in 1902 and, two years later was engaged for three days at the (Royal) Highland and Agricultural Society's Show at Perth and highly commend-

ed ; in the following year (1905) at the Edinburgh Highland
Gathering at Tynecastle in Open Competition it won First
Place.   The pipe-major at that time, Gavin C. Macdougall, and
his brother John were the last of four generations of pipe-
makers, their father, grandfather, and great-grandfather having
followed the same occupation, the last named from 1792 to
1834 (in Perth).   G. C. Macdougall, who while still in his teens
won the Gold Medal at the Northern Gathering at Inverness,
was, in his day, the only pipe-maker in Great Britain holding
the Royal Appointment to H.M. King Edward VII.   At one
time his father, Duncan, was piper to Edward VII when he
was Prince of Wales and, afterwards, to Lord Breadalbane ; it
was he who started the Aberfeldy business which supplied
pipes to the Army and Navy and to Scottish Societies all over
the world, Indian potentates, etc.

In the early part of this year a silver cup—The Macdougall
Cup—was presented for annual competition in solo piping.
It was the gift of the sisters of the late Mr Gavin C. Macdougall,
Miss Macdougall, Perth, and Mrs W. Anderson, Aberfeldy, and is
open to all players in the County.

Before the days of the Town Band the piping needs of the
population were met by the pipers of the 5th V.B.R.H. and by
Macdougall's Band run by the pipe-making family.   This
latter band used to meet and play, in the 1890's, beside the old
bowling green.

In Victoria Park there is a metal drinking fountain which,
in addition to the date July 1885, bears an inscription to the
effect that it, together with certain other improvements, was
presented to the town by Lord Breadalbane as a memento and
in recognition of the great ovation given to himself and Lady
Breadalbane by the residents on his arrival home from London,
where he was Treasurer to the Household under a Liberal
Government, after the restoration of the Marquisate which had
lapsed in 1862.   It was first erected in the centre of The Square
where it stood, crowned with a street lamp, for a number of
years till, proving an obstruction to traffic, it was removed ;
after that for some time it lay derelict in the Town Hall yard
until re-erected, but without the lamp, in its present site.

ABERFELDY "PRIZE" PIPE BAND. 1905.

In the Park also are swings for the children which give excellent service.   It was found, however, that as a playground
it was not conveniently situated for children living at the east
end of the town, and a second, the JUBILEE PARK, was officially opened in 1935, the year of King George V's Silver
Jubilee, at the east end of Breadalbane Terrace almost directly
opposite the County Council Highland District Road Depot.

*   *   *   *   *   *

FOOTBALL, though now with a strong local following, is a
game of comparatively recent introduction in Aberfeldy, and
of a growth covered almost by my own lifetime.   Kennedy, in
his *Old Highland Days* reports that in his boyhood in the
town football was unknown, a kind of shinty being played,
and the late J. C. Campbell wrote :   "Football was played in
1878/9 but the first club was not formed till 1880, and it was
called Aberfeldy Breadalbane.   Shortly after, another club
was formed in the east end of the town—Aberfeldy Rangers.
After a period of great rivalry these clubs eventually amalga-
mated.   Enthusiasm from the start was tremendous, but
business had to come first so that in the short winter days the
long shop hours left little time for practice.   It was therefore
resolved to have early morning practice, starting about 6 A.M.
The captain borrowed the bugle of the local Volunteers (5th
V.B.R.H.) and at 5.30 A.M. went through the town blowing
a blast here and there awakening many more than the football
team.   Those for whom this hour had no appeal met for
practice in the Cour Park after dark in the evenings.   For
illumination they had such light as six showman's lamps, purchased for the club, could provide."   Those were the days !

It was a Breadalbane player, Robert Campbell, who introduced the game into Perth.   He brought the Breadalbane team
to the Fair City to play an exhibition game against a combined
Perth team, and beat them by five goals.

For a time around the beginning of this century the field west
of Tomghiubhais was the ground in use, the slope of the hill

making an ideal terrace for onlookers. The playing pitch is now once again down by the river, in that part of the golf course lying east of the Moness Burn.

The CURLING Club, founded in 1853, finding that the pond at Pitilie in mild winters was not always willing to oblige, opened, in 1925, a 'sprinkle' pond—asphalt, and only calling for spraying—in the field behind the gardens on the west side of Taybridge Road. For a time here play after dark was under the light of paraffin flares ; electricity is now installed.

The Pitilie pond dates from about 1885, the estimate for construction (£53 16/-) having been considered and passed by the Committee in November 1884. Prior to this time, for over thirty years, the Club had played, as well as on the Duntuim mill dam aready referred to, at Bolfracks and elsewhere.

The traditional garb, as I remember it—Breadalbane tartan trousers, blue pilot jacket, and balmoral bonnet— no longer lends colour to the curling scene, but the old enthusiasm still flourishes. That times are changing is borne out by the fact that only last year the local club, before sending a chosen rink to Perth to take part in a match against a touring Canadian team, searched high and low for balmoral bonnets for their players—without success !

To-day our open-air ponds tend to see less service than of old ; the 'luxury' conditions and freedom from weather vagaries of the covered rink in Perth are a strong counter-attraction. Many of our local curlers, men and, of late years, women too, either own cars or have friends who do ; and buses are very handy.

Next year, 1953, is the centenary of the club and preparations for suitable celebrations are now under consideration. If a precedent for a 'roaring' time is required, the Minutes of the Club provide one for on 10th January, 1859, "The Committee discussed the best means of supplying players with refreshments on the ice and came to the unanimous conclusion that the players supply themselves with eatables, and Messrs. Monro, McLean, and J. Wyllie are instructed to lay in a stock of four or five gallons of whisky which the Secretary will deal out as required !"

The Aberfeldy Boy Scouts, Girl Guides, etc., have their meetings in an ex-army hut close to the artificial curling pond for which they pay a nominal ground rent of 1/- per year, and the first-mentioned at least seem more likely to survive than the Aberfeldy Company of the Boys' Brigade which was started in the 1890's, only to expire after a semi-comatose existence of two or three years. I think the youngsters, of whom I was one, preferred to run wild in their spare time, and the straightforward drilling, forming fours, etc., and the anti-smoking rule (!) which seemed to us to be the be-all and end-all of the business, did not appeal to us as boys in the same way as does the Scout training to our successors of to-day.

The Scout hut was used during the 1939-45 War as an auxiliary schoolroom (as were also three rooms in the Town Hall Buildings) when the influx of children from Glasgow and elsewhere increased the numbers beyond the capacity of the Academy buildings.

The nine hole GOLF course was opened on 5th June, 1895, by Lady Currie of Garth. A contemporary newspaper reported as follows : "There was a very large attendance. All the shops in the town were closed for two hours and the Police Commissioners, headed by the Volunteer Pipe Band, marched to the north end of the bridge where they received her Ladyship, accompanied by Sir Donald Currie, M.P. and Mr E. H. Carson, Q.C., M.P., ex-Solicitor General for Ireland"—later Sir Edward Carson, first Premier of Northern Ireland. The ceremony then proceeded along the usual lines—speech-making, and so on, in course of which Lady Currie was presented with a silver-mounted putter bearing a suitable inscription.

Some time after this, with a view to giving things a further boost, and to putting the course definitely on the golfing map, the club brought two well-known professionals of the day, Alex. Herd and Andrew Kirkcaldy, to play an exhibition game and make suggestions. Since then the lay-out of the greens has been altered from time to time ; it now follows the plan drawn out in the 1920's by the late James Braid, one of the 'Big Three' who dominated the tournaments in the early years of this century and who was in the district in connection with the laying out of the newly opened course at Taymouth.

Sunday golf is not allowed.

In the early days the game in Aberfeldy was something of an undertaking and far removed from what it is to-day. Before the introduction of motor-drawn mowers the fairways had to be hand cut with the scythe and as for a number of years the greenkeeper was an elderly man who found the bunkers ideal places for a snooze on sunny afternoons the result, as was to be expected, was not conducive to good golf or good tempers. The fairways were narrow—in most cases little more and in some cases less than half their present widths; the way to the first green particularly was almost lane-like, for a fence ran down the middle of what is now the fairway, and on the other side of the fence was a cultivated field ; pulling or slicing meant either the river or this field. The 'rough' was rough in the roughest sense, and all the way round it was per- petually a case of 'lost ball,' and for the average player the niblick—number 7 iron it is now called—the most useful club in the bag !

Fore-caddies were practically a *sine qua non* and amply repaid the 6d. a round charge. On one occasion, about ten years after the course was opened, after a round (nine holes) without one of these boys I was able to announce in the club house that I had lost eight balls. I was immediately capped by a man who had been round before me, "I can beat that. I lost eleven—and a *club* !"

Of course at that time clubs were wooden-shafted and cost only from 7/6 to 12/6 or thereabouts ; 'gutties' ran at 6d. or 9d.

each—less for 're-mades'—and the man who played silvertowns at 12/-per dozen was really in the top class, of money if not necessarily of golf. In those days, however, one was on more intimate terms with one's clubs than is possible now. Each had its own name —driver, brassie, spoon, baffy, cleek, mid-iron, mashie, putter, etc. ; now it is a case of Number 1 wood, Number 2 wood, and so on up the scale, Number 1 iron, Number 2 iron, and so on up the scale again—I defy anyone to be on intimate terms with 'Numbers ;' I never yet met a 'Number' with any personality about it. To my mind the soul has gone out of the game !

Haskells, the first of the rubber-cored balls, were just begin-ning to be heard of here about the time I left school in 1898.

Before the Aberfeldy club came into being golf was almost entirely the monoply of a few retired and independent gentle-men, etc., who had four or five putting greens scattered about the Weem Park (so-called, though nowhere near Weem) and there, clad in red jackets—*de rigeur* in those days—they were wont to go through the evolutions of the Royal and Ancient Game.

* * * * * *

At the further end of Weem Park, at the end of a right of way from Wade's Taybridge to the Killiechassie Road and crossing a small ditch-like stream, is a bridge to the neighbourhood of which clings the name 'Stair Ghòrach.' At one time there was a ford (Gaelic, 'stair') over the Tay near here which was frequented by a kelpie called Gòrach that used to cry before a death, "Thainig an uair, ach cha d'thainig an duine !" —"The hour has come but not the man !" Invariably after this someone was drowned at the ford.

At Cuil Farm near by tradition has it that a 'Bocan' or 'Tannasg' (apparition) disturbed the farmer and his family for many years until finally exorcised by one of the ministers of the neighbourhood. What form the apparition took does not transpire.

On the right of the farm road to Cuil is one of the two of the seven old lime kilns within a mile of Aberfeldy as yet unmentioned. The other lies on the west side of the Tighnault Burn, between the burn and Easter Boltachan. Behind Tighnault (house), at one time there was in operation a sawmill ; the building and the mill dam are still there but the saw has long been silent.

The farm next eastward from Cuil, 'cuil' 'a nook,' is Borlick (Killiechassie). The significance of the name has already been explained in reference to the other Borlick just across the valley.

Further eastward still is the mansionhouse of Killiechassie which, though considerably more than a mile from Aberfeldy by road, is less as the crow flies, and so calls for a word here.

'Killiechassie', 'the Church of the steep face,' takes its name from a church which once stood on the ground of the farm of Tombuie—'Tom buidhe,' 'yellow knoll'—on the hillface further east above the row of four (joined) cottages of Chapelton, in the name of which the memory of the sacred building is preserved. It is said that the church was in existence 700 years ago but there is no sign now either of it or of the adjacent burial ground except a single standing stone, uninscribed, though burials are said to have taken place here up to about the 1740's. According to tradition some of the descendants of Alexander Stewart the Wolf of Badenoch were among the number. Tradition also has it that on one occasion a funeral party was crossing from the other side of the river, when the people of Killiechassie, believing that the deceased was not entitled to burial here, assembled on the bank to prevent their landing. In the scuffle which ensued the boat was upset and the occupants drowned. The horror of this event caused such an impression that no further burials took place in the churchyard.

A little way to the west of Chapelton are the Canon's Knoll, the Canon's Pool, and also the Killiechassie school. This school, no longer in use as such, is occupied as a dwelling house, the children of the district coming in to the Academy in Aberfeldy. It last functioned in the role for which it was cast during the 1939-45 War, when it was attended by Roman Catholic children evacuated from Glasgow and resident in Cluny House, a hostel for the time being. A former school, also now in use as a dwelling house, stands on the hillface just west of Killiechassie mansionhouse.

Killiechassie house was erected in 1865 to replace an older house which occupied a site on a level piece of ground on a natural terrace about 100 yards further east, and a little way up the drive there is an old plane tree which is called Prince Charlie's Tree, the story being that, during his wanderings in the Highlands, Prince Charlie spent a night under its shade. The stone lintel of the front doorway of the old house is built into a rockery facing the front door of the new. It bears a religious inscription.

Long ago the proprietors of Killiechassie were Robertsons of the famous house of Struan, but it is said that at a still more remote period the Stewarts had some association with the place —as witness the Wolf of Badenoch tradition of the old burial ground at Chapelton. From the Robertsons the property passed into the hands of another family of Stewarts. In the Fasti of the Presbytery of Dunkeld reference is made to a Rev. Robert Stewart who was admitted to Killin in 1680, at which time the Cure was still held by an Episcopal incumbent. Stewart, who had earned for himself the nickname 'Curam'—a Gaelic word meaning 'care' —was able before he died in 1729 to set up his four sons as lairds in Strathtay : James, the eldest, in Killiechassie; Duncan, in Blackhill; Alexander, in Cloichfoldich ; and Robert, in Derculich. A son of Duncan married the daughter and only child of Robertson of Edradynate and, on succeeding to the Edradynate Estate, took the name of Stewart-Robertson.

Until the late J. Stewart-Robertson, Esq., of Edradynate, who died in 1940, arranged a new burial place for himself and his wife in the grounds of Edradynate, all these Stewarts used the small private burial ground in Killiechassie, which stands by the side of the main road where the hill-road to Tombuie branches off. This burial ground is now in a sadly neglected state, untended and weed-overgrown, and the inscriptions on most of the stones are quite illegible ; the oldest, the dates on which can still be read, stands in memory of an Adam Stewart, born 1733, died 1811. Also within the walls is a monument, giving many names but unfortunately few dates, which was erected in 1884 by the then James Stewart-Robertson of Edradynate to the memory of his ancestors and kinsfolk. From the inscriptions it may be deduced that Killiechassie came into the hands of the Flemyngs of Moness through the marriage of Margaret Flemyng, the last of her line, to Robert Stewart of Killiechassie in the earlier part of the 18th century. Their son is named James Stewart-Flemyng of Killiechassie and Moness. The son of the next generation is noted as Robert Stewart-Flemyng of Killiechassie only. Moness, sold in 1787, had evidently passed from his hands therefore by the time of his death.

From the Stewart-Flemyngs the property came into the ownership of a Mr H. G. Gordon, who built and lived in the present mansion house, but in the course of a year or two it was purchased by Mr E. O. Douglas ; Mr and Mrs Douglas have already been referred to, as benefactors of the Aberfeldy and District Cottage Hospital. A relative of Mrs Douglas was Principal Shairp of St. Andrew's University who built and spent his summer holidays in Cuilaluinn for many years. In this house he composed some of his finest poems and essays.

Within the past thirty or forty years the Estate has shrunk somewhat in size and changed ownership a number of times, the present proprietor being Captain G. E. Coles, who took possession this year.—(L). During the interval it was held successively by Lord Barnby of Blyth, Captain J. E. B. Radcliffe, Mr William Hood, and Mr Walter Nicoll.

*　*　*　*　*　*

When Wade's Taybridge was in process of construction and during his road making operations in these parts the General is said to have resided, at all events for some of the time, in the lower east wing of what is now Weem Hotel. According to *Take Note*, the propaganda magazine issued by the Scottish Tourist Board, this part, an inn in those days, was one of Wade's 'King's Houses,' as was also the King's House at Balquhidder. Where his men were quartered is not recorded, but it is believed that the present hotel at Coshieville (Gaelic, 'Cois-bhile,' 'thicket's foot') was built by him as a barracks to accommodate them, probably while they were engaged on the road that crosses the hills to Tummelbridge.

It was Wade's practice to erect barrack huts at intervals along his roads. Wooden at first these were later completed in stone and, when no longer required as barracks, functioned as inns or change houses, some of which were called King's Houses. Whether the inn which stood where the Bank of Scotland now is ever served as a barracks is uncertain.

Wade's road from Taybridge to Coshieville did not follow the line of the present road but struck off to the left just beyond the bridge and, taking a more direct course, rejoined it 180 yards west of Weem Hotel.

Incidentally the small earthworks (trenches) in the parks on either side of the road at the north end of the bridge were constructed at the time a German invasion was considered a possibility early in the 1939-45 War.

The Lombardy poplars which line the present main road to the other side of the valley and make such a fine approach to Aberfeldy from the north were planted by the late Sir Robert Menzies in 1897, the year of Queen Victoria's Diamond Jubilee. This stretch is still sometimes spoken of among the older folk as 'The Hedges,' a name which recalls the time, 50 years ago and more, when it ran narrow and lane-like between hedges of beech, thorn, and brier, ten to twelve feet high on either side.

At the northern end of the poplar avenue, standing just across the east-to-west road from the Weem Toll, is a red roofed cottage of the bungalow type. This was built about fifty years ago by the late Miss Egidea Menzies of Menzies as a saleroom for dairy produce, etc., from the Castle Menzies Home Farm. She gave it the name of 'Record Reign Cottage' but it was better known to the people around as 'the Creamery.' Its life as such was short however as the idea never seemed to catch on in the neighbourhood. After that, for some years, it was occupied by the District Nurse and re-christened 'Altrumas' (Gaelic, 'banaltrumachd' 'nursing,' 'ban' 'a woman' and 'altrum' 'to nurse'), until accommodation was found for her in a house in Aberfeldy, in Moness Terrace almost opposite the Masonic Temple ; since then it has served as a private residence. It is still known as 'Altrumas' though occasionally even to-day in the mouths of some of the older people one hears it referred to as 'the Creamery.' During this year (1952) it has been altered and extended somewhat.

* * * * * *

Beside Weem Hotel, the oldest part of which is said to date back to 1527, is the East Gate of the policies of Castle Menzies, ancient home of the Chiefs of the Clan, and just inside, beyond the Lodge, there hung for many years high up in one of the trees a bell which used to be rung to warn the people at the Castle of the approach of visitors. It was set up there by Sir John and Lady Menzies in the year 1790, which date it bore. Somewhere about 1919 this tree with its bell fell before the woodman's axe during timber operations which were being carried out by order of the trustees of the estate between the date of the death of Sir Neil Menzies, the last male chief hereditary in direct line, in 1910, and that of its purchase by Lord Barnby of Blyth, or Mr Francis Willy as he was at that time.

Head of a large woollen manufacturing company in Bradford, Mr Willy paid £69,000 for the Castle and 16,000 acres of the old Menzies Estates. Not long after his death the property was re-sold, in 1930, by his heirs to a firm of land agents and broken up mostly into small holdings bought by the sitting tenants.

The Poplar Avenue.

ABERFELDY IN THE 1890's (FROM THE NORTH WEST).

SHOWING THE TAY IN FLOOD, WEEM TOLL IN THE FOREGROUND AND "THE HEDGES" ON THE RIGHT.

At one time the lands of the Menzieses of Weem reached over to the shores of Loch Rannoch, into Glenlyon, westwards into Breadalbane as far as Glen Dochart and both sides of Loch Tay, Bolfracks, Wester Aberfeldy, Borlick and Murthly. Among other Baronies held by them in the far past were those of Durisdeer in Dumfriesshire, Vogrie in the County of Midlothian, and Culter in Lanarkshire. Of all this vast tract of country, not one acre now remains in the hands of any member of this ancient family who came as land-owners in these parts from Durisdeer towards the end of the 13th century.

In 1510 the then laird obtained a Charter from James IV consolidating his scattered estates into a free Barony. The Baronetcy, which dates from 1665, was conferred by Charles II "in memory of the losses of life and property so nobly sacrificed for our illustrious ancestors—" etc. Various off-shoots of the family still survive, but no claim to the Baronetcy has so far been sustained in the Law Courts.

Castle Menzies, now in alien hands and unfortunately half derelict, was built about 1571 and renovated, with the addition of a west wing, in 1840. It lies outside the scope of this Account.

In the early 1700's the Kirktown of Weem was a more important centre than Aberfeldy. There were three important Fairs on that side of the valley, one of which, St. Ringan's or Ninian's Fair, carries one back to the earliest introduction of Christianity into Scotland before the time of St. Columba. Adamnan, St. Columba's biographer, was commemorated in one of the biggest markets at Dull, and a couplet has been handed down showing that the retailers of cakes, sweets, etc., at this market used to put up at Weem :—
   "On the night of Adamnan's Fair in Dow (6th Oct., O.S.)
   Of huckster wives will Weem be fou."

A curious entry in the Records of the Parish of Weem about that time mentions the Provost's Herd. Unless it is concluded that the official scribe was mixing jest with more serious matters the Kirktown must have been a Burgh many generations before Aberfeldy attained that dignity !

* * * * * *

Though Weem has not many buildings altogether it can boast at least two very much older than anything Aberfeldy has to show—its hotel and its 'Auld Kirk' (pre-Reformation). This latter, dedicated to St. Cuthbert and named after him, is believed to be one of the oldest structures in the kingdom. In the first *Statistical Account* it is written, "The Church of Weem was probably built about the time of or before King Robert the Bruce—," but it would seem to be older than that, being included in Charters as far back as 1235. Some however question the accuracy of records placing the erection so far back into the past and suggest that the building as it now stands dates from about 1510.

The first mention of Weem as a Parish is in *Boiamund's Taxatio*, preserved in the Vatican. In this record, popularly known as *Bagimont's Roll*, is set out a list of parishes and tithes collected from them in 1275 and 1276 by Boiamund de Vicci, Nuncio sent out by the Pope to gather funds for the relief of the Holy Land. Among others there is this entry : '*Ecclesia de Weem, 30 sols., giving revenue of 15 lib.*'

According to the writer of the *Statistical Account* the church was altered and repaired in 1609 (?) and repaired again in 1752. Re-roofing and re-slating were carried out in 1936. Whether it was ever fitted with pews is not now certain, but in its early days these were unknown in churches in Scotland. The first permanent or fixed pew in any church in this country would appear to be the 'Baxters' (bakers') seat in St. Nicholas Church, Aberdeen, which bears the date 1607. In the cities prior to that time wealthier people and trade guilds had seats which stood in the church, but poorer people brought their stools ; remember Jenny Geddes who threw her stool at the minister in St. Giles. As an additional note : It was in or about 1560 that every church was ordered to have a pulpit, a bell (a hand bell to begin with in many cases), and communion tables.

The Auld Kirk ceased to be used as a place of worship in 1839 and was handed over by the heritors of Weem Parish to the then Sir Neil Menzies, to be used by him and his successors exclusively as a family mausoleum ; up till then only the east wing had been so used. In return for this gift Sir Neil granted a site for a new Parish Church halfway between Weem and the old toll-house.

This new church, erected at a cost of £700, was in use until 7th July, 1921, when it became the Menzies Clan Society Hall on the gift to the heritors by Miss Egidea Menzies of that Ilk, Chieftainess for a short time after her brother's death, of what was formerly St. David's Episcopal Church of Weem (built 1870) ; it was intended to be used for holding annual Clan meetings, housing Clan relics, etc., and also as a meeting place of the Menzies troop of Boy Scouts. It was re-roofed by the Clan Society in 1930 but to-day its appearance of utter neglect —weed-overgrown enclosure, broken windows, etc.—makes it an eyesore, and certainly no credit to any Clan.

Regarding the stretch of road between the Weem Toll and Weem : In November 1778 the Presbytery of Dunkeld met to examine the glebe of the Minister at Weem on the proposal to cut through it a road along the line of the present road past the site of the 1839 church, to take the place of the old high road which passed behind the manse. To compensate the minister the glebe was extended to take in the field between the present road and the canal just south of it.

Over one of the doors of the Auld Kirk (the one that faces towards the main road) is sculptured the marriage heraldic shield of Sir Alexander Menzies and Lady Margaret Campbell of Glenorchy, his wife, and the date 1600 (commemorating the birth of their second son, Duncan). The family motto is there, VIL GOD I SAL, and the following inscriptions in Latin, CONTENDITE INTRARE PER ANGUSTAM PORTAM ("Strive To Enter In At The Strait Gate") and SANCTIS MORO JANUS VITAE EST. MEMENTO MORI ("To The Godly Death Is The Gate Of Life, Remember Death"). The initials of Sir Alexander and his wife figure on either side of the shield.

The interior of the church consists of an aisle running east and west (70 feet), with an offset to the north (north-south—40 feet). The altar is supposed originally to have stood in this recess, but it would seem that it has been moved about somewhat ; it now stands against the north wall though at one time it is said to have stood against the west gable facing east. The fine mural monument, one of the most peculiar and remarkable in Scotland, which forms the back of the altar was erected in 1616 by Sir Alexander Menzies in memory of the ladies of the House ; it is carved from the same durable chlorite schist as was used in the construction of Wade's Taybridge, and the sculpture is at the present time in as perfect a condition as it was the day it was completed. It measures 16 feet high by 12 feet broad. Some parts of it appear to be much older than others, especially the two large figures, almost life size, at the sides. It is supposed that the oldest part was originally in the Monastery of Dull.

Within the church are other objects of interest in the shape of memorial tablets of departed chiefs and their ladies, an iron collar or 'jougs' for confining the necks of evil-doers, two recesses used in the time of Sir David for keeping the 'Host' or the 'Holy Communion Wafer,' and two of the stone crosses which at one time, with two others, marked out the Sanctuary of Dull within which debtors could not be taken and imprisoned. The recesses for the Host are each about 1 foot square and have once had doors, one of them having carved on the upright lintels, right and left, the ringed initials of one of the old chiefs.

Regarding the Crosses of Sanctuary : About 120 years ago a Mr Campbell, who was factor at Castle Menzies, took two of these Crosses from Dull for use as gate-posts at his house at Tom-na-Dashan (the knoll of the stackyard), as Camserney Cottage was then called. Canon Bowstead, in his *Facts and Fancies Concerning Kilmaveonaig*, continues the story thus : "On the day same that the factor removed the Crosses he attended a farmers' dinner at the Breadalbane Hotel in Aberfeldy, after which he rode home in the small hours of the morning, and his lifeless body was found at his entrance gate

Monument in the Auld Kirk o' Weem

the same morning. The two Crosses were then restored to their original place at Dull.''

It is a pity that such a story should be perpetuated in print for, in addition to the fact that the Crosses were not so restored, the truth of the matter is quite otherwise. The factor did take the Crosses, and for the purpose given but, according to an old man who died within the last year or two in Aberfeldy who in his boyhood had the story from an eye-witness (one Archie Menzies, Balachroich, Gaelic, 'Bail-'a-chroich,' 'the town of the gibbet,' Keltneyburn), what happened was this : One night Mr Campbell went into Coshieville Inn and asked for a good horse to take him to Rannoch. He was told that there was one in the stable but advised not to take it as it was fresh and mettlesome. He replied, "I will ride it to Rannoch or Hell !" The horse bolted, turned down the old road to Fortingall and leapt the wall at the right-angled turn at the old bridge. Its feet scrambled on the rocks, but it fell back on Mr Campbell and killed him. There is no suggestion here that the accident had any connection with the removal of the Crosses.

* * * * * *

In August 1797 the peace of the countryside was shattered by anti-Militia riots. Under the terms of the Militia Act every parish was called upon to furnish a quota of men, chosen by ballot, to serve in the Militia—e.g., 18 in the case of Dull— with, in the unsettled state of France at the time and the fear of war with that country, the liability of being called upon for active service. In Weem, which was one of the storm centres, several men set about stirring up a resistance movement, even going the length of carrying out a house to house search for arms. Excitement ran high and, though no actual violence was done in this district, the mob, among other activities, "seized the schoolmaster at Dull and carried him a horse-prisoner to Aberfeldie and obliged him to give up his lists and session books and then dismissed him." This was less harsh treatment than that meted out to Forbes the schoolmaster at Fonab who had one of his ears cut off so close to his head that he bled to death. A detachment of dragoons arrived to quell the disturbances and, soon after, a detachment of the Sutherland Fencibles. The instigators of the riots, one of the chief of whom lived in the cottage which lies between the Auld Kirk and the road at the east end of the village, were arrested and taken to Edinburgh for trial. Apparently the trial extended over a considerable time for it is noted in the Parish Records that the minister was absent from his duties over several Sundays for the purpose of giving evidence.

*　*　*　*　*　*

Steeply behind the village rise the tree-clad slopes of the Rock of Weem, once a beacon station of the Clan Menzies from which the Chief summoned his men in times of trouble ; according to an old tradition the death of one of the heads of the Clan was immediately preceded or followed by a fall of a portion of the Rock. Access to its fastnesses is by the road which branches off immediately to the west of the present Parish Church by the doorway of which in the form of an Iona Cross stands the local War Memorial and, some fifty yards beyond, passes on the left one of the three last thatched cottages not only of Weem and Aberfeldy but of the whole 'Circle of one mile radius' covered by this Account. (The other two are in Tighchraggan and Boltachan respectively). It was in the small annexe at the eastern end of this cottage in Weem that the District Nurse lived before more suitable accommodation was found for her in Altrumas.

A few yards further on, where the road swings sharply eastward it is overlooked on the left by what was once the old school of Weem, but now altered out of recognition and occupied as a private house. As already told, it was discontinued as a school about the beginning of the present century.

In Weem Rock are, of course, the famous Cave and equally famous St. David's Well. It is from the former that the village derives its name—Gaelic, 'uamh,' 'cave.' Dr Mac-

millan in *The Highland Tay*, writes : "Weem is sometimes
called Balclachan, 'the town of the Stones,' which may indicate
that a Stone Circle once stood here." If so, there is no sign
of it now nor is there any tradition that such ever existed ; in
any case he would appear to be wrong for, though 'clachan,'
the plural form of 'clach,' certainly means 'stones,' in the
singular it means 'hamlet,' generally a hamlet in which there
is a church. 'Bail-'a-'chlachain,' therefore, is simply 'the town
of the church,' in short, Kirktown.

Both the Cave and the Well are a little way up the steep
slope almost directly behind the hotel but, owing to the spread
of undergrowth, etc., that followed the felling of the bigger
trees, access is no longer so easy as it was twenty years ago.

The so-called St. David's Well is one of the ancient Wishing
Wells of the district, into which devotees were wont to drop
money and articles of value while invoking the blessing of the
Patron Saint. Tradition relates that the Saint in question was
one of the lairds of the place, Sir David de Meyners or Menzies,
8th Baron, 1377-1449, who in the 15th century retired here in
disgust with the world after resigning his patrimony to a
younger brother. To this day one may from time to time find
trifling objects in the little basin into which the water flows —
buttons, pins, an occasional halfpenny or penny, and so on.
Probably long ago the gifts were of more value and proved a
source of wealth to the priests of the district. Ill luck is said
to dog the footsteps of the visitor who departs without dropping
some sort of donation into the waters.

Sir David Menzies was one of the hostages for James I in
1423. Later he was made Commissioner of Orkney and
Shetland by Erik, the Scandinavian King. He ended his days
as a monk in Melrose Abbey. In his memory the annual
March fair or tryst at Weem was called 'Feill Dhaidh.'

In the Bishop of Brechin's *Kalendars of Scottish Saints*
it is stated that the Celtic dedications to St. David must be
attributed to Dabius, or Davius, an Irish priest who preached

with success in Ireland and Alba (Scotland) ; his 'Day' was 22nd July. There is no St. David Menzies in any of the Calendars, and the first ascription of the Well and Church of Weem to him would seem to be in the *New Statistical Account*, probably from someone having inadvertently used the term *St*. David for *Sir* David. In old documents *Sir* was often written *Sr*., easily mistaken for *St*.

In front of the Well, but now overgrown with trees, is a considerable space of level ground which is said to have been used at one time as a burial ground.

Beside the Well there is a stone slab on which is crudely carved the figure of a cross. The Well occupies one corner of a great hollow under an overhanging rock ; this hollow is capable of accommodating about fifty persons and is believed to have been used for religious purposes. The Well and the rock at one time were known as 'Fuaran Creig a' Chaibeal,' 'the Chapel Rock Well,' and 'Creig a' Chaibeal,' 'the Chapel Rock.' The late Rev. R. G. Dunbar, in his *Notes on the Parish of Weem*, wrote in 1897 that these names were known to some of the old people at that time, but I question if they are known to many now.

In *The Irish Life of St. Cuthbert* (Latin M.S.) there appears the following : "In Scottish land Cuthbert came to a town called Dul and dwelt in a richly wooded hill at Doilweme —" (the Weme or Cave of Dull ; Dull being at that time the name applied to the whole district) "—about a mile distant. Here he brought from the hard rock a fountain or well of water, erected a large stone cross, built an oratory of wood, and constructed for himself out of a single stone a bath in which he used to immerse himself and spend the night in prayer to God. He remained here for some time until, being accused by the daughter of the king of that province of having seduced her, he prayed to God and the earth opened and swallowed up the young woman. He could not continue to dwell longer there but removed to other parts of the country." 'Corruen' is the name of the place where the young woman is said to have disappeared, but its locality is not known now. ('Corruen,' 'Steep or precipitous hill').

The writer of the Latin M.S. goes on to narrate, in accordance with ideas of the time, that notwithstanding the small opening of the Well there was connected with it inside the Rock a huge reservoir of water which was always full to the very top, and that if the covering stone was removed for any length of time or altogether, then, according to the tradition of the people of the country, the water welling up would overflow and speedily submerge the district. In another part of the account the writer tells how the Devil, jealous of the doings of St. Cuthbert, constructed another bath for himself of enormous dimensions, until the Saint, no longer able to endure such comradeship, seized one day a huge cudgel like a fuller's pole and, rushing upon his antagonist, knocked him about from place to place and drove him away. St. Cuthbert is supposed to have lived here between the years A.D. 651 and 661. He died in the Farne Islands in 687.

* * * * * *

The Cave, almost directly below the Well, is particularly difficult to find for anyone who does not know where to look and, even if the search be successful, the result will prove scarcely worth the trouble, for, apart from being accessible now only to a child or a very small adult, the passage penetrates no further than some 12 or 14 feet from the entrance, the result, it is said, of a rock fall which occurred many years ago. It is more than doubtful if there was ever any true passage for the rock formation here is not of the type in which caves with long underground passages are likely to occur.

It is its story however that makes it still a place of interest, and this is the story : In times past it was asserted to have subterranean communication with Loch Glassie, 1¾ miles distant and about 700 feet higher, where it was said to open at the bottom of a rugged crag on the north shore and to have within it many curious windings. This long tunnel had nine iron gates which opened and closed of their own accord, and at parts widened out into large roomy chambers with gem-studded roofs. One of these chambers contained treasure of untold value, guarded by the Devil in person.

A common legend attached to caves in the Highlands is that of the piper who entered the underground and marched away into the bowels of the earth playing his pipes; the sound of the music grew gradually fainter as he penetrated farther and farther and finally died out altogether. The piper never returned. This story is told of three caves in this district—one near Balnaguard, another on the slope of Schiehallion, and that of the Rock of Weem.

Some of these beliefs appear in a legend, however, which is peculiar to the Weem Cave : The wife of a laird who at one time lived near by sent her two daughters and a step-child to find a heifer which had strayed into the Rock. Attracted by bellowing, the two daughters were induced to enter the Cave ; the step-child had in her possession some leaves of the Bible and was safe from harm. They never returned, and nothing was heard of them till some time afterwards their two mangled bodies were found floating in the waters of Loch Glassie.

In another version of the legend only one sister went into the Cave and disappeared. Here too the story has it that the body was eventually found in Loch Glassie, and goes on to tell that for long afterwards her lifeless body might be seen floating on its back in the middle of the Loch with a long spiral of fiery light ascending from each of her breasts, which apparition caused the natives of the place to give Loch Glassie a wide berth after sunset.

Yet a third version tells that the girls were sent to gather kail and while so engaged heard the lowing of a calf and were so induced to enter the Cave. Oddly enough part of the Rock used to be called Creag Chail (Craig Kail), but the exact location of this appears to have been forgotten though the Rev. R. G. Dunbar, in his *Notes on the Parish of Weem*, wrote— in 1897—that its situation was known at that time.

A full account of this legend, quoted from Ferguson's *Rambles in Breadalbane*, is given in Appendix—(K).

The interesting question arises whether the two legends of the Rock, that of the King's daughter who, after accusing St. Cuthbert, was swallowed up by the ground, and that of the laird's daughter who disappeared into the ground (cave) never to return, did not in the beginning stem from a common root, the disappearance of the daughter of a laird or chief (Chiefs easily became 'Kings' in these old legends), and, by a process of accretion over the centuries, acquire all the trappings in which they have come down to us.

Though Loch Glassie falls outside the prescribed circle limiting this Account there is a story told of it in *Folklore and Reminiscences of Strathtay and Grandtully* by the late Mr James Kennedy, F.E.I.S., one-time schoolmaster, Ballinluig, which further illustrates the credulity of the people in the Highlands long ago and is worth re-telling : Loch Glassie was inhabited by an 'Each Uisge'—a malignant spirit in the form of a horse which frequented fords and hill lochs— Gaelic, 'Each,' 'horse,' and 'Uisge,' 'water'—which, on summer evenings, was to be seen roaming at large on a green meadow by the shore. One afternoon six girls and a boy from Strathtay set out from their homes to inspect it for themselves. They found it, patted it on the head and neck and apparently made friends with it for it lay down and allowed them to sit on its back. The boy stood at a little distance and watched developments. He concluded that this animal was not the genuine horse it seemed to be, and thought that it grew considerably larger than it was at first. When the 'Each' had the six girls comfortably seated on its back it suddenly rose, plunged into the loch, and drowned them all. The boy immediately took to his heels and, spurred by fear, managed to escape from the 'each' which was soon in pursuit. When he got home, terrified and breathless, and told what had happened the parents of the girls hastened to the spot but all they found were parts of the dead bodies of their daughters floating on the surface of the waters.

Another 'Each Uisge,' 'Water Horse,' or 'Kelpie,' for they all signify the same thing, was Gòrach, the evil spirit which used to frequent 'Stair Ghòrach,' as already told, and here seems as good a place as any to add a few remarks on the subject of old Highland superstitions, practices, and beliefs to those others already mentioned in these pages. I have written of the 'Urisks' of the Den of Moness, the Fairies of Tomchaldon, the superstitions and practices connected with Hallowe'en, so pass on now, to the old customs, etc., associated with 'Beltain' or May-day in the Highlands as described by Thomas Pennant in his *Tour in Scotland, 1769.* He writes :—"On the 1st May, the herdsmen of every village hold their Bel-tein, a rural sacrifice. They cut a square trench on the ground, leaving the turf in the middle ; on that they make a fire of wood, on which they dress a large caudle of eggs, butter, oatmeal and milk ; and bring, besides the ingredients of the caudle, plenty of beer and whisky ; for each of the company must contribute something. The rites begin with spilling some of the caudle on the ground, by way of libation : on that everyone takes a cake of oatmeal, upon which are raised nine square knobs, each dedicated to some particular being, the supposed preserver of their flocks and herds, or to some particular animal, the real destroyer of them : each person then turns his face to the fire, breaks off a knob, and flinging it over his shoulders, says, 'This I give to thee, preserve thou my horses ; this to thee, preserve thou my sheep ;' and so on. After that they use the same ceremony to the noxious animals : 'This I give to thee, O Fox ! spare thou my lambs ; this to thee, O hooded Crow ! this to thee, O Eagle !'

"When the ceremony is over, they dine on the caudle ; and after the feast is finished, what is left is hid by two persons deputed for the purpose ; but on the next Sunday they reassemble, and finish the reliques of the first entertainment."

As already told the fire and the 'caudle' still survived here in Dr John Kennedy's young days, but now all the old observances have died out.

Pennant goes on :—"A Highlander never begins anything of consequence on the day of the week on which the 3d. of May falls, which he styles 'La Sheach-anna na bleanagh,' or 'the dismal day'."

On funeral customs he has to say :—"On the death of a Highlander, the corps being stretched on a board, and covered with a coarse linnen wrapper, the friends lay on the breast of the deceased a wooden platter, containing a small quantity of salt and earth, separate and unmixed ; the earth, an emblem of the corruptible body ; the salt, an emblem of the immortal spirit. All fire is extinguished where a corps is kept ; and it is reckoned so ominous for a dog or cat to pass over it, that the poor animal is killed without mercy."

In 1893 Mr John Christie published a booklet of extracts from the Kenmore Kirk Session Records entitled *Witchcraft in Kenmore in the 1700's*. Unfortunately no one has thought to do this for Aberfeldy, but Kenmore is not very far away and as Christie's selected cases are no doubt typical of what went on in all the surrounding district at that time I feel that no apology is necessary for the inclusion here of a few extracts from his work.

(1)   "Kenmore, Aug. 30, 1730.

Margaret M'Grigar forsd called, compeared and denied she slandered John Lumsdan as guilty of ye death of her children by witchcraft."

(2)   "Kenmore, Jun. 11, 1747.

Margaret Robertson in Rumuckie compeared before the Session complaining she was unjustly charged with witchcraft and enchantments——" etc., etc.

(3)   "Kenmore, Jul. 19, 1747.

Janet M'Intaggart, daughter to Gilbert M'Intaggart in Wester Aucharn, was charged with using charms and inchantments against Alexander Fisher in Wester Aucharn." After the Kirk Session had duly deliberated on the case the charge was found proved and Janet was "ordered to stand before the Congregation against this day eight days to be rebuked for her base practices." She did, and was "rebuked and exorted." (*sic*.)

(4)   "Kenmore, Jul. 1, 1753.

——Donald Thomson, his wife, were charged with using charms
and Janet M'Nicol his present servant was said to have been
practising some unbecoming things earlie of a morning, crossing back and fore over a burn, and bowing herself to the ground,
as if she was taking up something out of the ground, or putting
something into it. At the same time Donald Thomson, his
wife Margaret Walker, and said maid were scandalised, as if
they had been using some unlawful charms ; that some of his
nighbours alleged his cows had too much milk as if she used
some diabolical act to get more milk than her own. Farther
that it was said her servant maid was practising some charm
earlie upon Belton day this year——" etc. Janet M'Nicol was
found guilty and received the same sentence and punishment
as Janet M'Intaggart.

There is no record of any witch having suffered the extreme
penalty in this neighbourhood but Charles Kirkpatrick Sharpe
in his *History of Witchcraft in Scotland* tells that a witch
was strangled and burned on the Knock of Crieff somewhere
between 1668 and 1683. In his *History of Crieff* Alexander
Porteous gives the date as 1663 and makes no mention of
strangling. Poor old Kate Macnevin (Kate Nike Neiving),
she was said, among other heinous crimes, to have committed
that of jumping from the top of the Knock (911 feet) to the
Manse of Monzie about one mile away ! Black, in his *Calendar
of Witchcraft in Scotland from 1510 to 1727*, gives the
date as '1615, but uncertain' and believes that Porteous is
confusing the Crieff case with that of Nic Neville, burned at
St. Andrew's in 1669.

Though, as I have just said, there is no record of any case
of witch-burning in this district, tradition has it that a heap
of stones on the top of the hill beyond Loch Hoil commemorates
such an event. It is known as the Wicked Woman's Cairn
('Carn na Mna Uilc') and stands by the side of the now rarely
used track from Urlar to Glenquaich. In the old days it was
customary for every passer-by to add a stone to the heap.

Before the passing of the Statute of June 1563 there is little mention of witchcraft in Scotland.   This Statute, in its wording, did not imply that the legislature believed in sorcery but aimed at the punishment of people pretending to believe in such supernatural powers rather than the actual crime of witchcraft.   In time the Church assumed the role of prosecutors and became so vindictive that the Law had to step in again. After the repeal of the Statute in 1736 little more was heard of witchcraft.

To our twentieth century minds these recordings may seem fantastic, but even now from time to time one comes across reminders of the old witchcraft days.   The following incident occurred in the 1890's but I feel sure that the idea at the back of it still survives in many parts of the country.   A man who came to live in Aberfeldy about that time spoce of it as a personal experience to the late Mr Donald MacCallum: A neighbour came in one morning and said to his landlady, "You have a new calf ?" — "Is it a grey calf ?" — "Is it a black calf ?" — "Is it a speckled calf ?"—and so on.   The landlady replied in monosyllables without giving any information.   When the woman took her departure the listener asked, "Why didn't you let her see the calf ?"   " 'Deed no !" was the answer, "She would have put the Evil Eye on it !"   If the owner had first taken the precaution to tie a chip or 'cnag' of rowan wood to the animal's tail, of course all would have been well, for is not this the recognised preventive treatment, tried and proved, in just such cases ? !

When I was a small boy there lived in Tayside Cottages a very stout old man, known to us irreverent young ruffians as 'Barrel-Guts,' of whom it is told how once, when his cow turned sick, he sent Mr Donald MacCallum's sister to fetch pails of water from a stream which formed the dividing march between two properties—no other kind would do ; even then, for the cure to be effective, a sixpenny piece had to be dropped into the water before it was given to the invalid !   (The two 'march' streams available at the time were the Tighnault Burn separating the lands of the lairds of Killiechassie and Weem, and the burn between the Breadalbane and Grantully properties about a mile east of the town.)

We are inclined nowadays to poke fun and sometimes to sneer at the superstitions of our forebears but, though the *belief* in witches may be extinct, the subconscious fear of them seems still to persist. To cut down a rowan tree at one's gate is still to invite trouble and horseshoes are still hung up over doorways to ward it off—generally in the reversed position, heels up, with the additional object of catching and retaining good luck.

Some present day superstitions are of recent birth, *e.g.*, the belief that it is unlucky to be third to light a cigarette off one match, the gremlins of the R.A.F., etc., but most have come down to us through the ages and show little sign of weakening. Thus :—

Probably there are more people than are willing to admit it who dislike sitting down thirteen to a table. Why? Because 'thirteen' is an unlucky number—I have even sailed on modern liners in which there was no Cabin 13—and this because, almost 2,000 years ago, Christ and his disciples sat down thirteen to the last Supper.

To spill salt is considered unlucky. Again, why? Because salt used to be considered the emblem of the immortal spirit. It was placed on the heads of victims designed for sacrifice and to spill it was taken as a bad omen. In Da Vinci's picture of the Last Supper Judas Iscariot is represented as having knocked over the salt cellar with his left arm.

It is unlucky to marry in May. Why? Beacause in this month in ancient Rome were celebrated the Festival of the Goddess of Chastity and the Feast of the Dead.

Friday is often held to be an unlucky day. Once again, Why? Because it was the day of the Crucifixion.

To extend the list : Even in this present 'enlightened' age of atom bombs, television, and strato-cruisers, there are many who hate to see the new moon through glass and rapidly turn over their money when they see it under suitable conditions, who are delighted when a black cat chances to cross their path, who walk off the pavement rather than pass under a ladder, who shiver with apprehension if they crack a mirror or have a picture fall from its place, who hasten to lay two pennies over the eyes of the recently dead (I have seen this done), and who carry charms, mascots, and so on, to bring good luck or ward off bad.

How some of these superstitions originated is obscure but others, as shown, trace back to the beginning of the Christian era and even earlier. How old the legend of the Cave in Weem Rock is or how the Cave and Loch Glassie came to be linked together in the story no one can tell, but the Loch by night, lonesome and isolated in its hollow in the moorland, must have been an eerie and frightening place to those who believed it. Why people should have found it necessary to be there by night may seem strange, yet not so strange perhaps when it is remembered that in the not very remote past many more people lived and worked on the higher levels of our Highland valleys than do so now.

On the hill near Glassie, as elsewhere in the Highlands, are to be seen traces of old ditches and turf walls. Long ago, 250 years and more, cultivation was carried on in the low grounds in patches but a little more was successfully tried on the higher grounds ; the ditches or furrows served as drains and the compact arable land thus formed was fenced in with feal-, fal-, or fold-dykes, a system and a name that Celtic scholars suppose to have been derived from the practice of the Romans who carefully surrounded their camps with an earthen rampart or *vallum*.

That cultivation was once carried on here on a wider scale and at a higher altitude than it is now is borne out by the very name of the place : Gaelic, 'Glasaidh,' for 'Glasaghaidh' 'green face,' from the comparative lateness of the crops.

About a furlong to the north-west of Glassie farmhouse there is a pyramidical rock with pronounced cup- and ring-markings of a somewhat uncommon character, in that several of the cups, instead of showing the usual saucer-like depressions, stand up in inverted relief, and they occur on both sides of the stone ; also, the rings or 'channels' are unusual in that they pass from one side of the rock to the other, crossing the dividing ridge where it forms an angle of 140 degrees.

* * * * * *

There is not much more to add.   As anyone will gather who has read thus far, Aberfeldy is, comparatively speaking, of recent date—almost an upstart indeed—for, as indicated at the outset, it has no 'personal' history reaching far back into the past such as have, say, Dull with its ancient Culdee settlement and its association with the foundation of the University of St. Andrews, and Weem with its Auld Kirk and Castle ; even its one real legend, that of St. Palladius is open to doubt.

But what of it ?   As he looks down from Glassie on Aberfeldy snuggling 700 feet below, the native born cannot help but feel stirring within him emotions such as can be evoked by no other place.   Other towns and cities may have their appeal, but his home town must always occupy a corner apart ; the the old familiar landmarks, too, must all have their place in the picture and their individual effects on his mind.

Straight across from Glassie he looks, almost with level eye, on the wooded eminence of the Dùn with its ancient fort, and round it he feels that a story, many stories, might be woven were the facts but known.   A little to the west he sees the Den of Moness like an axe-cut in the hill-face and conjures to his mind the legends of St. Palladius and Peallaidh an Spuit, and the vision of Robert Burns deep in its recesses writing his immortal song.   Slanting down the hill from the south-east he picks out the two roads from Crieff, the old and the new, and, on the hill-face, the sites of the many now vanished and half forgotten clachans which once echoed to the sounds of

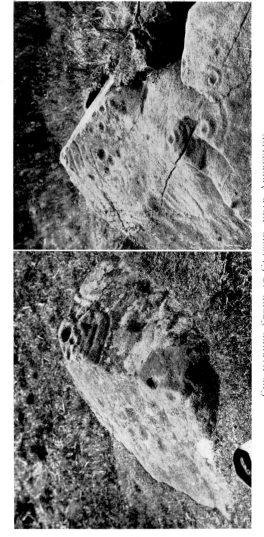

Cup marked Stone at Glassie, near Aberfeldy.

South Easterly Face.

Northerly face.

human life and endeavour. He sees Aberfeldy, with the bridge which helped to set it on the road to prosperity, with its Black Watch Memorial and all it stands for, with its people whom he has lived among and known, and with all its other memories and associations which have grown into him and become part of his very being.

That everyone born in Aberfeldy cannot be expected to live all his life in it is natural, but there are not many of its children who have gone forth into the world but feel it tugging at their heart-strings and come, and come again.

Surely all this counts for something—intangible, but none-theless real—so perhaps he and they for whom this Account has been written may feel, after all, that the writing has been worth while.   I hope so.

APPENDIX

———

Appendix A.

Saint Palladius : (Refer to page 12).

As well as Aberfeldy, Fordoun in Kincardine (The Mearns) lays claim to Palladius, it being held there that, as A. P. Forbes, Bishop of Brechin, in his *Kalendars of Scottish Saints*, writes, if tradition is correct, on leaving Ireland, he (Palladius) sailed round the north coast of Scotland, landing on what is now called The Mearns where he found the principal scene of his labours. He is said to have settled in Fordoun and to have been buried there. The yearly market is (or was) held on his Day, 6th July, and is known as Paldie's Fair, and a well near by bears his name as does part of the building in the local churchyard.

* * * * * *

Appendix B.

The Aerial Ropeway : (Refer to page 47).

The ropeway was constructed by J. Henderson & Co., Aberdeen, and cost £4,000, the rope alone accounting for £350. There were 38 steel trestles, several of which between the Cottage Hospital and the Railway Station are still standing, varying in height from 35 to 40 feet, set about 100 yards apart ; the road metal came down ready for use in buckets or skips each of which was fixed to the moving cable by means of a finger-and-thumb clip or clutch gripped by its own weight and did the round trip, down with 3 cwt. of metal and up empty, in one hour and five minutes. The whole ropeway had a carrying capacity of 10 tons per hour.

* * * * * *

Appendix C.

NOTES ON CHARTERS FOR TRANSFER OF WEEM AND ABER-
FELDYBEG FROM THE ATHOLE FAMILY TO THE MENZIESES.
(Refer to page 54).

1. From *Reports of The Royal Commission on Historical
Manuscripts.* 1877 :

> Ancient "Charter by John, Earl of Athole, son and heir of
> David, Earl of Athole, in favour of Sir Alexander de
> Meyners, son and heir of umquhile Sir Robert de Meyners
> and his heirs, for his homage and service, of all the granter's
> land of Weem and Abyrfeally-beg in Atholl, extending to
> three davachs of land—" etc. This Charter bears no date.

2. From *The Earldom of Atholl.* J. A. Robertson (1860) :
Charter dated 1301 by which "the Earl of Atholl gives
to Sir Robert de Meyners the whole of his lands of Weem
and Abyrfealdybeg ; namely two and a half davates of
the lands of Abyrfealdybeg ; the Earl retaining the patronage of the Church of Weem. Sir Robert is to render
to the Earl and his heirs one penny, and one suit at his
court of Rath in Atholl." ('Rath,' now Logierait).

Note : 1 davach — 416 old Scottish acres — 524 English
acres ; 'as much land as two ploughs could till in a year.'

* * * * * *

Appendix D.

THE TABLETS ON WADE'S TAYBRIDGE :   (Refer to page 64)

(a)   Latin Inscription :

MIRARE
VIAM HANC MILITAREM
ULTRA ROMANÆ TERMINOS
M. PASSUŪ CCL. HÂC ILLÂC EXTENSĀ
TESQ͠IS & PALUDIB⁰ INSULTANTĒ;
PER RUPES MONTESQ; PATEFACTĀ
ET INDIGNANTI TAVO,
UT CERNIS INSTRATAM.
OPUS HOC ARDUŪ SUA SOLERTIA,
ET DECENNALI MILITUM OPERA
AN, ÆR: Xᴬᴱ 1733. PERFECIT G.WADE
COPIARUM IN SCOTIA PRAEFECTUS.
ECCE QUANTUM VALEANT
REGIA GEORGII 2ᴰⁱ AUSPICIA!

The Latin inscription was composed by Dr Friend, headmaster of Westminster School, of whom Pope wrote :

"Friend, for your epitaphs I'm grieved
  Where still so much is said,
One half will never be believed,
  The other never read."

English Translation of the Latin :

ADMIRE

THIS MILITARY ROAD

STRETCHING ON THIS SIDE AND THAT

250 MILES BEYOND THE LIMIT OF THE ROMAN ONE

MOCKING MOORS AND BOGS

AND AS YOU SEE

CROSSING THE INDIGNANT TAY.

THIS DIFFICULT WORK

G. WADE, COMMANDER IN CHIEF

OF THE FORCES IN SCOTLAND

ACCOMPLISHED BY HIS OWN SKILL

AND THE TEN YEARS LABOUR OF SOLDIERS

IN THE YEAR 1733.

BEHOLD HOW MUCH AVAIL

THE ROYAL AUSPICES OF GEORGE II.

(b) English Inscription :

At The Command
of His Maj^{ty} King George
The 2^d This Bridge was Erected
in the Year 1733.
This with the Roads & other
Military works for Securing a
Safe and Easy Communication
Between the High Lands and the
Tradeing Towns in the low Country
Was by His Maj^{ty} Committed
to the care of Lieu^t General
George Wade Commander
in Chief of the Forces in Scot-
Land who Laid the first Stone
of this Bridge on the 23^d of
April And Finished The Work
in the Same Year

Appendix E.

'POEM' BY ALEXANDER ROBERSONE* OF STRUAN "TAYBRIDGE
TO THE PASSENGER" :   (Refer to page 65).

"Long has old SCOTIA Desolation fear'd,
Pensive, 'till an auspicious Star appeared ;
But soon as the Celestial Power came down,
To smile on Labour, and on Sloth to frown ;
SCOTIA reviving, rais'd her drooping Crown :
Discord and Barrenness confess'd their Doom ;
One closed her Feuds, and t'other ope'd her Womb ;
Rocks inaccessible a passage knew,
And Men, too fond of Arms, consent to plow.

Not less surprising was the daring Scheme,
That fixed my station in this rapid Stream.
The North and South rejoice to see Me Stand,
Untiring in my Function, Hand in Hand,
Commerce and Concord, Life of every Land !
But—who could force rough Nature thus to ply,
Becalm the Torrents and teach Rocks to fly ?
What Art, what Temper, and what manly Toil,
Could smooth the rugged Sons of Abria's Soil ?

Methinks the anxious Reader's at a stand,
Not knowing, George for GEORGE (to bless the Land
Averse t' Obedience) spoke the stern Command.
And still he seems perplex'd till he is told,
That Wade was skilful, and that Wade was bold.
Thus shall his Fame, with GEORGE'S Glory rise
Till Sun and Moon shall tumble from the Skies."

*Robertson signed his name as spelt.

*   *   *   *   *   *

Appendix F.

UNVEILING OF THE BLACK WATCH MEMORIAL : ORDER, ETC., OF PROCESSION : (Refer to page 73).

2nd. Perthshire Highland Rifles, preceded by the Regimental Pipe Band, Major Munro commanding. There were 89 men present belonging to the Aberfeldy Company, with 56 from Pitlochry under the command of Major Fisher.

42nd. "Royal Highlanders" Guard of Honour from 1st. Battalion (Black Watch) Perth Depot, consisting of 39 men (a large proportion of them wearing medals), under Lieutenant MacLeod. Colonel Ralston, C.B., commanding the Perth Regimental District, and Colonel Kidston, 2nd. Battalion Royal Highlanders, were also present.

Detachment of 60 men belonging to the Glasgow Highland Volunteers, preceded by 10 pipers, under Majors James Menzies and Williamson, ex-Major Wright, Captain and Adjutant Grant, Captain Macpherson, and Lieutenants Birrell and Henry.

The 3rd. Forfarshire Rifle Volunteers (Dundee Highlanders) —Represented by Colonel Smith, Captains Laburn and Adam, Sergeant-Instructor Kilgour, and Pipe-Major Donald Bain.

Perth Troop of Fife Light Horse—represented by Sergeant-Instructor Masterton and Sergeant James MacLeish.

Queen's Edinburgh Volunteers—represented by Colonel Robert Menzies, Major Cranston, Captain Archibald Menzies, and Quartermaster Henry.

Military Officers in Uniform.

Magistrates and Commissioners of the Burgh of Aberfeldy.

Taymouth Brass Band.

Edinburgh Society of High Constables—represented by Vice-Moderator Bruce, Mr P. L. Henderson, Treasurer : Captains James Grieve and Linton.

Edinburgh Breadalbane Association—Dr H. Stewart, Buccleuch Place, President ; Mr J. M'Dairmid, Treasurer ; Mr James Grieve, Mr W. Stewart, Mr H. Stewart, Mr Donald Fisher, Mr J. Middlemas, Mr Donald Robertson, Mr James Robertson, Dr Urquhart, Mr Archibald Menzies.

Perthshire Junior Association—Mr J. Henry, Architect, Mr McGlashan, S.S.C.

Celtic Society of Glasgow—represented by Mr Edwards, President.

Glasgow Perthshire Society—Mr John Macgregor and others.

Crieff Subscribers—Provost Macgregor and Bailie Cochrane.

Freemasons—Lodge Tay and Lyon (No. 276) 50 members present ; Lodge Breadalbane (No. 657) 20 ; Royal Arch, Aberfeldy, and Provincial Lodge of Perthshire West.

Ancient Order of Foresters—Court Hope of Dunkeld (No. 6537) 25 ; Court St. Idan's, Kenmore (No. 6756) ; Court Breadalbane (No. 6774) ; Representatives from Perth.

Good Templars.

General Public.

* * * * * *

Appendix G.

INSCRIPTIONS ON THE BLACK WATCH MEMORIAL :

(a)   On the north-west Panel :   (Refer to page 74).
TIR N-AM BEANN NA-N GLEANN S-NA-N GAISGEACH
CHAIDH AN CARN SO A THOGAIL
MAR CHUIMHNEACHAN
GU'N DEACHAIDH NA SE BUIDHEANNAN GAIDHEAL-
ACH
D' AM BAINM
AM "FREICEADAN DUBH"
AONADH AIR AN FHAICHE SO ANNS A'BHLIADHNA
1740.
AGUS O'N LATHA SIN CHOISINN AN REISIMEID SO
IOMADH BUAIDH
ANNS GACH CEARN DO'N T-SAOGHAL
A' DEARBHADH
GAISGE AGUS DUINEALAS NAN GAIDHEAL
1887.

"Rinneadh gnìomhradh leò
Anns' gach tìr chum an deach ;
Bhios n'an iognadh, 's na'm mìorbhuile,
Gu brath do gach neach ;
Cha leig an saoghal aìr dearmad,
An treubhantas go sìor
'm feadh bhios spéis agus mòr-mheas
Do shaighdeireachd fhìor."

English translation of above :

The Land of the Bens and the Glens and the Heroes (an
old Highland toast)/   This Cairn has been erected/   to
commemorate/   the forming into one Company/   at this
spot/   of the six Highland Companies/   called/   The
Black Watch/   1740./   And from that day this Regiment
won/   many battles/   in different parts of the World,/
proving/   the valour and patriotism of the Gael./   1887./

(The markings correspond approximately to the ends of the
Gaelic lines).

"They performed many noble deeds
In every land to which they came,
Which shall be to every one
A wonder and a marvel.
The world will not forget
Their patriotism
While respect and regard are held
For the true soldier."

(These lines are the 12th verse of the Black Watch song, a Gaelic poem of 16 verses, composed by Alexander MacGregor, Schoolmaster, Dull).

(b)   On the south-east panel :

THIS CAIRN IS ERECTED BY
GRATEFUL AND ADMIRING COUNTRYMEN
IN COMMEMORATION
OF THE ASSEMBLING TOGETHER AT TAYBRIDGE
IN OCTOBER 1739
OF THE SIX INDEPENDANT* COMPANIES
(AFTERWARDS INCREASED TO TEN)
OF THE "FREICEADAN DUBH" OR BLACK WATCH
WHO, AFTER SERVING
IN VARIOUS PARTS OF THE HIGHLANDS
WERE EMBODIED INTO A REGIMENT
DESIGNATED THE 43RD, AND AFTERWARDS
THE 42ND ROYAL HIGHLANDERS
WHOSE FIRST MUSTER
TOOK PLACE IN MAY, 1740, NEAR TAYBRIDGE,
AND ALSO IN RECOGNITION
OF THE VALOUR AND PATRIOTISM
WHICH HAS EVER SINCE DISTINGUISHED
THE SOLDIERS OF THIS CORPS
DURING ITS ILLUSTRIOUS CAREER IN MANY LANDS.
A.D. 1887.

* This spelling is as on the panel.

(c) On the north-east panel :

Fontenoy. Fort Sandberg. Ticonderoga. Martinique.
Guadeloupe. Havannah. Bushy Run. Brooklyn.
Fort Washington. Charlestown. Aboukir. Alexandria.
Egypt. (1801) Corunna. Busaco. Fuentes-d'Onor.
Cuidad Rodrigo. Burgos. Salamanca. Pyrenees.
Vittoria. Nivella. Nive. Toulouse.
Orthes. Waterloo. Alma. Sebastopol.
Lucknow. Egypt. Ashantee. Nile.
Tel-el-Kebir. Kirbekan.

*　*　*　*　*　*

Appendix H.

"THE BIRKS O' ABERFELDY"—SONG BY ROBERT BURNS ; AIR
TRADITIONAL :   (Refer to page 116).

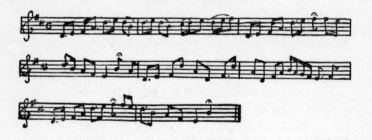

(Chorus)　Bonnie lassie, will ye go,
　　　　　　　Will ye go, will ye go,
　　　　　Bonnie lassie, will ye go
　　　　　　　To the Birks o' Aberfeldy ?

　　　Now simmer blinks on flow'ry braes
　　　And o'er the crystal streamlet plays,
　　　Come let us spend the lightsome days
　　　　　　In the Birks o' Aberfeldy.

(Chorus)　Bonnie lassie, will ye go,—etc.

The little birdies blythely sing
While o'er their heads the hazels hing
Or lightly flit on wanton wing
         In the Birks o' Aberfeldy.

(Chorus)   Bonnie lassie, will ye go,—etc.

The braes ascend like lofty wa's,
The foamy stream deep roaring fa's,
O'erhung wi' fragrant spreading shaws,
         The Birks o' Aberfeldy.

(Chorus)   Bonnie lassie, will ye go,—etc.

The hoary cliffs are crowned wi' flowers
White o'er the linn the burnie pours
And rising weets wi' misty showers
         The Birks o' Aberfeldy.

(Chorus)   Bonnie lassie, will ye go,—etc.

Let Fortune's gifts at random flee,
They ne'er shall draw a wish frae me,
Supremely blest wi' love and thee
         In the Birks o' Aberfeldy.

(Chorus)   Bonnie lassie, will ye go,—etc.

*   *   *   *   *   *

Appendix J.

"The Smiths of Aberfeldy" :   (Refer to page 143).

(English translation of some of the verses of a poem composed in Gaelic by John Campbell, 'The Bard of Morenish,' shortly before the time of Burn's visit).

    Convey from me a kindly hail
      To homes that loves abide in,
    To Aberfeldy in the vale
      The town the smiths abide in.

(Verse omitted)

Yes, if I be as I desire
  With health and strength my guerdon,
I'll go and at that town enquire
  That sound of smiths is heard in.

(Several verses omitted)

Where is there found within the land
  A smith whate'er his station
In hammering with a cunning hand
  Could beat you on occasion?

Steel shoes, the product of your forge,
  For strength with smoothness blended
The choicest horse that's owned by George
  Might wear a year unmended.   (Geo. III)

And for your tenant farmer carls,
  Well served at every visit,
To give you both reward and arles
  Most reasonably is it.

With auger, adze, or other tool,
  Or shovel needs repairing,
If they supply a little coal,
  Of pains you won't be sparing.

Ah, fine and joyous is the sight
  When you your tools are plying—
Steel vices with their grip so tight
  Their will there's no denying.

And sweeter is to me the sound
  Than harper's tuneful playing,
When bellows blow and hammers bound
  While with the smith I'm staying.

*   *   *   *   *   *

Appendix K.

THE LEGEND OF THE CAVE IN WEEM ROCK : (Refer to page 182).

Long ago a certain laird had a fine old castle with beautiful grassy lawns around it and situated somewhere along the base of the precipitous Rock of Weem. This laird had married a beautiful and accomplished young lady, daughter of a landed proprietor in Argyll. About a year after a daughter was born in the castle and the following day, sad to relate, the young mother died and was deeply mourned by her loving and bereaved husband.

Not long afterwards the laird married again, and in due time his second wife presented him with a baby daughter. The two half-sisters grew up and had great affection for each other. The step-mother took a bitter dislike to the older girl, who was heiress to the estate and who was as beautiful as she was kind-hearted, and entered into some secret and unholy pact with a black-hearted villain who had his abode in the gloomy 'Uamh' or Cave of Weem.

This monster is described by tradition as wearing a loose red hood or cloak and as possessing a ferocious savage scowl on his dark grim visage, and variously believed to be the Devil himself or some gigantic male brownie in the guise of a fierce-visaged monk.

In the execution of the fiendish plot a calf was seized by the monster and dragged into the Cave and inside the first iron gate. Shortly after,as pre-arranged, the stepmother sent the two sisters in search of the missing calf but, before they left the castle, the fond mother hung a beautiful miniature of the Virgin Mary around her own daughter's neck by which the monster was to know which of the two maidens he was to seize and take into the Cave. (Other versions of the legend have it that the lady put into the hands of the younger sister a Cross, some say a Bible, to protect her from mischance). While on the way to the Cave the younger sister took off the charm to examine it and playfully placed around her sister's neck.

By-and-by they were passing the Cave and heard the lowing of the lost calf within, and, being anxious to secure him, they both with cautious step entered the Cave, but had not proceeded far when the younger sister was cruelly seized by the hooded monster and rudely borne inside several iron gates which stood open and which, one by one and of their own accord, closed instantly the poor captive was carried past.

At this point begins the pathetic old song by the elder sister at the mouth of the Cave imploring her sister to come home. The story and the song have been rendered into English in the following ballad by the late Principal Shairp of St. Andrew's University, at one time resident in this district :

On the Sabbath morn from the Castle green
The young calf was gone, and no more was seen ;
And the lady said "Lassies, tho' the Sabbath it be,
"Ye'se gang and fetch hame my calfie to me."

The daughters they were of an ancient house,
The eldest the child of a long dead spouse,
And oft, 'neath her stern step-mother's sway
She sighed for her minnie that long was away.

At the lady's word they boun to go,
And they sought all day both high and low,
Till, passing the Cave in the Rock of Weem,
They were ware of a lowing faint as a dream.

Lightly the younger entered in,
No thought had she of sorrow or sin,
But the elder could not, though much she would,
For she held in her hand the Holy Rood.

When home came her step-daughter not her child
I wot the lady waxed savage wild,
And drave her forth, with a curse on her head,
To bring back her sister living or dead.

> "Oh woe in the going
> > we went yon day,
> "Oh woe in the lowing
> > brought us this way."

Elder Sister : Little sister, sweet sister, my sister dear,
When will we go home, when will we go home ?

Younger sister : I shall not go, I cannot come ;
I shall not go home till the Day of Doom.

Elder sister : But thou'lt come, sure thou wilt come home with me
To the old big house where the great planes be.

> There the lady stands, ever wringing her hands,
> > with crying so wild,
> That her step-daughter's come, not her own dear child.

Elder sister : My sister, gentle sister, sweet sister dear,
When will you come home,
When will you come home ?

Younger sister : When the time of seed-sowing
And lint-pulling combine,
Then home I'll be going,
Sweet sister mine,
Then home I'll be going.

Elder sister : But sister, gentle sister, sweet sister dear,
When will you come home,
When will you come home ?

Younger sister : There are five iron locks
Between me and my home—
Five strong locks of iron—I cannot come.

Elder sister : But sister, gentle sister, sweet sister dear,
When will you come home,
When will you come home ?

Younger sister :	There's a man in scarlet stands at the door,
	He keepeth me in, for evermore.
Elder sister :	Ah gentle sister, my sister dear,
	When will you come home,
	When will you come home ?
Younger sister :	There's an old high road
	Runs underground
	From the Cave to Loch Glassie,
	That way I'm bound.
Elder sister :	But sister, gentle sister,
	How for thee we yearn,
	Gentle little sister,
	Wilt thou not return ?
Younger sister :	No, dearest sister, I will not come
	To the Church in the Clachan
	Till the Day of Doom.

The lady has risen, and all alone
Gone to the hills making her moan,
And found at the head of Loch Glassie there
The white breast of her dead child floating fair.

The following is the original Gaelic version which however
would appear to be incomplete, and it would seem that the
language has been altered and adapted in repetition from age
to age. The version given is from Dunbar's *Notes on the
Parish of Weem*, for which it was taken down from recitation
by the late Rev. John MacLean, Pitilie, the air to which it is
sung being taken down by the late William McLeish, musician,
Aberfeldy :—

(As there is a great deal of repetition in this song, the first line
of most of the verses being repeated once or twice, I have
found it convenient in these cases to write out only the first
line in full but with an indication, where necessary, of how often
it is repeated in the original).

Elder sister :   A phiùthrag mhìn   (repeat twice)
                      Cuin theid sinn dhachaidh ?

Younger sister :   'Se geum an laoigh chrìn,   (repeat **twice**)
                      'Thug mise an car so.

Elder sister :   A phiùthrag mhìn   (repeat twice)
                      Cuin theid sinn dhachaidh ?

Younger sister :   Cha teid gu la bhràth   (repeat twice)
                      Cha teid mise dhachaidh.

Elder sister :   Ach, theid thu, nach teid,
                      O, theid thu, nach teid   (repeat once)
                      Theid thusa dhachaidh ?

Younger sister :   Muime gun ghras,   (repeat once))
                      Chuir sinn bhuain Cail
                      'S nach teid sinn dhachaidh.

Elder sister :   A phiùthrag mhìn,   (repeat twice)
                      Nach till thu dhachaidh ?

Younger sister :   Cha till ghu bràth,   (repeat twice)
                      Gu baile a' chlachain,

Elder sister :   A phiùthrag mhìn,   (repeat twice)
                      Nach tig thu dhachaidh ?

Younger sister :   Gu grìn an tigh mhòir,   (repeat twice)
                      'S gu lòn a chaisteil.
                      Tha an t'aon rathaid mòr   (repeat **twice**)
                      Eadar Uaimh's Loch Ghlasaidh.
                      Tha bean an tigh mhòir   (repeat twice)
                      'Sior 'bhual' a basan.
                      'Si glaodhaich thar a ceill   (repeat twice)
                      Gun d'thain' a dalta.

Elder sister :   A phiùthrag mhìn,   (repeat twice)
                      Cuin theid sinn dhachaidh ?

Younger sister :   Dar thig àm cuir an t'sìl
                      Aig àm buain an lìn,
                      Dar thig àm cuir an t'sìl
                      'Sann theid mise dhacaidh.

Elder sister :   Ach a phiùthrag mhìn,   (repeat **twice**)
                      Cuin theid sinn dhachaidh ?

Younger sister :   Tha cuig glasan iaruinn,   (repeat **twice**)
                      Eadar mi's dol dhachaidh.

Elder sister :	Ach a phiùthrag mhìn, (repeat twice) Cuin theid sinn dhachaidh?
Younger sister :	'Se fear a chleoc dheirg, (repeat twice) A tha 'gam bhacadh.
Elder sister :	Ach a phiùthrag mhìn, (repeat twice) Cuin theid sinn dhachaidh?
Younger sister :	'Se geum am laoigh chrìn, (repeat twice) Thug mise an car so.
Elder sister :	Ach a phiùthrag mhìn, (repeat twice) Cuin theid sinn dhachaidh?
Younger sister :	Cha teid gu la bhràth, (repeat twice) Cha teid mise dhachaidh.

* * * * * *

Dar dh'eirich a màthair
'Sa chaidh i 'an aird
Fhuair i 'broilleach a' snàmh
Air ceann Loch Ghlasaidh.

Elder sister :	A phiùthrag mhìn, (repeat twice) Cha tig thu dhachaidh?

* * * * * * *

Appendix L.

STOP PRESS NEWS.   JUNE 1954.

(1) (Refer to page 74). A second Presentation Seat was added last year to those already in the grounds of the Black Watch Memorial. It carries a tablet inscribed : "Coronation 1953. Presented by the 1st Aberfeldy Girl Guides."

(2) (Refer to pages 139 and 144). The new Police Station in Kenmore Street came into occupation in May 1953.

(3) (Refer to page 133). The burned out ruin of Number 12, Dunkeld Street, was demolished and cleared away in December 1953. At the moment the site is vacant.

(4) (Refer to page 170). Killiechassie is now once again for sale.

* * * * * *

BIBLIOGRAPHY

Aberdeen Ecclesiological Society.—Transactions of 1896—1898.

Antiquaries (Scotland).—Proceedings of Society of Vols. XVIII. XXXIV. XLIV. XLV. LXXXII.

Atholl and Tullibardine Families.—Chronicles of

Black (George) : *Calendar of Witchcraft in Scotland from 1510 to 1727.* (1938).

Bowie (William) : *The Black Book of Taymouth* (1598 etc.) with Introduction by Cosmo Innes, one-time Professor of History, University of Edinburgh.

Bowstead (Canon) : *Facts and Fancies Concerning Kilmaveonaig.*

Brown (Hume) : *Early Travellers in Scotland.*

Burns (Robert) : *Poetical Works*, etc.

Campbell (A.) : *Journey from Edinburgh.* (1802).

Campbell (Duncan) : *The Book of Garth and Fortingall.* (Published privately).

Christie (John) : *The Antiquity of Aberfeldy.* (1906).

Witchcraft in Kenmore. (1893).

Cornford (L. C.) and Walker (F. W.) : *The Black Watch.*

Cromwellian Soldier in Scotland, 1650.*—Letter from a*

Defoe (Daniel) : *A Tour through the Whole Island of Great Britain.* (1727).

Dunbar (R. G.) : *Notes on the Parish of Weem*. (1897).

Encyclopedia Britannica.

Ferguson (Malcolm) : *Rambles in Breadalbane.*

Forbes (A. P.), Bishop of Brechin : *Kalendars of Scottish Saints.*

Ford (Robert) : *The Harp of Perthshire.*

Fraser (W.) : *The Red Book of Grantully.*

Froissart (Jean) : *Les Chroniques de Froissart* (ed. Buchon, Paris).

Garnett (T.) : *Observations on a Tour through the Highlands of Scotland.* (1811).

Gillies (W. A.), D.D. : *In Famed Breadalbane.* (1938).

Gow (Alexander) : *Aberfeldy in the 18th Century.*

Haldane (A. R. B.) : *The Drove Roads of Scotland.*

Harleian Miscellany. Vol. VI. (1810).

Heron (Robert) : *Observations made in a Journey through the Western Counties of Scotland in the Autumn of 1792.*

Highland Roads and Bridges. Reports to the Commissioners (various years).

Historical Manuscripts. Royal Commission Report. (1877).

Hunter (Thomas) : *Woods, Forests, and Estates of Perthshire.* (1883).

Inverness. Transactions of Gaelic Society of Vol. XXV.

Irish Life of St. Cuthbert.

Kennedy (James) : *Folklore and Reminiscences of Strathtay and Grandtully.* (1928).

Kennedy (John), D.D., LL.D. : *Old Highland Days.*

Memoir of Rev. James Kennedy.

Mackay (J. G.) : *Romantic Story of the Highland Garb and Tartan.*

MacLaren (M.) : *Unrecorded Echoes of Recorded Lives in Aberfeldy.*

Macmillan (Hugh), D.D., LL.D. : *The Highland Tay.*

McNayr (James) : *A Guide from Glasgow.* (1797).

Marshall (William), D.D., : *Historic Scenes in Perthshire.* (1879).

Mitchell (Hugh) : *Pitlochry District.*

Morer (Thomas) : *A Short Account of Scotland.* (1689).

Oliver & Boyd's *New Edinburgh Almanac,* etc., (Various years).

Payne (Gordon) : *The Tay Valley Plan.* (1950);

Pennant (Robert) : *Tours in Scotland. 1769* and *1772.*

Porteous (Alexander) : *History of Crieff.*

Ray's Itineraries (about 1661) ed. by Dr Lankester.

Robertson (James) : *General View of the Agriculture in the County of Perth.* (1799).

Robertson (James) : *Survey of Perthshire*, etc. (1813).

Robertson (James A.) : *The Earldom of Atholl*. (1860).

Salmond (J. B.) : *Wade in Scotland*. (1938).

Scottish Geographical Magazine. (1911).

Scottish Notes and Queries. Vols. 1895 to 1938.

Sharp (C. K.) : *History of Witchcraft in Scotland*.

Skene (W. F.) : *Chronicles of the Picts and Scots*.

Skene (W. F.) : *History of Celtic Scotland*.

Smith (C. L.) : *Excursions through the Highlands and Isles of Scotland in 1835 and 1836*.

Southey (Robert) : *Journal of a Tour in Scotland*. (1819).

Statistical Account. 1791.

New Statistical Account. 1845.

Stewart (Alexander) : *A Highland Parish*. (1928).

Stewart (Charles) : *The Gaelic Kingdom in Scotland*. (1880).

Stewart (General David) : *Sketches of the Highlanders. A Short History of the Black Watch*.

Stoddart (John) : *Local Scenery and Manners in Scotland. 1799-1800*.

Townshend (C. H.) : *Descriptive Tour in Scotland*. (1840).

Tullibardine (Marchioness of) : *Military History of Perthshire*.

Wordsworth (Dorothy) : *Recollections of a Tour made in Scotland. A.D. 1803*.

INDEX

All Banks, Bridges, Burns, Hotels, Inns, Lime Kilns, Mills, Notable Visitors, Royalty, and Streets are grouped under 'Banks,' 'Bridges,' etc. : Churches, Chapels, Religious Meeting Houses, etc., under 'Churches, etc.' : Roads, not specifically indexed, under 'Roads' : Schools, Education, etc., under 'Schools' : and Wells, Springs, etc., under 'Water Supply' and 'Wells'.

B